Argentina
& Peron
1970-75

Argentina
& Peron
1970-75

Edited by Lester A. Sobel

Contributing editors: Joanne Edgar and Chris Hunt
Indexer: Grace M. Ferrara

FACTS ON FILE, INC.   NEW YORK, N.Y.

Argentina
& Peron
1970-75

Library of Congress Catalog Card Number: 75-20835
ISBN 0-87196-211-X

9 8 7 6 5 4 3 2 1
PRINTED IN
THE UNITED STATES OF AMERICA

982
Sob

Contents

MAPS & TABLES

Argentina & Peron

JUAN DOMINGO PERÓN, TWICE PRESIDENT of Argentina, exerted an almost hypnotic influence over his country's masses. Even during his 18 years of exile *peronismo* was a powerful force in Argentina, and rival political candidates could often differ on almost every issue except one—their loyalty to Peron.

Before he reached the presidency in 1946, Peron first earned the affection of Argentina's workers, whom he dubbed his *descamisados* (shirtless ones), by winning wage raises, social security and low-cost housing for them. The loyalty of the workers was the basis of Peron's power, but he had another important political asset—his second wife, the former Maria Eva Duarte, adored by the *descamisados* as Evita, a woman of great charm and political ability who made charity her monopoly in Argentina. Evita's death of cancer in 1952 marked the beginning of a downturn for Peron, who was overthrown in 1955 and forced into exile.

During his 18 years of absence from power, Peron slowly regained political strength. Economic adversity, labor strife, terrorism and other political violence, apparently combined with nostalgia for the old days of Peron and Evita, finally broke the opposition in Argentina and brought the aging former dictator back home in triumph. Not only was he elected president in 1973, but, on his insistence, his young third wife, the former Maria Estela (Isabel) Martinez, became vice president.

The Country Peron Ruled

Argentina, a landmass of 1,072,745 square miles, is the eighth

1

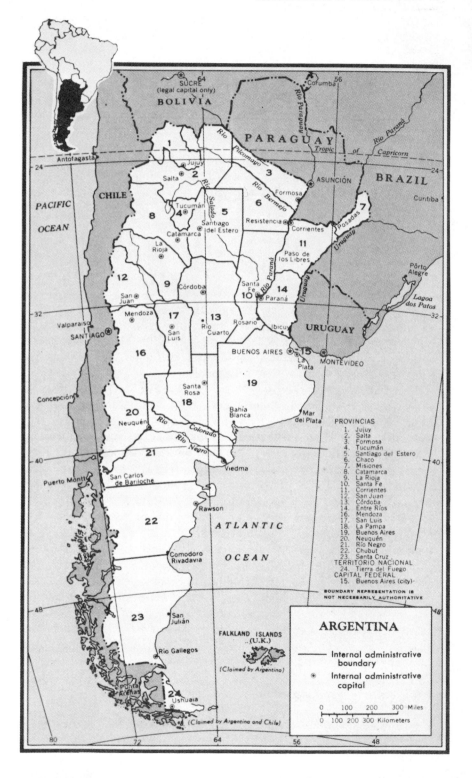

PROVINCIAS
1. Jujuy
2. Salta
3. Formosa
4. Tucumán
5. Santiago del Estero
6. Chaco
7. Misiones
8. Catamarca
9. La Rioja
10. Santa Fe
11. Corrientes
12. San Juan
13. Córdoba
14. Entre Ríos
16. Mendoza
17. San Luis
18. La Pampa
19. Buenos Aires
20. Neuquén
21. Río Negro
22. Chubut
23. Santa Cruz
TERRITORIO NACIONAL
24. Tierra del Fuego
CAPITAL FEDERAL
15. Buenos Aires (city)

BOUNDARY REPRESENTATION IS
NOT NECESSARILY AUTHORITATIVE

FALKLAND ISLANDS
.. (U.K.)

(Claimed by Argentina)

ARGENTINA

——— Internal administrative
boundary

⊙ Internal administrative
capital

0   100   200   300 Miles

0   100   200   300 Kilometers

(Claimed by Argentina and Chile)

largest country in the world. It is the second largest in South America, in population as well as in area. Argentina stretches more than 2,000 miles from the Bolivian and Paraguayan borders in the north to the tip of Argentina's part of Tierra del Fuego in the South. Bordering countries include Brazil on the northeast, Uruguay on the east and Chile on the west and southwest.

The major regions are: (1) Patagonia, a largely dry, windy plateau area covering the southern part of Argentina, stretching south from the Colorado River for 1,200 miles to the tip of rainy Tierra del Fuego. (2) The Pampa, northeast of Patagonia, a fertile 25,000-square-mile plain forming the heartland of Argentina. Stretching northwest, west and south of Buenos Aires, the Pampa is the home of more than half of the country's population and provides most of Argentina's livestock and farm and industrial production. (3) The Northeast, a subtropical lowland region north of the Pampa, east of the Andes and their foothills and bordering on Uruguay, Brazil and Paraguay. (4) The Northwest Andes and Piedmont, a region of mountains and foothills northwest of Patagonia, west of the Pampa and bordered by Chile on the west and Bolivia on the north.

The population of Argentina grew from 20,013,000 in 1960 to 23,354,000 in 1970. This 1.5% rate of population growth is the second lowest in Latin America. Seventy-two per cent of Argentine citizens live in urban areas. Greater Buenos Aires, which includes at least 10 major cities, has grown in recent years to a population of 5,380,000 (as of 1970) and surrounds the Federal Capital, which has a population (as of 1970) of 2,972,000. This megalopolis, with more than a third of Argentina's population, is South America's largest metropolitan area and one of the world's 10 largest.

Argentines are overwhelmingly (about 97%) of European descent. Citizens of Italian and Spanish origin predominate, but there are many residents of English, German, other European (both East and West), Jewish and Arab origin. The number of Indians is small, and there are several small Japanese enclaves. Spanish, the official and popular language, is spoken with several Argentine accents, particularly in the populous Buenos Aires area where the accent known as Rio Platense is in use. Most Argentines (about 94%) are Roman Catholic, but about 2% are Protestant and another 2% are Jewish.

Government

Argentina is governed under the Constitution of 1853, which includes many articles that are virtual translations from the U.S. con-

Population of Argentina 1960 & 1970

	1970		1960		Increase or Decrease	
	Number	Per-cent	Number	Per-cent	Number	Per-cent
Federal Capital	2,972,453	12.7	2,966,634	14.8	5,819	0.2
Buenos Aires	8,774,529	37.6	6,766,108	33.8	2,008,421	29.7
Catamarca	172,323	0.7	168,231	0.8	4,092	2.4
Córdoba	2,060,065	8.8	1,753,840	8.8	306,225	17.5
Corrientes	564,147	2.4	533,201	2.7	30,946	5.8
Chaco	566,613	2.4	543,331	2.7	23,282	4.3
Chubut	189,920	0.8	142,412	0.7	47,508	33.4
Entre Ríos	811,691	3.5	805,357	4.0	6,334	0.8
Formosa	234,075	1.0	178,526	0.9	55,549	31.1
Jujuy	302,436	1.3	241,462	1.2	60,974	25.3
La Pampa	172,029	0.7	158,746	0.8	13,283	8.4
La Rioja	136,237	0.6	128,220	0.6	8,017	6.3
Mendoza	973,075	4.2	824,036	4.1	149,039	18.1
Misiones	433,020	1.9	361,440	1.8	81,580	22.6
Neuquén	154,570	0.7	109,890	0.5	44,680	40.7
Río Negro	262,622	1.1	193,292	1.0	69,330	35.9
Salta	509,803	2.2	412,854	2.0	96,949	23.5
San Juan	384,284	1.6	352,387	1.8	31,897	9.1
San Luis	183,460	0.8	174,316	0.9	9,144	5.3
Santa Cruz	84,457	0.4	52,908	0.3	31,549	59.6
Santa Fe	2,135,583	9.1	1,884,918	9.4	250,665	13.3
Santiago del Estero	495,419	2.1	476,503	2.4	18,916	4.0
National Territory of the Tierra del Fuego, Falkland Islands, and Antarctic and South Atlantic islands[1]	15,658	0.1	11,209	0.1	4,449	39.7
Tucumán	765,962	3.3	773,972	3.9	−8,010	−1.0
Total Population ...	23,354,431	100.0	20,013,793	100.0	3,350,638	16.7

[1]Falkland Islands and South Atlantic islands are under British jurisdiction; population of Tierra del Fuego: 13,431.

Source: Adapted from Organición de los Estados Americanos, *América en Cifras, 1972, Situación Demográfica: Estado y Movimiento de la Población*, Washington, 1972, p. 23.

stitution. The charter provides for a representative, republican, federal system with powers divided between the federal government and the 22 provincial governments.

The federal executive is a president, who is elected for four years and who may not be reelected immediately. He governs with the aid of a presidentially appointed cabinet. Under the constitution, the president is the commander-in-chief of the armed forces, although there have been instances in the past decade in which someone other than the president has held supreme military command. The president usually introduces legislation, and he has veto power. He appoints members of the federal judiciary and has the right, subject to senatorial confirmation, to grant pardons and commute sentences. The president has the authority to declare a state of siege and to suspend constitutionally granted civil rights.

The legislature is a bicameral National Congress. The Senate has a membership of 69, comprising at least two senators from each province and the Federal District. Senators are elected by the provincial legislatures except in the case of the Federal District, where, since 1973, they are chosen by direct vote. The Chamber of Deputies has 243 members. They are elected directly, one for each 85,000 inhabitants in the provinces and in the Federal District. Members of Congress have immunity from arrest, but a member can lose this immunity by a 2/3 vote of his house.

Judicial matters are handled by a Supreme Court and by lower courts created by Congress. Congress has divided the nation into federal judicial districts, which are courts of original jurisdiction, and at least one justice is assigned to each district. Appellate courts are intermediate courts that handle appeals from the district courts, and the Supreme Court is the court of final appeal. In addition, each province has a judicial system to rule on non-federal matters.

Each province has its own provincial government. The elected provincial governors and legislatures serve, as specified by the constitution, as "regents of the federal government for the execution of the constitution and the law of the nation." The constitution gives the federal government the right to intervene in provincial matters to "guarantee the republican form of government, repel foreign invasion, and at the request of the constituted authorities, to support or re-establish those authorities, should they have been deposed by sedition or invasion by another province." Under this provision, the president or congress can remove a province's governor and other officials and replace them with a federal intervenor responsible only to the federal authority that appointed him.

Abbreviated History of Pre-Peron Argentina

The first Europeans known to have landed on the territory now called Argentina were members of a Spanish expedition commanded by Juan Diaz de Solis. They debarked on the northern bank of the Rio de la Plata estaury in 1516 but established no settlement, and de Solis was killed by a native. Part of Argentina's Atlantic coast was explored by Ferdinand Magellan in 1520. The Rio de la Plata was given its name by John Sebastian Cabot, who explored the area in 1526 and built a fort that he named Espiritu Santo. This was probably the first European settlement in Argentina.

Nearly a decade later Pedro de Mendoza received a large grant of land in the area from the crown of Castile. He financed an expedition that arrived at the Rio de la Plata area under his leadership in 1535. Mendoza founded Santa Maria del Buen Aire, later known as Buenos Aires, but the settlement was soon attacked and destroyed by Indians. Later explorers who came overland from other areas in South America were able to found more permanent settlements. But it was not until 1580 that Juan de Garay was able to build a second, permanent Buenos Aires.

Argentina was governed as a dependency of the Viceroyalty of Peru until 1776, when the Viceroyalty of Rio de la Plata was created. Until then, Buenos Aires had been forbidden to trade by sea. But the city quickly became an important and growing economic force when the Peruvian trade curbs were relaxed.

A movement for Argentine independence from Spain was sparked by the North American and French revolutions. It grew with Napoleon Bonaparte's overthrow of the Spanish government, and it received added impetus because of a British adventure. The British Commodore Home Popham, without his government's authority, seized Buenos Aires June 27, 1806. The militia, made up of settlers of Spanish origin, overpowered the British Aug. 12. A stronger British force of some 10,000 men under John Whitelocke attacked Buenos Aires in May 1807 but was defeated by an 8,000-man local militia force in a one-day battle. Following a peace agreement, the British left Sept. 9.

Under the brief British occupation, the merchants of Buenos Aires had received complete freedom of commerce and had enjoyed a drastic reduction of import duties. Virtually all were unwilling to be subjected again to Spain's oppressive commercial requirements, and the demand for independence became overwhelming.

The military leadership of the independence movement was entrusted to Jose de San Martin, an Argentine-born former officer in the Spanish army. A congress of representatives of the La Plata provinces took place in Tucuman in 1816, and a declaration of complete independence from Spain was issued July 9. In the first battle for independence, an Argentine force under San Martin defeated a Spanish force in the battle of Chacabuco in Chile Feb. 12, 1817. The Argentinians followed this victory by defeating the remainder of the Spaniards at Maipu April 5 and thus freed Chile from Spain. San Martin landed with an amphibious force on the Peruvian coast in 1820. Fighting his way into Lima in July 1821, he formally declared Peru independent. After returning to Argentina, San Martin retired from public life and has become one of Argentina's most venerated historical personages.

The early years of Argentine independence were marked by political confusion, disunity and violence. Bernardino Rivadavia, president in 1826-27, sought to improve commerce and agriculture and began a program for distributing public land, but his land plans failed and large tracts fell into the hands of a few powerful people.

Argentina's first *caudillo* (regional strongman), Juan Manuel de Rosas, arose from this chaos in 1829, when he became governor of Buenos Aires Province. After rejecting reelection in 1832, Rosas resumed office in 1835 and ruled as a dictator over most of Argentina, with a secret organization called Mazorca (ear of corn) helping to keep him in power by a rule of terror and violence.

Rosas was overthrown by a force led by Justo de Urquiza in 1852 in the Battle of Monte Caseros. Urquiza, hailed as a liberator and made provisional director of all Argentina, called a meeting of all provincial governors. The governors decided to convene a national assembly, which, under the guidance of Juan Bautista Alberdi, produced the U.S.-inspired Constitution of 1853, still the basic law of the land. Urquiza was elected the first president under the new charter.

The period that followed was one of occasional political confusion but continued economic and social growth. Under Presidents Bartolome Mitre (1862-68) and Domingo Faustina Sarmiento (1868-74), Argentina built the finest public school system in Latin America. Conservative forces ultimately won control of the country and remained in power until 1916, when Hipolito Irigoyen, heading the middle-class Radical Party, was elected president. Irigoyen kept Argentina neutral during World War I, a conflict that brought expanded markets to the country and from which Argentina emerged with a greatly enlarged industrial structure. Radical control continued until 1930, when it gave way to a conservative trend that led finally to military control, and the emergence of Peron.

Peron's Rise & Fall

Argentina had continued its policy of neutrality at the start of World War II. But under former vice president Ramon S. Castillo, who assumed the presidency on the resignation of ailing Roberto M. Ortiz in 1940, there was a definite turn toward the Axis, then at the height of its power. Although the war had brought record high prices for Argentina's food exports, a rising cost of living kept most workers from sharing this seeming prosperity. Criticism of the administration due to the economic situation and to Castillo's pro-Axis behavior preceded an army coup that deposed Castillo June 4, 1943.

The leaders of the coup were largely members of a rightwing army cabal called the United Officers' Group (Grupo de Officiales Unido, or GOU), whose leadership included Col. Juan Domingo Peron Sosa.

The future dictator, born Oct. 8, 1895 in Lobos, a rural town in Buenos Aires Province, was a product of both of Argentina's dominant ethnic strains. His father, Mario Tomas Peron, was of Italian descent, his mother of Spanish Creole origin.

Peron trained for the army at Argentina's national military academy, the Colegio Militar de la Nacion, and was graduated in 1913 with a commission as sublieutenant of infantry. Later he attended the Sargento Cabral officers' school and graduated with the rank of captain. He then took advanced courses at the Escuela Superior de Guerra, where he served as a professor of military history from 1930 to 1936. While serving in the latter capacity, Peron also acted as private secretary to the minister of war and as aide-de-camp to army leaders. He studied military tactics in France, Germany, Italy and Spain from 1939 to 1941, lectured, wrote several books on military history and strategy and is said to have become an admirer of Mussolini and Hitler.

Returning from Europe in 1941, Col. Peron became commandant of a mountain detachment in Mendoza, where he was in charge of training ski troops. It was at about this time that Peron joined the GOU, a group that sympathized with the Axis powers and wanted to make Argentina the dominant Latin American power.

After the successful GOU-engineered coup, in which Peron played a major role, Peron was appointed undersecretary of war in the cabinet of the next president, Gen. Pedro Pablo Ramirez. More important from the point of view of Peron's later rise to power, however, he was made director of the National Department of Labor, which, under his guidance, became the powerful Secretariat of Welfare & Labor.

Peron showed an early awareness of the significance of Argentina's transformation into an urbanized, industrialized society. As head of the labor secretariat, he won the allegiance of the workers, his *descamisados,* by successfully pressing for one labor benefit after another—higher wages, bonuses, social welfare reforms. He also welded the labor unions into a strong, politically significant unit under his control.

Supported by this power base, Peron was politically strong enough by February 1944 to force Ramirez to resign. Gen. Edelmiro Farrell, who then became president, was only a figurehead, however, and the real power was in the hands of Peron, who served as secretary of labor and welfare, as minister of war and as vice president.

It was in 1943 that Peron, a widower (his first wife, the former Aurelia Tizon, who he had married in 1925, had died of cancer in 1938), met the young actress Maria Eva Duarte—Evita. Evita became his mistress and a political aide of unrivaled value.

Although Peron had carefully built strong political support, his rise also created enemies opposed to his policies. These enemies included by-passed military leaders, landowners, businessmen, Radicals, Socialists and some union leaders. Foreign as well as domestic critics opposed his pro-Axis and anti-American position.

After Peron failed to come to terms with the victorious Allies at the end of World War II, his opponents in the military arrested him Oct. 9, 1945 and imprisoned him. It was at this point that Evita gave her first public demonstration of her political value. Under her prodding, the packinghouse workers and other unionists marched on Buenos Aires from the suburbs, and the General Confederation of Labor (Confederacion General de Trabajadores, or CGT) threatened a general strike unless Peron were freed.

The show of power awed Peron's opposition. President Farrell announced Peron's release and restoration to power. Peron began to plan for the election scheduled for the following year and for his ascent to supreme power. He also married Evita.

Peron was elected president in February 1946 by a vote of 1,474,000 to 1,207,000 for his liberal opponent, Jose P. Tamborino, candidate of the Democratic Union.

As president, Peron continued his program of worker benefits and his efforts to transform the Argentine economy and society under his philosophy of *justicialismo,* which he described as a middle way between capitalism and communism. Evita proved invaluable. She served as secretary of labor and welfare. She was in virtual command of the CGT. She sparked the movement that resulted in the extension of the vote to women, and she then organized the Women's Peronist Party. She created the Eva Duarte de Peron Foundation, which was given exclusive control of all charitable activity. Put in charge of the Ministry of Health, she founded hospitals and clinics and organized Argentina's first effective campaign against tuberculosis and malaria.

Under Peron's orders, Congress in 1949 amended the constitution to permit presidents to succeed themselves. Peron was then reelected easily in 1951. But with Evita's death in 1952, things started to fall apart for Peron. Criticism mounted because of his feud with the Roman Catholic Church over his proposals to legalize divorce and over his opposition to the church's growing influence in the labor unions. His opponents assailed his economic policies and his disregard for civil liberties. He was attacked for his deal to let North American oil companies develop Argentina's petroleum. He also earned the enmity of disgruntled military leaders.

The end came shortly after Peron was excommunicated by the Roman Catholic Church in June 1955.

Dissident armed forces officers revolted Sept. 16, 1955. Peron resigned Sept. 19 and fled on a Paraguayan gunboat. He lived in exile in Paraguay, Nicaragua, Panama, Venezuela and the Dominican Republic during the next five years before he found a more permanent exile headquarters in Madrid in 1960.

The Peronist parties were outlawed after Peron's ouster, but Peronism remained a potent political force. Peronists continued political activity in Argentina, and their leaders kept in close contact with Peron abroad and tried to follow his orders. As time went on, the memories of the good days under Peron seemed to grow stronger while the bitter antagonisms of the Peron era became weaker. Labor discontent mounted in Argentina as inflation eroded labor's gains. Political rivalries often exploded in violence, and incidents of terrorism mounted. As the 1960s ended, Argentina seemed ready for a change, and to many Argentinians, Peron represented that change.

THIS BOOK IS A RECORD OF events in Argentina during the years 1970-75, a period that covers the interval just preceding Peron's return, the brief interval of his resumption of power, the events surrounding his death and the period that followed when his widow succeeded him as president and tried to rule an increasingly dissatisfied nation. The material that follows consists largely of the record compiled by FACTS ON FILE in its weekly coverage of world events. As in all FACTS ON FILE works, care was taken to keep this volume free of bias and to make it a balanced and accurate reference tool.

LESTER A. SOBEL

New York, N.Y.
November, 1975

•

1970: Dissent Mounts

Peron Ready to Return

As political dissent and violence mounted in Argentina during 1970, the exiled Peron announced publicly that he was prepared to make another bid for power.

Peron urges revolution. Former President Juan D. Peron called for revolt in Argentina and pledged to return "at any moment I can be useful for something." In an interview published July 6 in the French magazine Africasia, Peron said that he had ordered his followers in Argentina to "go toward total confrontation, up to destruction." "Violence already reigns and only more violence can destroy it," the former dictator asserted. "The revolution will have to be violent." Prensa Latina, the Cuban news agency, conducted the interview with Peron, living in exile in Spain.

Evita's body found. In an apparent move to prepare for Peron's return, the ex-dictator's personal representative in Argentina, Jorge Daniel Paladino, announced in the fall of 1970 that the Peronist movement had located the body of Peron's late second wife, the popular Eva (Evita), who had died in 1952.

According to news reports Oct. 14, Paladino said the Peronist movement had conducted "its own investigation on the fate of Eva Peron's body," which had been missing since Juan Peron was overthrown in 1955, and that the movement knew where the body was. Paladino said: "The body will be delivered to the Argentine people in due time and when conditions are right," but he added that Peronists would not make any deal to give support to "any group anxious to remain in power."

Growing Dissent & Unrest

Peronist unions quit pro-government unit. The 62 Peronist labor unions had a delegation that had visited Peron in Spain in December 1969, expelled their voted to withdraw from the government-sponsored "Commission of 25" of the General Confederation of Labor (CGT), Le Monde reported Jan. 11. In addition, the unions, gathered to hear a report of some independent unions. The Peronists representatives on the "Commission of 25" (previously identified as the "Commission of 20") and called them traitors. The commission was left only with the support of the "participacionista" and issued several demands to the government including requests that the state of siege be lifted, that government-controlled unions be restored to their legiti-

13

mate authority and that prices be controlled.

The militant "rebel" CGT unions called off a mass meeting because of internal divisions between leaders Raimundo Ongaro, secretary general of the rebel faction, and Augustin Tosco, head of the Cordoba Luz y Fuerza (light and power) union, the Le Monde report stated; the meeting had been scheduled for Jan. 10 in Cordoba. Ongaro wanted to include the breakaway peronista unions, while Tosco favored relying only on already-existing support.

Regime controls Cordoba union—The government issued a decree placing under its control Tosco's Cordoba Luz y Fuerza union, according to a report by Le Monde Feb. 10. The government had previously prevented the holding Jan. 31 of a "labor and popular meeting for social justice and national liberation" in Cordoba. The meeting, organized by Tosco, was forbidden in order to "safeguard the atmosphere of tranquility" following the explosion Jan. 30 of bombs at the Cordoba offices of the Bank of London and South America, and the newspaper La Prensa and at the home of a wealthy Cordoba family.

Cordoba student protests. An estimated 5,000 Cordoba students, protesting against imposition of stiff university entrance examinations, clashed with police Feb. 23 and 24; one policeman was killed Feb. 23 and more than 75 persons were reported arrested during the violence. Demonstrations against the examinations, which, according to the students, limited popular access to higher education, had been staged throughout February and had resulted in the closing of the university. Cordoba officials charged that local Luz y Fuerza leaders had aided the students in planning the protests.

(Student-police clashes had erupted in Tucuman Jan. 20 when students staged demonstrations in support of textile workers occupying a nearby factory in opposition to the owners' decision to close it.)

Violence by protesting students and workers caused 16 deaths in Cordoba in March.

Three bombs exploded in Cordoba March 7, damaging the local army headquarters, the offices of a General Electric subsidiary and the Argentine-U.S. Cultural Institute.

Government controls Cordoba. Cordoba Province was put under direct government control April 8, following rumors that serious trouble was to break out the next week. Provincial Governor Roberto Huerta had resigned several days earlier and was temporarily succeeded by Gen. Juan Carlos Reyes.

Violent incidents at Cordoba, Rosario. Commemorative actions planned by workers and students to mark the anniversary of the "Cordobazo"—the events of May and June 1969—provoked in Cordoba May 29 intensified the civil strife.

A march of silence called to honor two students killed in Rosario in 1969 ended in clashes between police and students May 21.

In Cordoba, police broke into the university May 22 and routed students who were commemorating the death of a student shot by police in 1969. Students and worker groups took to the streets to protest alleged police brutality in connection with the incident. Demonstrators set fire to cars, smashed windows and erected street barricades throughout the night of May 22-23. The rioting reportedly resulted in the death of one student. Fifty-three were wounded. Police arrested 1,570 persons.

The University of Cordoba was ordered closed May 22 with all activities suspended until June 1. Two other universities also closed.

A May 24 report said the General Confederation of Labor (CGT) had called for a general strike to begin May 29. The French newspaper Le Monde reported May 26 that the CGT secretary general and several student leaders had been detained, according to student sources.

Some 4,000 workers and students, many carrying clubs and stones, clashed with police May 29 during the general strike demonstration. Police used tear gas to disperse the crowd, which broke up into smaller groups and went on a destructive rampage through the streets of Cordoba.

Dispute over return to democracy. Dispute continued early in 1970 over demands for the restoration of democracy.

Following several months of controversy over his attacks on government policies, Col. Juan Francisco Guevara, Argentina's ambassador to Venezuela, was forced to hand in his resignation, Le Monde reported Jan. 28. In a statement interpreted as a direct attack on Armed Forces Commander Gen. Alejandro Lanusse and former President Pedro Aramburu, both of whom had called publicly for a rapid return to democracy in Argentina, Guevara had said: "No one in Argentina, no matter how important his position, has the right to impose a return to any system whatever if the nation prefers a more highly-developed form."

Doctors' strike. Most of the nation's 33,000 physicians staged a 24-hour strike Jan. 23; the strike was called by the Argentine Medical Confederation to protest the government's public health policies. The doctors, who claimed that the government refused to consult with them in making public health decisions, opposed a government program to include the physicians' pension fund in the deficit-ridden state pension fund. In addition, the doctors objected to the closing of several state hospitals and to a government plan to sell state hospitals that operated at a deficit.

■About 30,000 Argentine doctors staged their second 24-hour strike in two months March 20 to protest state health policies.

El Chocon workers strike. Argentine military police were flown to Nequen Province the weekend of March 14–15 to end an 18-day strike of construction workers at the El Chocon hydroelectric project. The troops ousted some 400 strikers from huts in which they had barricaded themselves. The Interior Ministry later issued a communique stating that work had resumed and was progressing "normally." However, the French newspaper Le Monde reported

March 19 that about 1,000 of the 3,500 workers had left the area. The current strike, and an earlier work stoppage in December 1969, stemmed from workers' demands for higher pay and better living conditions, as well as workers' disputes with their union leadership. The El Chocon project was part of a huge public works project in northern Patagonia.

Leftists seized. Federal police investigator Col. Jorge Diotti announced May 7 the arrest of 17 members of an extreme leftist revolutionary group, according to an Agence France-Presse report.

The announcement said the group sought to mount "an armed insurrection against the government" in order "to set up an extreme leftist dictatorship."

The 17 were described as mostly young professional men and women as well as students. They reportedly were part of a group calling itself the Revolutionary Workers Party which was affiliated with the Fourth International, a Trotskyite organization headquartered in Brussels, Belgium.

Priests back revolution. The Priests for the Third World Movement May 2 issued a communique declaring their "formal rejection of the present capitalist system" and their adherence to the "revolutionary process." The movement had been founded by the Brazilian Archbishop Helder Camara.

The declaration came out of a meeting of the movement held in Santa Fe. The movement claimed 400 members of Argentina's 4,000 priests.

The communique called for "socialization of the means of production" and "the appearance of a new man" through the revolutionary process.

Five churches in Corrientes had been occupied by parishoners March 29 in protest against the excommunication of Rev. Oscar Marturet, a member of the Priests for the Third World Movement.

The conflict developed when Marturet brought legal action in which Corrientes Archbishop Francisco Vicentin was charged with complicity in alleged "police harrassment." An arrest order was issued for Vicentin March 23 when he refused to testify in the case, but an Argentine appeals court later annulled the order. Vicentin responded to the suit by excommunicating Marturet. Le Monde of Paris reported April 5 that Argentine police had removed the protesters from the churches.

Press crackdown. The January issue of the magazine Inedito was seized by the government several hours before its distribution to newstands, Le Monde reported Jan. 9. The edition included an article on divisions within the armed forces. The seizure of Inedito evoked comparison with the banning in 1969 of the magazine Primera Plana, which had also contained a report on armed forces disagreements. Inedito reappeared in February.

Three weeks later the government closed the pictorial magazine Asi, according to a Miami Herald report Feb. 7. The action followed Asi's publication of photographs of a railroad accident Feb. 1 in which 139 persons were killed.

The supreme court ruled March 5 that President Juan Carlos Ongania was authorized under the state of siege declared June 30, 1969 to prevent the publication of magazines he considered dangerous to the public order.

Before the court had issued its decision, the weekly political magazine Resumen had been suspended for an indefinite period, the Miami Herald reported March 6. The government gave no explanation for the action, although the last issue reportedly had contained an article critical of governmental officials.

Newspaper temporarily closed. The political police May 23 closed the daily newspaper Cronica, which claimed the largest circulation in Latin America. It was the first time the government of President Juan Carlos Ongania had banned publication of a newspaper, although seven other publications had previously been shut down. The ban was lifted May 26 with no comment.

The paper was charged with having falsely reported a student's death in antigovernment protests that took place in Cordoba May 22–23. A decree issued by the Secretariat of Information and Tourism said the "notoriously false" report was likely to contribute to unrest. The decree closed the newspaper indefinitely; editions already on the newsstands were seized by police.

Government control of broadcasting. The government published a decree Feb. 14 making the Interior Ministry responsible for "orientation and control" of all radio and television stations in Argentina. Private stations had previously been under the control of the government-sponsored National Council for Radio and Television, which, the decree said, had been found deficient. Under the new ruling, the Interior Ministry was to issue and renew licenses to commercial stations and to see that "the national style of life" was preserved in broadcasts.

Renewal of Terrorism

A new wave of terrorism swept Argentina during the early 1970s. This terrorism took form with the strengthening of the movement for the return of Peron. It has been characterized by terroristic activity by groups with often clashing ideology. Their political orientations range from far left to far right, but these often antagonistic groups frequently claim the same short-term goal— originally the return of Peron, later the continuation of his presumed program.

The ERP (Ejercito Revolucionario Popular, or Ejecerito Revolucionario del Pueblo, People's Revolutionary Army), an allegedly Trotskyist organization, is the largest, best known, most active and best organized terrorist group in Argentina. The FAL (Frente Argentino de Liberacion, also identified as Fuerzas Argentinas de Liberacion, Fuerzas Armadas de Liberacion and Argentine [or Armed] Liberation Forces [or Front]) is a terrorist group formed by dissident Communist Party members and described as both "Marxist" and "with no clearly defined ideology." Two terrorist groups, the Montoneros (which described itself as "Peronist and Christian") and the FAR (Fuerzas Armadas Revolucionarias, or Revolutionary Armed Forces), merged in November 1973 and kept the name Montoneros. Another Trotskyist terrorist group is known as the Red Faction (Partido Revolucionario de los Trabajadores [Fraccion Roja]). A rightwing terrorist group was identified as MANO (Movimiento Argentina Nacional Organizado, or Argentine National Organized Movement).

Aramburu kidnaped & slain. Lt. Gen. Pedro Eugenio Aramburu, 67, a former provisional president of Argentina, was kidnaped from his home May 29, 1970 by four men, two of them wearing army officers' uniforms. Aramburu's body was found July 16 in the cellar of an old farmhouse near Timote, about 300 miles west of Buenos Aires. He had been shot twice in the chest.

Following the abduction, at least a dozen communiques had been received from political organizations claiming credit for the abduction, but the Juan Jose Valle-Montoneros Command, named for a Peronist army general executed in 1956, offered what was called convincing evidence that it held Aramburu.

The Valle Command asserted in a May 31 communique that it had found Aramburu guilty of the execution of 27 Peronists accused of attempting a coup in 1956 to restore Peron to power.

A month-long search for Aramburu and clues to the kidnapers reportedly failed to turn up any substantial evidence until a July 1 terrorist raid on La Calera, a suburban town near Cordoba. Fifteen terrorists claiming to be members of the Montoneros group took over the town for about two hours, robbed a bank and occupied police and telephone offices. In a shootout with police following the raid, several of the terrorists were seriously injured, among them Emilio Angel Maza, 24, who died July 6. Maza was later identified as one of the Aramburu kidnapers. More than 10 arrests were made in connection with the La Calera raid, and these reportedly led to other arrests and the discovery of Aramburu's body near Timote.

Fernando Abal Medina, 23, described as having "received Communist training in Cuba," was identified by Argentine police July 11 as the mastermind of the abduction. The police announced Sept. 8 that Abal Medina and Carlos Gustavo Ramus, a second suspect in Aramburu's kidnap-murder, had been killed in a gun battle with police.

Inspector Osvaldo Sandoval, a key witness in the trial of five persons charged in connection with Aramburu's murder, was shot and killed in Buenos Aires Nov. 14. A group that identified itself as the Argentine Liberation Forces claimed responsibility for Sandoval's death.

(Carlos Raul Capuano Martinez, sought for alleged involvement in the Aramburu kidnap-murder, was killed in a shootout with Buenos Aires police Aug. 17, 1972.)

Paraguayan consul kidnaped. Joaquin Waldemar Sanchez, Paraguayan consul in the town of Ituzaingo in Corrientes Province, was abducted in Buenos Aires March 24, 1970 by a group of men who identified themselves as members of the FAL (Argentine Liberation Front). Sanchez was released by his kidnapers March 28 after the Argentine government refused to release two political prisoners. Argentina became the first Western Hemisphere government to defy kidnapers' demands in a recent wave of terrorist kidnapings in Latin America.

The kidnapers had demanded the release of two political prisoners—Carlos Della Nave and Alejandro Baldu—in exchange for Sanchez.

However, in an apparent attempt to force a showdown, the Argentine government announced March 25 that Baldu was "a fugitive from justice" who had not yet been captured and that Della Nave was being "processed for common crimes" and would not be released.

The kidnapers replied that they would execute Sanchez "by firing squad" and "begin the execution of all managers of American business" if their demands were not met. They also announced that they were extending their deadline for Sanchez' execution, originally set for 10 p.m. March 25.

Sanchez was released unharmed early March 28 in a suburb of Buenos Aires. His kidnapers said "humanitarian reasons" were behind their decision to spare his life. In an earlier statement, the kidnapers had cited their organization's previous unwillingness to shed unnecessary blood. "But now," they continued, "there has been killed, not in combat, but in cold blood, one of our dearest comrades [Baldu]. This changes our position and obliges us to adjust to circumstances." In a statement March 28 they warned that they were prepared to "undertake the execution of an undetermined number of police and officials."

Interior Minister Francisco Imaz hailed Sanchez' release March 28 and maintained that the government's decision to reject the kidnapers' demands "was the only position possible. Any other position would have been tremendously dangerous for the future of the country."

Soviet diplomat escapes. Right-wing kidnapers failed in an attempt to abduct Soviet diplomat Yuri Pivoravov March 29, 1970, when Pivoravov escaped from the getaway car as it was being pursued by police. Pivovarov, assistant commercial attache at the Soviet embassy in Buenos Aries, apparently was not seriously hurt in the incident. Police, alerted by the screams of Pivovarov's wife, shot and injured three of the kidnapers, who were later captured when the car crashed.

Argentine officials revealed March 30 that a deputy federal police inspector, Carlos Benigno Balbuena, was one of the three wounded kidnapers. The other two men, Guillermo John Jansen and Albert Germinal Borrell, were unconnected with the police, the government said.

Earlier, the right-wing Argentine National Organized Movement (MANO) had claimed responsibility for the kidnaping attempt and described the three wounded men as "war heroes." (MANO had threatened March 27 to kill Soviet Ambassador to Argentina Yuri Volski and his family in reprisal for the Sanchez kidnaping.)

Blast leads to bomb factory. An explosion April 4 in Buenos Aires led police to what was believed to be a terrorist bomb factory. Two persons were injured in the apparently accidental explosion. An address book found at the site led to more than 100 arrests April 5. A federal judge ordered trials for six arrested youths April 6.

The Parke Davis pharmaceutical plant near Buenos Aires was severely damaged by an explosion June 18; according to unconfirmed reports three employes were reported missing and feared dead. Nine bombs exploded June 27 in Buenos Aires, Rosario and Cordoba; U.S.-owned firms were among the targets.

Death penalty restored. The government June 2 reinstituted the death penalty, abolished in 1886, for kidnaping and terrorism.

Economic & Other Developments

'Heavy peso.' Argentina's currency was converted to a new "heavy peso" Jan. 1. The new peso, valued at 3½ to $1 U.S., was worth 100 old pesos.

Tax aid. Treasury Secretary Louis B. May announced the enactment of new legislation that increased the income tax deductions allowed for dependents from $170 to $274 each, an increase of 60%, with deductions of $515 allowed for university students. The law, reported Jan. 12 by the Journal of Commerce, also included provisions taxing certain carbonated beverages and setting an annual motor vehicle fee.

1970–74 development plan. The 1970–74 national development plan, published Feb. 1 by the Argentine National Development Council, called for rapid and sustained economic growth, accompanied by progressive redistribution of income. The plan forecast a 31% increase in the gross domestic product (GDP), resulting from an annual growth rate of 5.5%. Industrial production was expected to increase by 40% over the five-year period, while agricultural production was to rise by 19%. By 1974 total investment was expected to reach 22% of the GDP (compared with an average of 19% in recent years), and an annual increase of 4.2% was forecast for per capita income in real terms. Real wages were expected to increase by 5% annually.

The plan allocated top priority to expansion of exports, particularly manufactured products. Export increases were estimated at 7.4% annually, reaching $2.3 billion by 1974 or 43% more than in 1969. Export incentives were to be expected to promote sale of nontraditional manufactured products. Import increases were projected at only 10% over the five years, reaching $1.7 billion in 1974.

The plan estimated an increase in public investment from $1.4 billion in 1969 to $2 billion in 1974, a 40% increase. Appreciable increases in investment in education, housing and health programs would be emphasized.

Trade law sets tariff cuts. A new decree aimed at stimulating industrial production and authorizing reduction of import duties on some capital goods not manufactured in Argentina, was reported by the Journal of Commerce Feb. 13. The law also authorized preferential treatment for development of basic industries such as oil, energy and transportation and for the establishment of industrial parks in certain areas, particularly in the interior.

European trade mission. Economics Minister Jose Maria Dagnino Pastore concluded a European trade tour Feb. 20, following talks with trade and economic officials in West Germany, Switzerland, Italy, France and Great Britain. He had described the trip as part of an attempt "to set forth an economic program, the success of which depends in large measure on the access of Argentine products to external markets."

Inflation. Progress was reported in the battle against inflation.

In an effort to force meat prices down, the government forbade the serving of beef in restaurants on Thursdays and Fridays, the New York Times reported April 28. The decision, attacked by cattle interests as well as by ordinary Argentinians, who consume an average of four pounds of beef weekly, resulted in the resignation of Agriculture Minister Lorenzo

Raggio and his deputy minister Thomas J. de Anchorena.

Power expansion. Argentina continued efforts to bring electricity to additional users.

The Inter-American Development Bank announced May 7 approval of two loans equivalent to $30 million for the expansion of electric power systems in the Argentine interior. The loans, $9 million from the IDB's ordinary capital resources and $21 million from the Fund for Special Operations, were to help finance the first stage in a 10-year (1970–1980), $1.2 billion power expansion program.

200-mile sea limits reaffirmed. Nine Latin American nations which claimed 200-mile territorial sea limits upheld May 9 the right of all maritime states to "establish the limits of their sovereignty and maritime jurisdiction, in accordance with their geographical and geological characteristics. . . ." Meeting in Montevideo, Uruguay May 4–9, the participants adopted the Declaration of Montevideo on Sea Rights. The statement was signed by Argentina, Brazil, Chile, Ecuador, El Salvador, Nicaragua, Panama, Peru and Uruguay.

In addition to upholding the 200-mile sea limit, the declaration also affirmed "the right of maritime countries to dispose of the natural resources of the sea adjacent to their coast and the floor and sub-floor of the same sea, in order to promote the maximum development of their economies and raise the living standard of their peoples." The statement also asserted the right "to explore, conserve and exploit the living resources" in territorial waters "and to regulate the management of fishing and aquatic hunting."

Military Remove President

Ongania ousted by military. President Juan Carlos Ongania was forced to resign June 8 by the commanders in chief of Argentina's army, navy and air force. In assuming power, Army Lt. Gen. Alejandro Agustin Lanusse, Navy Adm.

Pedro J. Gnavi and Air Force Brig. Gen. Carlos Alberto Rey pledged to "establish order" in the country and to name a new president within 10 days. Ongania's ouster came four years after he had assumed power following a military coup overthrowing civilian President Arturo Umberto Illia. Ongania, a lieutenant general and former army commander, had been in retirement at the time he was named to replace Illia.

A crisis reportedly had been building up between the Ongania government and the military leaders for months. It erupted over the issue of how much power the military commanders should share with Ongania in governing the country. Ongania rejected a "political plan," submitted by Lanusse, demanding that presidential power be shared with the commanders, and dismissed Lanusse early June 8. Immediately after Ongania's action, the military chiefs announced their intention of taking over the government.

In a series of radio communiques June 8, the armed forces heads first "invited" Ongania to resign, but later announced that military commanders had "decided to reassume political power in the republic" and Ongania had "been removed from his duties as president of the nation."

At the same time, the military commanders sent troops to surround the presidential palace, where Ongania had barricaded himself under the protection of 1,200 cavalrymen serving as presidential guards. In addition, the commanders announced that troops were moving toward military bases in Buenos Aires reported to be loyal to Ongania.

In a resignation statement signed late June 8, Ongania said: "The events that the country has experienced in these final hours force me, under pressure of arms, to leave the post of president of the republic. I assume all responsibility for events that have occurred since the beginning of the Argentine revolution, while at the same time imposing on my successors the responsibility that may fall to them before the people and history for the events that may have just occurred."

Speaking for the junta June 9, Adm. Gnavi pledged "support for the demo-

cratic and representative system of government, based on the formation of truly responsible political parties," and promised that the new regime would establish "an authentic, democratic, republican, representative and federal" government in Argentina, though he declined to offer any date for elections. Gnavi praised Ongania for cutting the rate of monetary inflation in Argentina from 30% in 1966 to 6.6% in 1969, but he criticized him for his hard-line wage policy and his refusal to return the government to civilian rule.

In one of their first actions, the three-man junta June 9 dismissed Interior Minister Gen. Francisco Jose Imaz and federal police chief Gen. Mario Fonseca. Imaz's duties were temporarily taken over by Defense Minister Jose Rafael Caceres Monie, while Fonseca was replaced by Gen. Jorge Caceres Monie. The remainder of the cabinet, as well as provincial and municipal officials, were asked to remain in office. Banks and money-changing offices were closed June 9–10 to check possible speculation against the Argentine peso, but the nation was reported calm and most business was carried on as usual.

(The U.S. State Department announced June 12 that U.S. recognition of the new junta was not necessary "as there is no basic discontinuity in the military government of Argentina." "Diplomatic relations are continuing normally and there is no interruption in bilateral programs," a spokesman said.)

New Regime

Gen. Levingston president. The ruling three-man junta June 13 named Brig. Gen. Roberto Marcelo Levingston, 50, as the new president.

A military intelligence specialist, Levingston served as military attache in Washington, D.C. and as representative to the Inter-American Defense Board from September 1968 until June 11, when he was called to Buenos Aires by the new junta.

Described as a close friend of junta member Lanusse, Levingston was educated in the Argentine military college and later in the army intelligence school.

Levingston was sworn in June 18 and then delivered the oath of office to five of his cabinet ministers who had been named June 17.

The new cabinet members:

Economy and Labor—Carlos Moyano Llerena; Interior—Gen. Eduardo Francisco McLoughlin; Public Works and Services—Aldo Ferrer; Social Welfare—Francisco Manrique; and Foreign Relations—Luis Maria de Pablo Pardo. (Jose Rafael Caceres Monie remained as defense minister.)

Levingston's ministers of justice and education were sworn in July 3, completing the new cabinet. Jaime Luis Enrique Perriaux, a lawyer and businessman, was appointed to head the Justice Ministry, while Jose Luis Cantini was named education minister. (Juan Alejandro Luco, considered a neo-Peronist, was sworn in July 14 as labor secretary.)

Early actions. The new regime June 18 devalued the Argentine peso by 12.5%, shrinking the peso's value from 28.57 cents (U.S.) to 25 cents. Foreign exchange offices in the nation had remained closed since the June 8 coup. The devaluation was considered a political rather than an economic move.

In a statement outlining its policies, the new regime pledged June 20 to establish an "efficient and stable democracy" based on a representative system which "will ensure man's freedom and his fundamental rights." The document did not give a date for the holding of elections in Argentina, but promised to "maintain political pluralism, backed by an active participation of the population and its legitimate and authentic representation through political parties in the Congress."

The regime added that it would fight communism through "positive, preventive and not merely repressive measures" and that "in peace, a military power will be developed to be able to permanently disuade potential internal and external enemies." The document also stated that foreign relations with European countries, including the "Communist countries of East Europe" would be strengthened, along with relations with African and Asian nations.

In a formal decree issued June 19, the armed forces chiefs who had staged the coup stipulated that all important decrees and laws would require their signature as well as that of the new president, Gen. Levingston.

In his first speech to the nation, Levingston said June 23: "I, as president of the nation, have the full and exclusive responsibility for executive action. I do not share this power, I exercise it fully as established in the conditions under which I accepted the job." Levingston also indicated that although his government intended to return the nation to constitutional rule, "the process will not be short."

(Levingston issued a decree June 21 releasing seven political prisoners and lifting arrest orders which had been issued against three others. Most of the persons involved were labor leaders from Cordoba, where the local branch of the General Confederation of Labor had staged a successful general strike June 16.)

The government announced Aug. 31 that it was lifting the ban on four publications suspended during the regime of Juan Carlos Ongania. The four weekly magazines which were authorized to appear were Primera Plana, Ojo, Prensa Confidencial and Marchar.

The Argentine communications industry became a completely government-owned monopoly Sept. 25 when the nation took control of all telegraph and telephone communications with Europe. Communications between Argentina and other Latin American nations had come under government control Sept. 18, while communications with the U.S. became a government monopoly Sept. 22. The links to other parts of the world were already under the government-operated communications system.

Unrest continues. The armed forces took control of Rosario, the nation's second largest city, June 30, after the city's 3,500 policemen had seized their headquarters in a salary dispute. The wildcat strike ended July 1 when provincial authorities pledged to grant wage increases retroactive to January. During the police strike armed bandits stole $75,000 from messengers carrying money sacks to a Rosario bank.

The Parke Davis pharmaceutical plant near Buenos Aires was severely damaged by an explosion June 18; according to unconfirmed reports three employes were reported missing and feared dead. Nine bombs exploded June 27 in Buenos Aires, Rosario and Cordoba; U.S.-owned firms were among the targets.

Police clashed with students in Buenos Aires June 27; the youths were protesting the death of a leftist student leader killed a year ago in anti-government demonstrations. Student-police disorders continued in Buenos Aires as youths protested the arrest of student leader Daniel Laufer. Le Monde of Paris reported July 4 that 248 students of the architecture faculty had been arrested in the disorders.

In a nationwide speech Aug. 22, President Levingston sharply attacked "extremist groups" representing "ideological slogans of change and revision through spectacular violence." He charged that most of the groups' actions "correspond to an international plan of agitation which has chosen our homeland in the framework of its principal objectives on a continental scale." Pledging the government's intention to exert its authority over such groups, the president said that Argentines could "coexist with those who criticize our ideas, with those who fight them," but could not coexist "with those who refuse to reason, with those who pretend to negotiate the death of innocent individuals with the freedom of criminals ... [and] with those who wish to destroy the bases of justice...."

Labor leader killed. Jose Varela Alonso, 57, was shot to death Aug. 27 in suburban Buenos Aires as he was being driven to his office. Alonso, a supporter of former dictator Juan D. Peron, was head of the nation's Textile Workers' Union. He was considered a moderate and had cooperated with the government of Juan Carlos Ongania. He and the late Augusto Timoteo Vandor had clashed in the fight for leadership of the Peronist labor movement before Vandor's murder in June, 1969.

A police statement Aug. 27 said Alonso's driver had stopped the car after the occupants of another auto indicated he had a flat tire. The occupants of the other car knocked the driver unconscious and shot Alonso several times in the head.

In a speech to the nation that night, President Roberto Marcelo Levingston condemned the murder and pledged to find the guilty persons. He added that the offenders "deceive themselves if they believe they have eliminated an obstacle in their road, because they have reinforced another obstacle—the solidarity of the Argentine people, who, in their pain, tighten their ranks and surmount their differences."

Police said Aug. 29 that the Montoneros Command of the National Liberation Army had claimed responsibility for the murder and had said in a communique that Alonso had been killed because he "was a traitor to the motherland, to the working class and to the Peronist movement."

Elections delayed. President Levingston told a meeting of provincial governors Sept. 29 that general elections in Argentina would not be held for four or five years. He also reaffirmed the government ban on the existence of political parties. "Our first step has been to reopen communication with the genuine leaders of all currents of opinion." he said. But he added that the "parties that existed before 1966 are a thing of the past. It is the responsibility of their leaders, many of whom merit the nation's gratitude, to understand this."

In a related development, leaders of five political parties issued a joint declaration Nov. 11 calling for an immediate return to electoral democracy, legalization of political parties (which had been officially banned following the 1966 coup), and increased government action to prevent foreign economic domination of Argentina.

The signers of the document included Jorge Paladino, Juan D. Peron's official representative in Argentina, and Ricardo Balbin, a leader of the People's Radical party. Other signers represented the leftist Progressive Democrat party, the

Socialist party and the rightist Popular Conservative party.

Wage increase decreed. Economy Minister Carlos Moyano Llerena Aug. 15 announced an across-the-board 7% wage increase for the private sector, effective Sept. 1. The plan also called for additional selective wage increases, averaging 6%, for lower paid workers effective in January 1971. The government's economic advisers had argued that any increases higher than 5% would be too inflationary.

General Confederation of Labor Secretary General Jose Rucci denounced the increase and said that "regrettably, once again, the working class demands have been rejected." Labor leaders charged that cost of living increases had surpassed the 7% wage increase even before it went into effect.

In an Aug. 22 speech, President Levingston added that the government had drafted an overall "plan of wage and salary increases by stages with important complementary measures." "This plan will be adjusted periodically on the basis of the results that will be obtained," he said.

The CGT Sept. 14 presented President Levingston with an economic and social plan designed to avoid violence in the country. The plan called for the nationalization of banks and insurance firms, transfer of land to those who work on it, limitation of foreign ownership, and participation of Argentine workers in public and private firms. The document also called for decent salaries and exemption from taxes for workers, abolition of usury, and free elections.

CGT calls 3 general strikes. Argentine workers staged a 24-hour general strike Oct. 9 to protest President Levingston's economic policies.

The strike, called by the General Labor Confederation (CGT), was termed by union leaders 100% effective in industrial areas and about 90% effective elsewhere; government officials reported that 77% of the nation's factory and office workers stayed home. The workers were demanding an across-the-board wage increase of 20%.

Little violence was reported during the strike but 15 terrorist bombs were exploded in major cities Oct. 8.

A second CGT-called general strike took place Oct. 22. The fresh 10-hour strike, which paralyzed transportation and industry in major cities, led to more than 200 arrests and at least two deaths, including one policeman. Some militant trade union leaders had called for violent street demonstrations, but police managed to keep most of the violence under control.

A third CGT general strike, this one lasting 36 hours, was staged Nov. 12–13. The walkout virtually paralyzed Argentina, shutting down industry and businesses and halting transportation, including the national railroad system. Demonstrations and police clashes were reported in Salta, Cordoba and Tucuman. One man was reported killed in Salta. Buenos Aires was reported relatively quiet. Troops were called into Tucuman Nov. 12 to handle violent demonstrations which had erupted the previous day.

Cabinet crisis. President Roberto M. Levingston faced his first cabinet crisis with the resignations of Interior Minister Eduardo McLoughlin Oct. 13 and Economics Minister Carlos Moyano Llerena Oct. 14. The government closed all foreign exchange markets Oct. 15 in an effort to prevent a run on the peso in the wake of the resignations.

McLoughlin reportedly resigned over disagreements within the Interior Ministry on the status of former dictator Juan Peron. Assistant Secretary for Political Affairs Enrique Gilardi Novaro was reported to have drafted an amnesty law clearing Peron of all charges, opening the way for his return to Argentina. McLoughlin was also reported in disagreement with the government's economic policies.

Moyano Llerena's resignation reportedly stemmed from concern over McLoughlin's resignation, as well as disagreement with government policies. In his letter of resignation Moyano Llerena charged that Levingston's policies were weak and ambiguous.

Minister of Public Works Aldo M. Ferrer, a controversial economist considered to be left of center, was named economics minister Oct. 16. Ferrer reportedly favored a reduction of the role of foreign investment. Moyano Llerena and McLoughlin had favored increased foreign investment.

Levingston designated Oscar Colombo as the new minister of public works Oct. 22 to replace Ferrer. Leonardo Anidjar was named finance secretary, replacing Enrique Folcini who resigned. Jorge Haiek was named secretary of energy, replacing Daniel Fernandez,who was named president of the Central Bank. Fernandez succeeded Egidio Ianella.

Brig. Gen. Arturo Armando Cordon Aguirre was sworn in as interior minister Nov. 3 to succeed Brig. Gen. McLoughlin, whose resignation had triggered the cabinet crisis.

Unrest. New violence broke out in the northwestern city of Catamarca Nov. 17 when 300 policemen rebelled against the local government for its refusal to meet their pay demands and took over the city prison. Federal riot police were flown in from Buenos Aires as demonstrations began in support of the police. At least two persons were killed in gunfire Nov. 18 when mobs attempted to storm the provincial government building.

A nationwide 24-hour teachers' strike took place Nov. 18.

1971: Unrest Continues

Protests in Cordoba

Cordoba, generally regarded as a focus of Argentine labor and political dissent, continued to be a center of unrest and sporadic violence during 1971.

CGT general strike. Workers in Cordoba staged a 14-hour strike Jan. 29 in an attempt to put pressure on the government for higher wages and better working conditions. The strike, called by the General Confederation of Labor, was reported to have been almost total. Four small bombs were exploded during the day, but no casualties and little damage were reported.

Strikes & riots. At least three people were killed in riots in Cordoba as it was hit by general strikes and demonstrations March 12–19. The violence resulted in hundreds of injuries and arrests and in an estimated $4 million in damages.

Cordoba was declared an emergency zone March 18 and Gen. Lopez Aufranc of the Third Army Division took control of the city. The army also threatened courts-martial and possible execution by firing squad for demonstrators attacking soldiers.

Workers and students in Cordoba were protesting the government's wage policies and the general economic situation in Argentina, as well as the appointment of Jose Camilo Uriburu, a right-wing nationalist, as governor of Cordoba Province March 1, succeeding Bernardo Bas who had resigned Feb. 25. The Cordoba violence resulted in the resignation of Uriburu late March 16; he was temporarily succeeded by Helvio Gouzden, governor of La Pampa Province.

Economic Developments

Situation gets worse. The economic situation in Argentina had deteriorated sharply during late 1970 and the first two months of 1971. The rate of inflation, which had risen to 20% during 1970 from 6.6% in 1969, had reached 9.5% for January and February. Economy Minister Aldo Ferrer had originally forecast a 10% inflation ceiling for the whole of 1970, but had been forced to raise the prediction to around 30%, the newsletter Latin America reported March 12.

President Roberto Marcello Levingston announced March 7 that wage increases in 1971 would be held to a ceiling of 19%, of which 13% was to allow for inflation. (Unions had demanded raises of 40% to 200%.) Price controls on items critical to the cost-of-living index went into effect March 8.

An important element in the inflation was the increase in the price of meat by 130% during the past 14 months. The shortage of beef had almost decimated Argentina's traditional beef exports (down 10.1% in tonnage in 1970, though up slightly in value) and created a need for the importation of cattle. Levingston had announced Feb. 26 that the government, effective March 15, would intervene in the meat business by fixing a selling price of 14¢ a pound for live animals, above which special taxes would be instituted along with a possible cutoff of internal consumption for two weeks a month. In addition, credit facilities would be made available to meat packers and producers.

The bankruptcy of Deltec International Finance Corporation's Compania Swift de la Plata, the nation's largest private meat packer, in December 1970 followed by the collapse of the British-owned Anglo Meat Packing Co. in January and another British-owned house, Liebig's, in February, had diminished meat packing operations. The newsletter Latin America reported March 19 that Swift's Rosario plant had been reopened on a limited basis by a subsidiary of Campbell's Soup Co. the previous week.

(The Economy Ministry reported Feb. 5 that the gross domestic product had risen 4.8% in 1970, compared with 6.9% in 1969.)

Loans. The Inter-American Development Bank (IDB) approved a $40 million loan Jan. 7 to help Argentina expand and improve nine national universities and to help provide financial aid to needy students. The three-year program, with an estimated total cost of $71 million, was to aid the universities of Cordoba, Cuyo, La Plata, Litoral, Nordeste, Rosario, Sur, Tecnologica and Tucuman.

A month earlier the IDB had approved five loans totaling $38.3 million to aid in the construction of a three-mile bridge between Puerto Unzue, Argentina and Fray Bentos, Uruguay. The bridge was to be the first direct land link between Argentina and Uruguay. Funds were to be used to help construct a five-mile access road in Uruguay and to improve the highway network of northeastern Argentina. The loans, originally approved in December 1970, were reported by the Alliance of Progress Newsletter Jan. 18. The loans included $1.2 million in Argentine pesos, the first IDB

operation with the special funds provided by Argentina in 1970.

A group of banks led by Wells Fargo Bank of San Francisco granted a $50 million, five-year term loan to Argentina, it was reported Jan. 25. The loan was to help finance construction of a $100 million rail and road project across the Parana Delta in northern Argentina. The banks participating included Western American Bank (Europe) Ltd., London; Hambros Banks Ltd., London; and Security Pacific National Bank, Los Angeles.

President Levingston met with Uruguay President Jorge Pacheco Areco in La Barra de San Juan, Uruguay Feb. 17 and 18. The meetings resulted in agreements under which Argentina pledged to extend credits to Uruguay for financing bilateral development projects, including $2 million for the completion of a bridge from Colon to Paysandu across the River Uruguay.

The World Bank April 1 announced its approval of two loans to Argentina totaling $149.5 million for transportation projects. An $84 million loan was to help finance the first two years of a five-year railway rehabilitation program and was to be used mainly for the purchase of freight cars, rehabilitation of locomotives and cars, renewal and maintenance of tracks, and procurance of telecommunications equipment. The second loan, totaling $67.5 million, was to aid a project to construct and improve about 700 miles of highways, along with feasibility and engineering studies on another 2,200 miles of highways for future projects.

President Replaced

The Argentine armed forces in March 1971 again removed a president and chose a new chief executive to succeed him.

Levingston ousted. President Roberto Marcelo Levingston was ousted from his post March 23 by the commanders of Argentina's three armed services. The dismissal followed a week of severe riots in Cordoba and problems within the economy.

In an announcement broadcast over the government radio March 23, the three commanders—Adm. Pedro Alberto

Jose Gnavi (navy), Gen. Alejandro Augustin Lanusse (army) and air force commander Brig. Gen. Carlos Alberto Rey—said they would "resume political power until the Argentine revolution has been completed." In a statement issued later that day, Gen. Lanusse, speaking for the junta, called on "all Argentines, without distinctions or exclusions, to participate actively in the task of finding and consolidating solutions for the problems of the country through an ample and generous accord, rising above the antagonisms of the past." The junta also urged all officials and governors to remain in their posts.

In one of its first actions, the junta March 23 lifted the state of emergency that had been in effect in Cordoba since the recent riots. In addition, the military government restored Brig. Gen. Ezequiel Martinez as chairman of the joint chiefs of staff. Martinez, who had been named chairman March 3, had been dismissed by Levingston March 19 in a move which aggravated the crisis. Martinez, who was ousted, according to Levingston, for "a disciplinary infraction of grave character," was allegedly plotting with Gen. Rey against Levingston.

The junta also acted March 23 to lift the 19% ceiling on wage increases for 1971, while stressing the policy of "Argentinization of the economy." In addition, the junta March 23 reappointed Francisco Manrique as social welfare minister; and confirmed that Economy Minister Aldo Ferrer would remain in his post.

In a last ditch effort to avoid his ouster, Levingston March 22 had fired Gen. Lanusse as commander in chief of the army for not having "acted with sufficient authority" to quell the violence in Cordoba. However, the effort was futile since both Gen. Rey and Adm. Gnavi announced support for Lanusse, and his replacement—federal police chief Jorge Esteban Caceres Monie—announced he would hold the post only long enough to hand it back to Lanusse. Lanusse also received support from other key military leaders, particularly from Gen. Alcides Lopez Aufranc, commander of the Third Army, which was based in Cordoba.

Levingston left the presidential palace before dawn March 23. The three armed forces commanders officially announced their assumption of full governmental powers shortly after noon the same day.

Lanusse named president. Army Commander Alejandro Agustin Lanusse, 52, leader of the junta which ousted Levingston, was named president by the junta March 25 and was sworn in March 26.

After he was sworn in, President Lanusse, who reportedly retained his post as head of the army, swore in two new cabinet ministers—Social Welfare Minister Francisco Guillermo Manrique and Interior Minister Arturo Mor Roig. The six other ministers in the cabinet were retained from Levingston's administration—Economy Minister Aldo Ferrer, Foreign Affairs Minister Luis Maria de Pablo Pardo, Defense Minister Jose Rafael Caceres Monie, Justice Minister Jaime Perriaux, Education Minister Jose Luis Cantini, and Public Works Minister Oscar Colombo.

In a fresh attempt to solve the crisis over meat prices, the junta March 25 announced a ban on the sale of beef beginning March 29. The ban, instead of running two straight weeks of every month as envisaged under Levingston, would alternate every other week for an initial period of three months. (Argentines, for whom beef is the main staple, ate an estimated 184 pounds of beef per capita in 1969.)

Political parties legalized. Interior Minister Arturo Mor Roig announced April 1 the legalization of political parties in Argentina.

Mor Roig, a member of the People's Radical party, reported that the legal rights of political parties, their property and other possessions that had been taken from them by the military government would be restored. He added that rules governing the activities of the political parties would be issued within three months, explaining that the rehabilitation of the parties was intended to help the country prepare for a turn to democracy.

(President Alejandro Agustin Lanusse announced April 15 that he would hand over power to a constitutional government within three years.)

The government announced June 1 that the organization of political parties would be permitted beginning July 1.

Mor Roig announced June 11 that the Argentine Communist party would be permitted to organize and participate in future elections.

An Organic Law of Political Parties was accepted by the government June 30 with modifications. Each party must "express adhesion to the national constitution in its declaration of principles, programs or bases of political action." Judges, bank officials and presidents of state or mixed enterprises would be disqualified from holding directive positions in the parties.

Abortive coup against Lanusse. President Alejandro Lanusse retained control of the government after an attempted coup by what were described as "leftist-nationalist" elements failed May 11.

The central figure in the plot against Lanusse was reported to be retired Gen. Eduardo Rafael LaBanca, an anti-Marxist and nationalist. Despite LaBanca's anti-Communist stance, he had obtained the support of some left-wing groups, especially within the Peronist labor movement. In 1969, LaBanca had been forced to leave the army as the result of his activities in opposition to then-President Juan Carlos Ongania.

The conspiracy centered in Tucuman, where Capt. Jose Meritello attempted to rally the garrison on May 10 to support a "nationalist revolution." He was arrested by his commanding officer.

Cabinet reshuffled. Economy Minister Aldo Ferrer resigned May 29—apparently under compulsion—after President Lanusse had announced May 26 that his post would be abolished in order to create four new equal Cabinet posts: Finance, Commerce and Industry, Agriculture, and Labor.

Lanusse dismissed Pub. Works Minister Colombo and two men in charge of the state-run petroleum complex—Manuel Reimundes, president of the state oil company, and Secretary of Energy Jorge Haiek, according to a June 9 report. Lanusse named Gen. Jorge Raul

Carcagno to direct military supervision on the Yacimientos Petroleum Co. (YPF). The dismissals were reported to be the result of a controversy involving foreign investment in Argentine industry.

Pedro Antonio Gordilla was sworn in as minister of public works June 21.

Foreign exchange resumed. Argentine banks resumed foreign money transactions June 1. They had been suspended May 27 after speculation that the peso would be devalued. It had been devalued by 1% April 5. The devaluation, from 4 to 4.04 pesos to the U.S. dollar, was smaller than expected due to the start of a new policy of "mini-devaluations," a system which institutes small but frequent devaluations and thereby hopes to counter speculation against the currency.

The government devalued the peso 4.76% June 25 from 4.20 to 4.40 to the dollar.

Foreign Developments

Cuenca del Plata conference. The chancellors of Argentina, Bolivia, Brazil, Paraguay and Uruguay met June 1 for the fourth Cuenca del Plata conference in Asuncion, Paraguay. Twenty-seven resolutions of regional interest were approved in the three-day session.

Another agreement was concluded between Argentina and Brazil June 3 for the utilization and juridical regulation of contiguous international rivers.

Agreement on Falklands. Secret talks which began June 21 between Argentina and Britain on the opening of air and sea links to the Falkland Islands (called the Malvinas by the Argentines) ended in agreement July 1. Both sides had agreed to put aside the difficult question of sovereignty over the islands in order to settle other key issues. They stated in a communique July 1 that nothing contained in the agreement could signify renunciation by either government of its position on the question of sovereignty.

The agreement, signed by David Scott, British undersecretary of state at the foreign office, and Juan Carlos Beltramino, council minister of the Argentine embassy in London, called for creation of a special consultative committee to resolve any problems in communications and movement of persons from the islands; grant of a document to the islands' residents permitting them free travel within Argentina; exemption from taxes on certain equipment for islanders who pass through Argentina; and exemption from military service for island residents.

The agreement also provided for Argentina to establish a weekly air service for passengers, mail and cargo between the mainland and the islands and a similar maritime shipping service to be provided by Britain.

Britain announced July 1 that it would construct an airport at Port Stanley, capital of the Falkland Islands, as a first step in improving relations between Britain and Argentina.

Historic Argentine-Chilean meeting. Chilean President Salvador Allende and Argentine President Alejandro Agustin Lanusse held a two-day "summit" meeting July 23-24 in the northern Argentine city of Salta.

Accord on Beagle Channel—One day before the meeting began, an announcement was made in London that Chile and Argentina had agreed to a formula for ratification of the Beagle Channel dispute. The agreement, negotiated by the foreign ministers of both countries, consisted of three parts: a list of 18 articles providing for the border to be established by Britain's Queen Elizabeth on the basis of a technical decision by a five-man arbitration court composed of judges from the World Court; a modus vivendi to be applied while the court was deliberating; and a joint Chilean-Argentine declaration approving the eventual decision which would be binding on both sides. Both presidents subscribed to the formula during their meeting in Salta.

Friendship stressed—Lanusse welcomed Allende at the airport July 23, stating that the meeting was "a testimony of the firm friendship that unites Argentina and Chile." Allende replied that the countries shared common hopes and a common future which made possible a "juridical solution to the only difference existing between our common native lands."

During the meeting, the two heads of state reinforced the spirit of friendship in ceremonies in which each president decorated the other with his country's highest distinction.

Allende explained during the conference that, while his plans and objectives adhered to Marxist principles, they would be implemented to conform to the specific circumstances and characteristics of Chile. He added that "by means of the popular government over which I preside, Chile is building a humane and independent economy, inspired by Socialist ideals."

Lanusse replied by stating that "Argentina prefers to promote its development on the basis of all its people and the defense of free initiative in the private sector, reconciling this with the overall national interests."

Declaration signed—The conference concluded with both presidents signing the "Declaration of Salta" which ratified the arbitration agreement on the border dispute and expressed a "firm will to continue strengthening the bonds of amity" between the two nations. It stated that the friendship had its bases in the "respect for the principles of nonintervention in the internal and external affairs of each country and in the will to resolve their problems in a peaceful and juridical manner." The declaration also referred to the desire of both countries to maintain sovereignty over a 200-mile territorial coastal limit.

The statement also called for joint efforts to expand trade, transport, tourism and exchange of technology while declaring that the "human factor" would remain of "fundamental importance in the relations between the two states."

EEC trade accord. The European Economic Community (EEC) reached agreement with Argentina July 1 on a non-preferential trade agreement that would liberalize regulations on a number of items, including Argentine beef. The talks, which were held in Brussels beginning June 28, resulted in the creation of a commission of EEC and Argentine representatives to promote trade relations. This was the first non-preferential trade agreement between a Latin American country and the EEC. It was signed in Brussels Nov. 8.

Latins criticize U.S. economic policy. An emergency meeting of the Special Commission for Latin American Coordination (CECLA) was convened in Buenos Aires Sept. 3–5 at the request of Argentine President Alejandro Lanusse. Lanusse had proposed the meeting Aug. 21, urging other Latin nations to adopt a common front to combat recent U.S. economic policies that "gravely affect" the economies of Latin American nations.

The session, attended by representatives of 20 Latin American and Caribbean nations, ended Sept. 5 with the adoption of a document, the "Manifesto of Latin America," that asked for exemption from the new U.S. 10% surcharge on imports and outlined the position of Latin America in the face of U.S. economy measures.

It was reported Sept. 17 that Argentina had withdrawn from the Inter-American Committee on the Alliance for Progress (CIAP) to protest President Nixon's new economic policy. The announcement was made by Antonio Estrany y Gendre, Argentine undersecretary of foreign relations, at the 7th annual Inter-American Economic and Social Committee meeting in Panama.

Lanusse in Peru & Chile. President Lanusse, visiting Peru and Chile, defined his government as "center-left," supported the seating of Communist China in the United Nations and backed the Chilean government in its nationalization of U.S. copper interests.

Gen. Lanusse arrived in Lima Oct. 12 and was warmly greeted by Peruvian President Gen. Juan Velasco Alvarado. After days of negotiations, the foreign ministers of both countries Oct. 15 signed agreements on technical cooperation in educational medical rehabilitation programs, and on cultural exchanges.

At a news conference that day, Lanusse said there were "no tensions" in Argentine-Brazilian relations. Lanusse also asserted that Argentina would drop sanctions against Cuba "at the right time," and in collaboration with the Organization of American States.

Before leaving Lima Oct. 16, Lanusse and Velasco Alvarado signed a declaration expressing "their profound preoccupation" with the recent U.S. economic measures—specifically, the 10% surcharge imposed on imports which they called "prejudicial" to Latin America.

The two presidents also expressed fear over scientific advances that placed the environment in danger. Both supported the admission of Communist China into the U.N., stating that "the principle of universality in the relations between states would be enforced" by China's participation in the U.N.

One of the most important matters discussed was the possible entrance by Argentina into the Andean Group. In the joint declaration, the presidents called for the "progressive development of a permanent dialogue" between the Andean Pact nations and Argentina.

Lanusse arrived in Antofagasta, Chile, for a 28-hour stay which included talks with Chilean President Salvador Allende. Lanusse was returning a visit made by Allende to Argentina in July.

Lanusse said Oct. 17 that he did not expect or want the U.S. to impose sanctions against Chile as a result of the nationalization of U.S. copper properties. In that event, he said, Argentina would intervene to look for a solution as a friend of both Chile and the U.S.

Lanusse meets Banzer. Lanusse met with Bolivian President Hugo Banzer Suarez Nov. 19–20 in Jujuy, Argentina to discuss social and economic problems shared by the two countries.

A declaration signed by both presidents Nov. 20 reaffirmed the "principle of non-intervention in the self-determination of the nations, the territorial integrity of the states, and respect for party pluralism."

They also mapped a program of scientific and technical cooperation that included cost studies of a railway connecting Argentina and Bolivia and the construction of a roadway and bridge connecting the two countries.

Argentina also agreed to extend an $8 million credit to Bolivia for construction of hospitals in return for Bolivian surpluses of natural and liquid gas. Argentina also proposed expansion of its banking activity in Bolivia, with new branches of Banco de la Nation to be built in La Paz, Santa Cruz, and other large Bolivian centers.

The two presidents also agreed to combat drug traffic and discussed the problem of displaced Bolivians who work in Argentina.

Six-nation tour by Finch. U.S. Presidential Counselor Robert H. Finch Nov. 25 ended a 14-day, six-nation tour of Latin America, which he said was undertaken to choose between two schools of thought in the Nixon Administration on the 10% import surcharge—whether "to waive it country-by-country" or cancel it commodity-by-commodity."

Observers saw Finch's trip to Peru, Ecuador, Argentina, Brazil, Honduras and Mexico as a gesture by President Nixon to demonstrate U.S. interest in Latin America at a time when many Latins were concerned over the effects of the surcharge.

Finch met with President Alejandro Lanusse in Argentina Nov. 17. They discussed the U.S. surcharge and tourism in Argentina. According to reports Nov. 19 Argentina had asked that its meat exports be exempted from the U.S. surcharge.

Although Finch defended the surcharge before a meeting of the U.S. Chamber of Commerce in Buenos Aires Nov. 18, sources close to him indicated there were areas in which the surcharge could be lifted for some Latin American products, according to the Miami Herald Nov. 25.

Finch also told the meeting that President Nixon did not agree with the approach that creates a Good Neighbor Policy or an Alliance for Progress. "We are trying to deal country-to-country . . . We recognize that each country is very different . . . We do not want to lump the Latin American countries together because this is not the reality."

(On the eve of his departure for Latin America Nov. 10, Finch had said: "We don't have any litmus paper tests as to whether they're democracies or republics or dictatorships. They make decisions on their economic and political systems for themselves.")

Four of the countries visited by Finch —Peru, Ecuador, Argentina and Brazil— had authoritarian governments, heavily influenced by the armed forces.

According to reports in the Washington Post Nov. 21, Peru, Ecuador, Argentina and Brazil had informed Finch they were interested in purchasing U.S. military materiel available after the end of U.S. involvement in the Vietnam war.

Four countries exempted from surcharge. Argentina announced the exemption of goods exported from Bolivia, Ecuador, Paraguay and Uruguay from a 15% import surcharge. Although Argentina had claimed that the surcharge was compatible with rules of the Latin American Free Trade Association rules because of its balance of payments difficulties, there had been strong protests from the organization's four "less developed" members, according to the London newsletter Latin America Nov. 26.

Violence, Terrorism & Action Against Dissent

Assassination foiled. More than a dozen young men and women were arrested after police discovered a plot to kill both Argentine President Alejandro Lanusse and Uruguayan President Jorge Pacheco Areco while they reviewed a military parade on Argentine Independence Day, July 9.

The youths, members of a self-proclaimed Revolutionary Peoples' Army composed of both Argentines and Uruguayans, were found with arms and explosives, according to police reports July 11. Police said a tank truck loaded with gasoline was to have been exploded near the reviewing stand.

An attempt by 10 youths to kidnap Julio Rodolfo Alsogaray, ex-commander in chief of the army, failed Aug. 17 in Buenos Aires.

British consul kidnaped. Stanley Sylvester, honorary British consul in Rosario, was kidnaped May 23 by members of a left-wing guerrilla group, the People's Revolutionary Army (ERP).

A message from the group said that the kidnaping was carried out "in homage" to Luis N. Blanco, a left-wing university student killed in riots in Rosario in May 1969. The guerrillas said Sylvester would be "tried before a people's court of justice."

Sylvester was the director of a Swift Co. meat packing plant in Rosario, Swift de la Plata. The firm had been the target of considerable leftist criticism.

A demand by the kidnapers for distribution of $62,500 in food to the poor of Rosario was carried out by the de la Plata meat-packing plant May 29. Sylvester was released unharmed May 30.

Peronist rebels strike. A band of guerrillas invaded the town of Santa Clara de Saguier in Santa Fe province July 15 and held up the bank, the police station and other municipal buildings. Unconfirmed reports said they fled with $30,000 and that at least four were arrested near the city of Rosario.

The group claimed to be supporters of former dictator Juan Peron.

Cordoba unrest. Residents of the poorer sections of Cordoba occupied the Archdiocese of Cordoba July 16. A member of the group said they had come to ask the intervention of the archbishop, Msgr. Raul Francisco Primatesta, "to mitigate the effects that the rising cost of living has on the less capable segments of the population." A similar message was transmitted on the city's radio stations.

Members of a subversive command unit of the Revolutionary People's Army Aug. 18 raided an armory in Cordoba, fleeing with a large quantity of arms.

A 14-hour general strike called by the General Confederation of Labor in Cordoba Oct. 22 virtually paralyzed the city, closing down radio and television stations, newspapers, transport and other essential services, the Argentine newspaper La Prensa reported Oct. 23. The federal government had imposed strict security measures in Cordoba's central district to impede disorders.

The strike, however, provoked clashes between provincial and the federal police who had been mobilized in Cordoba to maintain order during the strike activities. The clash began when federal police, placing a roadblock on a principal city street, shot at and destroyed a car that ignored the barrier. The car's driver, Eduardo Romero, 25, was severely injured.

The provincial police immediately issued statements condemning the assault, claiming that the federal police had abused their powers. The federal police responded Oct. 23 by attacking the Cordoba police headquarters, wounding several officers and damaging the building. Federal police also detained Cordoba Police Chief Alberto Villar and other police officials who were charged with obstruction of federal police activity.

Military police moved into two Cordoba factories Oct. 26 to halt union meetings that were held after the government had withdrawn the unions' legal status.

The Labor Ministry had charged that the unions, Sitrac at the large Fiat-Concord factory complex and Sitram at the Materfer locomotive factory, had been used for Communist political purposes. Both unions were considered to be openly revolutionary.

The French newspaper Le Monde reported Oct. 29 that 20 workers were arrested in Cordoba Oct. 27 during violent demonstrations following the government's move against the two unions. All police leaves in the city were canceled and the CGT met in emergency session Oct. 27 to consider calling an indefinite general strike.

Terrorism & counter-terrorism. Various other acts of terrorism were reported as well as actions to counter terrorism.

The New York Times Aug. 9, 1971 reported estimates of Argentine authorities that armed subversive groups in Argentina had 6,000 active members. The report said evidence indicated that, as in Brazil and Guatemala, "death squads" linked to security forces had been responsible for the killing of persons suspected of subversive activities.

Police in Rosario arrested four members of subversive groups Aug. 18 and said this would lead to the arrest of more members of clandestine groups. At the same time, the police seized medical equipment used by the guerrillas, literature of the Revolutionary Armed Forces (FAR), arms and explosives.

Members of a subversive command unit of the Revolutionary People's Army Aug. 18 raided an armory in Cordoba, fleeing with a large quantity of arms.

A 27-year-old navy canteen maid became the first Argentine to be sentenced by a special military tribunal to combat rising left-wing guerrilla activity. Louisa Velosa, who told the tribunal that police had tortured her with electric shocks, was given a seven-year sentence Nov. 3 after being found guilty of participating in an armed attempt by guerrillas to seize weapons from the Buenos Aires police July 20.

La Prensa reported terrorist assaults and other disorders in Buenos Aires Oct. 29. One policeman was killed, others injured and businesses and banks were damaged in the unrest.

Police officials said bombs were placed throughout the central district by students demonstrating support for striking Cordoba workers.

One policeman was shot and killed in a subway station. A total of 18 people were arrested during the disorders, including Pedro Viano, a Buenos Aires priest.

In related developments, terrorists of the Armed Forces of Liberation Oct. 29 kidnaped bank president Jorge Vasquez Iglesias while he was leaving his Buenos Aires home. Vasquez was released the next day after his kidnapers had received 90 million pesos from the Vasquez family.

A command unit of the People's Revolutionary Army Oct. 28 assaulted a Cordoba hospital seizing equipment worth 15 million pesos.

'Third World' priests arrested. Four priests, members of the Third World

Priests Movement, were arrested by the army in Rosario Aug. 3, 1971 with 13 other suspects in a roundup of "terrorist elements." The priests were Jose Maria Ferrari, Nestor Garcia, Juan Carlos Arroyo and Ruben Dri. Army officials said they had seized arms, explosives, subversive literature and narcotics in raids on the priests residences.

In a related development, the permanent commission of the Argentine Episcopate in Rome issued a statement, reported in the French newspaper Le Monde Aug. 19, affirming that the country's problems "have engendered violence on the attitudes, remarks and acts [kidnapings, crimes, tortures and assassinations] that are absolutely unjustifiable and condemnable."

The statement was understood as marking a schism in the Argentine church, with the Catholic bishops condemning both the violence of the "oppressors" and that of the "oppressed."

In response to questioning about the detention of the priests, Interior Minister Arturo Mor Roig said Aug. 17 that the government would act no differently toward these than toward any other persons who committed similar acts.

Three of the arrested priests were released Sept. 4.

The three priests, Juan Carlos Arroyo, Nestor Garcia Gomez and Jose Maria Ferrari, said their treatment by the military had been "correct, but severe."

Forty-seven more "third world priests" were arrested in Rosario Sept. 25 while participating in a peaceful demonstration for the release of parish priest Santiago MacGuire and other political prisoners. The protest had taken place in front of the cathedral.

The 47 priests were released Sept. 28 by order of Municipal Court Judge Hugo Castagnino. They had been detained in local firehouse headquarters.

Sixty priests had gathered from all parts of the country to attend a national "third world movement" conference.

Besides demanding the release of political prisoners, the arrested priests made a public statement to the press criticizing the "growing participation of the army in investigation without proper legal controls."

Argentine bishops condemned the

priests' arrests. Msgr. Antonio Basca, bishop of Santa Fe province, called the incident a persecution of the church, the Miami Herald reported Sept. 30.

Jurists complain. It was reported Dec. 23 that the International Commission of Jurists in Geneva had expressed its "deep concern about the growing disrespect for the rule of law in Argentina." It made its concern known in a letter to the Argentine government.

A commission statement said it had acted on the basis of numerous reports of "serious obstruction, intimidation and persecution suffered by Argentine lawyers in the exercise of their professional duty."

Politics & Peron

Meetings with Peron reported. The New York Times reported June 9 that top Peronist political and labor leaders, after weeks of discussions with President Alejandro Lanusse, were in Madrid discussing government offers with former President Juan Peron. Talks between the government and Peronists concerned Lanusse's desire to gain support from the followers of Peron in exchange for certain concessions, including grant of an Argentine passport to Peron, permitting him to return, grant of a pension received by all former presidents and the restoration of Peron's former rank of general.

Peronist demands election date. Jorge Daniel Paladino, the personal delegate of Peron, demanded in a Buenos Aires speech July 9 that election dates be set promptly as a condition for Peronist support of Lanusse's plan to legalize political parties and hand over power to a constitutional government by 1973.

Eva Peron's body taken to Spain. The Argentine government Sept. 3 returned the body of Eva Peron to Juan Peron in Spain. The silver coffin was turned over to Peron by Argentine embassy of-

ficials for reburial near his Madrid home. The office of Argentine President Alejandro Lanusse issued a statement Sept. 3 confirming the delivery.

It was disclosed Sept. 7 that Eva Peron's body had been kept in a Milan, Italy, cemetery for 14 years before its transfer to Madrid. Italian press reports said Sept. 5 that the late Pope Pius XII had given permission for the secret burial on a request by President Pedro Aramburu, who headed the Argentine government after Peron was overthrown.

The government banned a six-hour general strike called for Sept. 10 by the General Confederation of Labor (CGT) in a memorial to Eva Peron. Interior Minister Arturo Mor Roig said Sept. 8 that the strike had "a definite political motive."

It was reported Sept. 12 that police used tear gas to disperse a crowd that gathered after a memorial mass for the late Mrs. Peron.

Lanusse meets opposition leaders. Leaders of the opposition group, the Hora del Pueblo, composed of six leftist parties dominated by the Peronists, held a conference with Argentine President Lanusse Aug. 26 to ask the government to fix a clear date for the upcoming elections in order to re-establish institutional normalcy in the country.

An official communique following the meeting said Lanusse would take into account the opinions of the leaders and would make more concrete announcements concerning the "Political Plan for the institutionalization of the country" before Oct. 15.

Lanusse Sept. 17 announced the junta's decision to hold general elections March 25, 1973 and to hand over power to the elected constitutional officials May 25, 1973.

Speaking Sept. 2 at the National War School, Interior Minister Arturo Mor Roig said that, at the end of the process of "political institutionalization," there would not be more than four or five structured political parties that would be able to fulfill the rules outlined by the Organic Law of Political Parties.

Peron picks new representative. The French newspaper Le Monde reported Nov. 5 that Jorge Paladino, Peron's personal representative in Argentina, and head of Justicialist party there, had resigned because he did not wish to divide the Peronist movement. The London newsletter Latin America reported Nov. 11 that Peron had dismissed Paladino, fearing that he was gaining too much influence on his own, and because Paladino had backed President Lanusse during an abortive army revolt in October. Peron appointed Hector Campora to replace Paladino.

Peron's wife arrives in Argentina. Mrs. Maria Estela (Isabel) Martinez de Peron, wife of Juan D. Peron, arrived in Buenos Aires Dec. 7 in an attempt to unify the faction-ridden Peronist movement. It was reported that Mrs. Peron, who had represented her husband at political meetings in Argentina and elsewhere, would try to resolve a dispute between orthodox Peronists of the Justicialist party and younger, more independent elements in the labor unions and in a militant women's group.

Military Unrest, Government Changes

Army revolt quelled. Two army regiments south of Buenos Aires Oct. 8 declared their rebellion against the military government of Gen. Alejandro Agustin Lanusse. The rebellion ended 20 hours later with only a few shots fired and no casualties when the rebel commanders surrendered to loyal government forces.

Soldiers in the garrisons in the towns of Azul and Olavarria, both about 200 miles south of the capital, seized control of the local radio stations and called for the immediate resignation of Lanusse, claiming "the people have lost confidence and faith" in the president. The rebels, under the command of Lt. Col. Florentino Diaz Loza in Olavarria and Col. Manuel Alejandro Garcia and Lt. Col. Fernando Amadeo Baldrich in Azul, said the Lanusse government was guilty of creating "political and economic chaos,

and moral disaster." The rebels described the recently announced government plan to hold elections in March 1973 as "a farce" that would betray the army's nationalist goals.

Lanusse announced that loyal units of the 1st Corps had been sent to quell the insurrection. He said the rebellion had sought to establish a "rightist, totalitarian regime" and called it a "lamentable incident that will be useful, however, in showing the determination of the armed forces" to pursue the president's goal of democratic rule.

While 10,000 troops converged on the rebel zone, commanders of several units of the 85,000-man Argentine army issued statements declaring their allegiance to the president. Lanusse also received considerable support outside the military. The General Confederation of Labor, Argentina's largest labor union dominated by the followers of Juan Peron, condemned the revolt. The Hour of the People, a coalition of leftist parties, described the rebellion as "fascist" and declared its support for Lanusse.

The revolt collapsed Oct. 9 with the surrender of the three rebel leaders, and the government announced that their units "have returned to their barracks and placed themselves under the command of the army high command."

Former President Roberto M. Levingston was placed under arrest Oct. 10 as the suspected organizer of the uprising, the New York Times reported Oct. 11. The Times also reported that Lanusse emerged with stronger support from all public sectors as a result of the rebellion.

Navy crisis resolved—The revolt came one day after a crisis in the leadership of the navy was resolved Oct. 7 by the decision of the navy commander in chief, Adm. Pedro J. Gnavi, to retire in December. Gnavi was a member of the military junta that ruled with President Lanusse.

The crisis in the naval command was the result of Gnavi's attempt to dismiss several other high-ranking officers. Five senior naval officers were dismissed Oct. 3 by Gnavi. No reasons were given for the dismissals, although a reference was made to an "internal situation without any implication outside the navy."

It was reported Oct. 7 that five admirals had applied for early retirement, a move believed to have been an attempt to force the resignation of Adm. Gnavi. Sources said the rebel naval officers wanted to oust Gnavi as a result of his cooperation in government overtures to supporters of former President Juan Peron. The naval crisis was reportedly linked with the navy's traditional refusal to admit negotiations with Peronist supporters. The navy had a prominent role in the overthrow of Peron's regime in 1955.

Lanusse announced Nov. 4 that Vice Adm. Carlos G. N. Coda would replace Gnavi as navy commander and member of the country's ruling three-man junta.

Two ministers replaced. President Alejandro Lanusse accepted the resignations Oct. 11 of two conservative ministers, Juan A. Quilici, finance minister, and Jaime Perriaux, minister of Justice. He immediately named two liberals, Ismael Bruno Quijano and Cayetano A. Licciardo, to the justice and finance positions.

The New York Times reported Oct. 12 that the appointment of Licciardo, an economic technician, was welcomed by both businessmen and labor leaders who were dissatisfied with the country's deteriorating economic situation.

2 new posts. Lanusse Oct. 23 created two new Cabinet portfolios, splitting the former Ministry of Industry, Commerce and Mining into two separate ministries for Commerce and Industry and Mining.

The minister of industry, commerce and mining, Gen. Oscar Mario Chescotta, resigned Oct. 22 and Lanusse named Alfredo Jose Girelli to the Ministry of Commerce and Carlos Gerardo Casale to the new Ministry of Industry and Mining.

Economic Plans & Problems

Lanusse proposes new economic plan. President Alejandro Lanusse proposed July 7 a new moderately nationalistic economic program that he said would strengthen his efforts to restore an elected government.

The program was designed to facilitate the creation of a Cabinet with the participation of the political parties, including those allied with Peron.

According to the plan, announced by Lanusse in a speech at an armed forces dinner, the real wages of workers would be maintained in the face of continued inflation and prices of essential goods would be regulated. Prices of pharmaceuticals would be cut 40%. Lanusse also said that "special regulations" would prevent the purchase by foreigners of Argentine-owned industries "in key sectors of the economy."

Lanusse asserted that tax structures would be changed "radically so that those who earn more, pay more" and that in the future those who evaded tax payment would be imprisoned without bail.

The government announced Aug. 4 that, beginning Aug. 9, alternate "beefless weeks" would go into effect again. The action was seen as an attempt to increase lagging beef exports.

Wage increase, price freeze set. The Argentine government invoked a "social accord" Sept. 2 which would consist of "a truce between those sectors that perform functions in both the economic and social fields."

To solidify the accord, the following measures were announced: prices and taxes were frozen at their Aug. 24 level; tariffs from state enterprises would be maintained for the next 60 days; a family allowance for wives was increased by $6,000 pesos (national money); compensation to retired people and pensioners was readjusted beginning Oct. 1.

Other measures announced by the government included an increase of $5,-000 pesos (national money) in wages for workers in collective enterprises beginning Sept. 1. During the time of the "truce," the peso would not be devalued nor would taxes be increased.

During the time the measures would take effect, the government would study the necessary means to place economic and social factors in equilibrium. Any abuses of the measures would lead to either a censure or a closing by the government of the companies involved.

It was also announced that the length of the "truce" would depend on the effectiveness of the measures.

It had been announced Aug. 24 that the government would reopen the financial exchange market it closed after U.S. economic measures were announced Aug. 15. A devaluation was announced, fixing at 5 pesos parity with the U.S. dollar. The government also announced the application of an additional duty of .15 peso per dollar on exports whose shipments had been authorized to leave before Aug. 24 and would establish a system of reimbursements to stimulate the sale of goods and services to the exterior.

Central Bank President Ricardo Gruneisen was forced to resign under government criticism of his suggestions of a major devaluation. Carlos Santiago Brignone, who succeeded him, became the fifth Central Bank president in a year.

Import ban imposed. In an effort to avert a balance-of-payments crisis and to stop the outflow of hard currency from the country, the Argentine government Sept. 13 imposed a ban on all imports.

Gen. Oscar Mario Chescotta, minister of industry, trade and mining, said the decision was made after a three-hour meeting of economic officials with President Alejandro Lanusse. He called it an "emergency measure to counter Argentina's unfavorable balance of payments" and indicated that the ban might last 60–90 days.

(Trade figures for the past seven months showed a deficit of $76.3 million compared with a surplus of $291 million for the same period of 1970.)

Brignone warns on foreign debts. Dr. Carlos S. Brignone, president of Argentina's Central Bank, warned Nov. 18 that the country was on the brink of being forced to freeze all foreign payments. He said that in the last year there had been "the most violent flight of capital in the history of the country," with over $1 billion sent abroad.

As a result, economic activity had been sustained by the most massive creation of money in Argentina since the 1890s.

Argentina had estimated her total foreign debt at $3.5 billion–$4 billion. Independent economists had estimated her payments deficit at about $500 million.

Eximbank loans. Two separate loans were announced by the U.S. Export-Import Bank (Eximbank) to Argentina.

The first, signed Sept. 20, called for $6.8 million in credit to help finance the operation of a factory producing cellulose and white sulfur.

The other loan, signed Sept. 30, was for $12 million for the purchase by Aerolineas Argentinas of two Boeing commercial jets. A similar loan by Eximbank to Chile was recently rejected.

Illegal CGT strike called success. A 24-hour strike Sept. 29 called by the General Confederation of Workers (CGT), the country's largest labor union, was called a success by union leaders who claimed nearly 100% support by the union's 3.5 million members. The strike, seen as a protest against the military government of President Alejandro Lanusse, had been declared illegal by government authorities Sept. 27.

The CGT, dominated by supporters of former President Juan Peron, ostensibly called the strike to protest inflation and the decline of real wages and to demand increased salaries, pension benefits and family allowances. Police took no action against the illegal strikers.

Swift declared bankrupt. Swift de la Plata, Argentina's financially troubled and largest meat packer, was declared bankrupt Nov. 8.

A civil court judge ordered the government to appoint an administrator/liquidator within 24 hours. At the same time he recommended that the official bank provide sufficient funds for the company to continue running those sections of the company currently in operation. President Alejandro Lanusse took the necessary legal steps for the state takeover.

Swift, owned by Deltec International,

a U.S.-European consortium based in the Bahamas, employed about 10,000 workers and provided about 30% of Argentina's meat exports.

Railroad contract to Japan. Argentina awarded a $150 million dollar contract to electrify and modernize the Buenos Aires suburban railway system to a consortium of 22 Japanese companies Nov. 24.

New economic plan invoked. The government invoked a new economic program Dec. 3 designed to combat inflation and help balance an adverse balance of payments. The plan would be in effect until May 1973, the date set by President Alejandro Lanusse for election of a restored constitutional government.

The new plan, consisting of 25 measures, would stimulate the flow of exports, provide periodic salary raises up to 25% while holding price increases to 20%, and increase the cost of public services by 40%. It would also lift the 15% import surcharge in steps, beginning with the removal of the entire surcharge on basic industrial and iron and steel imports.

Salary increases for the public sector would take place Jan. 1, 1972 and July 1, 1972. The plan also provided for an increase of 30% in family allowances and an adjustment in the wages of all workers to reassure maintenance of real salaries.

Under the new plan, the Central Bank would not be able to issue more than two billion new pesos until May 1973, in an effort to stem the rising rate of inflation, reported to have been 40% in 1971. (It was reported Nov. 26 that the peso had been devalued to its lowest point ever, 10.05 pesos to the dollar.)

Pay raises announced. The Argentine government decreed a 25% wage increase Dec. 30 for all workers, payable in two installments.

All state and private employes would receive a 15% raise Jan. 1, 1972 and another increase of 10% July 1, 1972.

1972: Before Peron's Return

Political Activity Intensifies

During 1972, the year before Juan Peron was restored to power, there was a marked intensification of political activity as competing groups sought to improve their chances in the 1973 election. There appeared to be no improvement in the economic climate. Civil unrest continued at a high level, and the current wave of terrorism was unabated. With these problems adding to the heat of the approaching political campaign, Peron interrupted his 17-year exile to return briefly to Argentina late in 1972 for 28 hectic days of political activity.

Election plans reported. Interior Minister Arturo Mor Roig Jan. 6 reported government plans to hold democratic elections March 25, 1973, with installation of a new president May 25, 1973.

In an interview in La Prensa of Buenos Aires, Mor Roig said the next government would have to have the backing of the armed forces and reaffirmed their role in the re-establishment of institutional normalcy in the country.

Mor Roig also said it was necessary to continue the state of siege in Argentina.

Sometime later in January, two bombs damaged the headquarters of the women's branch of the Peronist movement where Isabel Martinez Peron, Peron's wife, had an office.

A Peron spokesman said Feb. 10 that the former president was willing to run in the March 1973 general elections "if that's what the people want." Peron's Justicialista party was recognized as a legitimate political organization Jan. 24 by the federal judge of Buenos Aires.

The British newsletter Latin America noted Feb. 18 that Peron had met in Madrid with Rogelio Frigerio, of ex-President Arturo Frondizi's Desarrollista movement, and that an accord between followers of Peron and Frondizi might be arranged. Both leaders were said to believe that any elected government would be extremely vulnerable to military intervention during its first year in office, and that they would have to be looking to the round of negotiations between civilians and the military which could follow a coup after the elections.

Although there were formidable political obstacles to a Peron-Frondizi accord, two military men were mentioned as candidates who could enjoy the support of both ex-presidents: Gen. Osiris Villegas, currently ambassador to Brazil, and Gen. Jorge Carcagno, chief of operations of the general staff.

The army's cooperation, however, was uncertain. Chief of staff Gen. Jose Herrera Feb. 10 filed libel proceedings against an article signed by Peron and published in the Justicialista magazine Las Bases, claiming that it "insulted the honor of the army." The article scored the armed forces' involvement in the government's anti-guerrilla campaign.

Frondizi announced April 1 that he and Peron had agreed to form a National Front for the projected 1973 elections. Frondizi said the front would bring together "all people in their different social sectors and political groups to produce a fundamental change in the direction of the country."

According to Le Monde April 4, Frondizi said the front would exclude "only those small groups tied to policies which would keep Argentina in the old structure of foreign domination."

Frondizi and Peron had conferred in Madrid March 14 and 29.

Peron and the Lanusse government had begun negotiations to pave the way for an electoral accord, El Nacional of Caracas reported April 4.

According to El Nacional, the Buenos Aires weekly Confirmado, which often reflected government opinion, said that in the past month representatives of Peron and Lanusse had held weekly meetings in Madrid. The magazine said the negotiators had no formal agenda, but did discuss Peron's Justicialista movement, the issuance of a passport to Peron and the reinstatement of his military rank.

The Miami Herald reported March 24 that Peron had been cleared of fraud charges filed against him after he was overthrown. A Buenos Aires judge April 7 removed the last legal obstacle to Peron's return to Argentina by dismissing a 1955 charge of treason against him.

The Spanish government declared April 18 that Peron, who lived in Madrid, would no longer be considered a political exile, but an ordinary Argentine citizen. Peron would be allowed to make political statements and to leave and re-enter Spain freely.

Peron candidacy announced. The candidacy of ex-President Juan Domingo Peron in the 1973 presidential elections was announced April 30 at a Buenos Aires luncheon attended by about 2,000 prominent members of Peron's Justicialista party.

(Peron had granted powers of attorney to two Buenos Aires lawyers to seek authority for him to vote and run for election in Argentina, the London Times reported April 14.)

Persons attending the luncheon heard a recorded message from Peron, who said President Alejandro Lanusse had an "obligation" to hold the elections.

According to the London Times May 2, Peron's candidacy might have been set to test the reaction of the armed forces, among whose right-wing elements there was considerable opposition to Peron's return to office.

The Justicialista party, at its convention in Buenos Aires June 25, proclaimed Peron its presidential candidate. A federal court June 27 cleared Peron to vote and run in the 1973 election.

In an apparent challenge to Peron to return to Argentina, Lanusse declared July 7 that all potential candidates in the elections must take up residence in the country by Aug. 25. Lanusse added that members of the military government who wished to run for office must resign from their positions by the same date.

Peron said July 22 that, for "security reasons," he would not return to Argentina by Aug. 25 but would conduct his election campaign from exile.

Ex-President Roberto M. Levingston was placed under 30 days' detention July 6 after publicly criticizing Lanusse's attempts to reach an electoral accord with Peron. Levingston had charged Lanusse and Peron were negotiating behind the backs of the armed forces and the people of Argentina.

Levingston's arrest followed the dismissal of another critic of the negotiations, Foreign Minister Luis M. de Pablo Pardo.

Union funds blocked—The government July 7 blocked the bank accounts of all labor unions and the personal accounts of union leaders in apparent response to a belligerent communique from the General Confederation of Labor (CGT).

The communique, scheduled for release July 8, warned the armed forces that if the 1973 elections were not carried out with scrupulous fairness, there would be a violent revolution. The statement had been approved by the CGT's national congress July 6 along with a call for the union's nomination of Peron as its presidential candidate.

Bombings in Eva's memory—Terrorists burned a country club in Corrientes and set off more than 20 time bombs in other parts of the country July 26, on the 20th anniversary of the death of Peron's wife, Eva Duarte de Peron. At least three police officers were seriously wounded when a bomb they were trying to disarm exploded in the Buenos Aires suburb of San Isidro.

Among the bombing targets were the homes of two Buenos Aires newspaper directors, Alberto Gainza of La Prensa and Jacobo Timerman of La Opinion.

Cabinet resigns. All 12 Cabinet ministers and the president of the Central Bank resigned March 3, leaving President Alejandro Lanusse free to form a new administration. Lanusse, who had announced plans for a major reorganization of the government Feb. 24, was reportedly seeking a Cabinet able to control the current economic crisis and prepare for election of a constitutional government in March 1973.

The Miami Herald reported March 4 that the governors of Argentina's 21 provinces had also submitted their resignations.

Three new ministers were sworn in March 10. Daniel Garcial replaced Alfredo Girelli as commerce minister; Enrique Juan Parellada succeeded Carlos Casale as industry and mining minister; and Ernesto Jorge Lanusse replaced Antonio Americo Di Rocco as agriculture and livestock minister.

According to La Prensa of Buenos Aires March 8, the resignations of all other Cabinet officials except Defense Minister Jose Rafael Caceres Monie had been rejected by Lanusse. The government announced May 9 that Eduardo E. Aguirre Obarrio, a Buenos Aires attorney and law professor, had been appointed defense minister.

Foreign Minister Luis Maria de Pablo Pardo resigned June 19 and was succeeded June 22 by retired Brig. Gen. Eduardo McLoughlin.

Justice minister resigns. Justice Minister Ismael Bruno Quijano resigned July 4, claiming he did so to protect himself from a charge that he had sought to influence an appeals court in the bankruptcy case of Swift de la Plata.

The charge was made by the presiding' judge in the case, Salvador M. Lozada, who ruled against Swift's plan to return to solvency after being forced into receivership in 1971. The ruling was made despite testimony by representatives of Swift's numerous creditors and employes, who had voted overwhelmingly to accept management's recovery pledge.

Gervasio Colombres was sworn in July 11 to replace Quijano.

Manrique resigns. Social Welfare Minister Francisco Manrique resigned Aug. 9, facilitating a possible presidential candidacy in the elections scheduled for March 1973. His post was taken Aug. 13 by Oscar R. Puiggros, a founder of the Christian Democratic party and former labor and social security minister.

Manrique had frequently been mentioned as the government's presidential candidate in the event that President Alejandro Lanusse chose not to run. His resignation complied with a requirement that officials wishing to run in the elections leave their posts by Aug. 25.

Another possible government candidate, Gen. Osiris Villegas, had resigned as ambassador to Brazil.

Manrique announced his candidacy Aug. 31 after having reportedly secured the support of the Popular Alliance, a coalition of groups in several provinces.

New party approved. A Federal court in Buenos Aires recognized the Leftist Popular Front (FIP) and declared it eligible to compete for political posts in future elections, according to the Miami Herald June 17. The FIP became Argentina's fourth political party.

The electoral court had recognized the right-wing New Force as a political organization and declared it eligible for elections, the Herald reported May 12. The group was headed by Alvaro Alsogaray, a former economy minister and ambassador to the U.S.

Regime Vs. Peron

Lanusse attacks Peron. President Alejandro Lanusse, responding to Juan

Domingo Peron's refusal to accept his terms for a political settlement, delivered a scathing personal attack on the ex-dictator July 28.

Speaking to 1,000 officers at the Military College in Buenos Aires, Lanusse charged that Peron would not return to Argentina because he was afraid to. As for Peron's contention that he could better conduct the overall strategy of his Justicialista movement from the relative isolation of his exile in Spain, Lanusse remarked that even Christ did not stay away as "commander of strategic policy," but came down to earth in person.

In a moderately worded reply reported Aug. 4, Peron said he would not return to Argentina until the government lifted the national state of siege, released all political prisoners, abolished the judicial police apparatus, and took emergency measures to relieve economic pressures on the ordinary Argentine worker.

According to the London newsletter Latin America Aug. 4, Lanusse was seeking to isolate Peron from the Justicialistas, Argentina's most powerful political party. After attacking the ex-dictator, Lanusse added that he had nothing against the party, which could not be denied "the right to be definitely included in the nation's affairs." Both Lanusse and Peron were reportedly also maneuvering for the support of the moderate Radical Civic Union party, whose key figure was Interior Minister Arturo Mor Roig.

A recent Buenos Aires opinion poll indicated that Peron would win the 1973 elections, and Lanusse, if he ran, would receive a mere 6% of the vote, the French newspaper Le Monde reported Aug. 1.

Constitutional amendments set. President Alejandro Lanusse Aug. 24 decreed a series of constitutional amendments designed "solely to guarantee the stability of authorities elected by the people" in the projected March 1973 general elections. The measures, altering the constitution of 1853, included:

■ Direct election of the president and vice president, abandoning the old system of electoral colleges similar to that of the U.S.

■ Reduction of the presidential term of office from six to four years, with a limit of two terms to any president.

■ Establishment of four-year terms of office for governors, national and provincial legislators, and municipal intendants and councilmen.

■ Allocation of three Senate seats, instead of two, to each province and the federal capital. One of the three senators from each area would represent the minority of voters.

■ Extension from four to seven months of the normal Congressional session, with provisions to facilitate quorums and allow the government budget to encompass projects lasting more than a year.

The amendments, reportedly opposed by most political parties and lawyers' organizations, would remain in effect until May 24, 1977—the end of the first four-year legislative term—and for four years after that if a special constitutional convention was unable either to incorporate them into the constitution or overturn them.

Announcement of the amendments followed promulgation Aug. 24 of a press law which established prison terms of six months to three years for anyone who "by any means broadcast, divulged or spread messages or ideas attributed or attributable to illegal associations or persons or groups notoriously dedicated to subversive activities or terrorism."

Elections proclamation hastened. Interior Minister Arturo Mor Roig announced that the official proclamation of elections for 1973 would be updated to Oct. 1 from Nov. 25, the London newsletter Latin America reported Sept. 8.

The move, according to the newsletter, was designed partly to offset widespread rumors than a recent upsurge of civil disturbances might prevent the elections. However, prospects for the elections taking place had reportedly been improved by a recent statement by Gen. Alcides Lopez Aufranc—once rumored to be plotting against Lanusse—to the effect that the elections would take place "even if only three people vote."

The conversion of Lanusse's right-wing enemies within the army to support for his political strategy went back to a promise by Lanusse in May that the armed forces would continue to play a part in political decision-making even after the installation of a constitutionally elected government, the newsletter reported. Lopez Aufranc's new enthusiasm for the elections was also said to be attributable to recent suggestions that Lanusse would retire after the elections and Lopez Aufranc would succeed him as commander in chief of the armed forces. Aufranc, a bitter opponent of Peron, was installed by Lanusse Oct. 20 as army chief of staff.

Lanusse, meanwhile, was improving relations with the General Labor Confederation (CGT), which was dominated by followers of ex-dictator Juan Domingo Peron, the newsletter reported Sept. 15. The CGT had reportedly issued a policy document suggesting social and economic measures which could provide a basis for cooperation with the government, and had agreed to drop its traditional positions in favor of land reform and against foreign investment. CGT Secretary General Jose Rucci had even condemned the union's Cordoba branch, recently closed by the government during civil disturbances.

The government Oct. 18 called the general elections for March 11, 1973, moving up the date by two weeks.

Peron's proposals. An outline of Peron's ideas for Argentina's political future was made public Oct. 4.

Peron's proposals for action by the regime were set forth in a 10-point "minimal basis for an accord for national reconstruction," presented to an Argentine government representative by the former dictator's chief spokesman, Hector Campora. Peron's proposals:

1. Argentina must resist military, economic and political imperialism in the hemisphere.
2. New Cabinet ministers must be appointed to implement new social and economic policies on the basis of the minimum program drawn up by the General Labor Confederation (CGT) and the General Economic Confederation, and the new Cabinet should include Peronist representatives.
3. The Social Economic Council should immediately convene to discuss the plan for national reconstruction which would be the first concern of the constitutional government elected in 1973.
4. The military should make an explicit statement on the nature and extent of its participation in the future government.
5. There should be a re-examination of the government's recent constitutional amendments and of the rules governing participation in the 1973 elections (including the August 25 deadline by which candidates were supposed to have returned to Argentina).
6. All decisions on special laws, suspension of constitutional guarantees, etc. should be left to the future government and to the legislative branch in particular.
7. A senior officer of the armed forces should be immediately appointed minister of the interior to replace Arturo Mor Roig.
8. A multi-party commission should be appointed to ensure the impartiality of state-controlled information media, and to guarantee equal access to the media by all political parties.
9. The state of siege must be lifted and all political prisoners (particularly trade unionists) released.
10. All political sectors should be consulted on the new electoral law and the calling of elections.

President Alejandro Lanusse reacted warily to Peron's proposals, saying the ten points would be discussed by the political leadership of the armed forces, and a decision would then be reached on the possibility of further discussion with the ex-dictator, the London newsletter Latin America reported Oct. 13. However, Lanusse went on to attack Peron, asserting he would not forget "what has happened, happened to me, and happened to us."

Peron bars immediate return. Peron increased the confusion about his political plans Oct. 28, telling a reporter there was no possibility of his "immediate return" to Argentina. A Peronist spokesman said that rather than return to Argentina Nov. 17, as reported earlier, Peron would call political leaders to Madrid to form an anti-imperialist, anti-military coalition which would take power through a plebiscite.

Peron's statement followed announcement by the government Oct. 26 that a plane presumably chartered by Peron would be permitted to fly to Argentina Nov. 17.

Peron had said Oct. 13 that there was a threat of civil war in Argentina, and that "the moment is near" for his return to seek the presidency. In an interview broadcast by the Italian state television network, Peron said "my men are preparing my voyage. . . . I think it will be very, very soon."

Peron in Argentina,
Leaves After 28 Days

After repeated reports and denials (some by Peron himself) that the former dictator would return to Argentina in 1972, Peron arrived in Buenos Aires in mid-November. But he left in mid-December after nearly a month of disappointing political negotiations.

Peron returns. Ex-President Juan Domingo Peron returned to Argentina Nov. 17, ending 17 years of exile, the last 11 in Spain. His arrival followed months of negotiations with the military government, which reportedly believed an arrangement with Peron's Justicialista party was necessary to insure the success of the March 1973 elections and a return to institutional rule.

Only 300 officially cleared supporters were admitted to Buenos Aires' Ezeiza airport to greet the ex-dictator, who was reportedly accompanied by 130 labor leaders, politicians, models, boxers and tango singers. Soldiers using tear gas dispersed Peronists marching to the airport, which was cordoned off by tanks, cannon and 30,000 troops. Among other security measures:

Police and army patrols were increased in Buenos Aires and other cities to prevent large demonstrations and quell raucous celebrations.

A paid holiday was declared to prevent factory workers from massing to march on the airport, and to defuse a general strike called by the Peronist-dominated General Labor Confederation (CGT). All public and private schools were closed.

Radio and television stations, especially those owned directly by the government, carried spot replays of President Alejandro Lanusse's assurances that order would be maintained and that all Argentines dedicated to their homeland were welcome. When Peron arrived, Lanusse was 375 miles from Buenos Aires, inaugurating a petrochemicals complex.

Upon arrival, Peron was rushed to the heavily guarded airport hotel, where he canceled a scheduled press conference and message to the country to protest the strict security measures. A spokesman charged the ex-president had been made a "prisoner," but the government maintained the measures were for Peron's safety. Peron was allowed late Nov. 18 to move to a new home in the well-to-do Buenos Aires suburb of Vicente Lopez, where he was cheered by thousands of young men and women. Thousands of other supporters invaded the neighborhood over the next few days to stage noisy celebrations.

Political leaders contacted—Peron immediately took control of the Justicialista party and then met with leaders of a wide range of civilian groups. He conferred Nov. 19 with Ricardo Balbin, leader of the Radical party—the second largest in Argentina after the Justicialistas—and Nov. 20 with 50 political, union and business leaders.

All political parties except the right-wing New Force and backers of independent presidential candidate Francisco Manrique were given invitations to the Nov. 20 meeting, which took place in a suburban restaurant and lasted nearly six hours. The Socialist party and the outlawed Communists chose not to send representatives. Peron said early Nov. 21 that the meeting had achieved "a united attitude representing the whole of Argentine civiliandom," implying concerted opposition to the military in the 1973 elections.

A few thousand Peronists clashed with police and soldiers Nov. 20 near the site of the meeting in the first violence reported since Peron's arrival. One demonstrator and one policeman were reported wounded by gunfire.

Peron met Nov. 21 with Radical party leader Ricardo Balbin and Dec. 1 with ex-President Arturo Frondizi, whose support he needed for an effective coalition. He also conferred Dec. 1 with ex-President Roberto M. Levingston.

Hopes for a united civilian front began to fade Nov. 27 with the nomination of Balbin as the Radical presidential candidate. Frondizi was nominated Dec. 2 by his Desarrollista party. The government asserted Nov. 29 and again Dec. 8 that the residency requirement for candidates was irreversible, ending Peron's presidential prospects. A Peronist appeal against the requirement was rejected by the Supreme Court Dec. 10.

(The right-wing New Force nominated Julio Chamizo as its presidential candidate Dec. 17.)

Lanusse, meanwhile, announced Dec. 14 that he would retire from active service in the armed forces and all public life May 25, 1973, the day he was scheduled to hand over power to an elected government. Lanusse's tenure in power until then was assured Nov. 28 when Brig. Gen. Carlos Alberto Rey, the air force commander, agreed to give up the chairmanship of the joint chiefs of staff and thus the presidency of Argentina, which were due to him in the military rotation in January 1973.

Peronist candidate killed—Francisco Ripoll, who sought the Justicialista nomination for governor of Misiones, was shot to death Dec. 10 by a local party member. The shooting took place shortly before the local Justicialista leadership convened to select a gubernatorial candidate.

The incident followed a clash Dec. 3 between police and young Peronist demonstrators in the Buenos Aires suburb of San Miguel, in which one of the youths was killed. Thirteen other Peronists were reported injured when police dispersed them with tear gas and rubber bullets. The demonstrators were protesting the 1970 killing of two Peronists.

Priests banned from politics. The Roman Catholic archdiocese of Buenos Aires Dec. 8 prohibited all priests under its jurisdiction from participating in political parties or accepting political office. More than 70 members of the Third World Priests Movement met with ex-President Peron Dec. 9, declaring afterwards that "the Argentine people's desire for liberation and justice is expressed . . . through the Peronist movement."

Peron leaves country. Peron left Argentina Dec. 14, ending 28 days of political consultations. A statement released as he departed said he would not accept the presidential nomination offered by the Justicialista Liberation Front, a coalition formed Dec. 5 by his Justicialista party and some 14 minor parties and political groups.

Peron arrived in Asuncion, Paraguay Dec. 14 for a visit with President Alfredo Stroessner, an old friend. He flew Dec. 18 to Peru, from where he would travel to Europe and Asia. An aide said he would return to Argentina in January 1973 to campaign for his party in the March elections.

Peron's statement Dec. 14 was written in conciliatory terms, calling for continued political peace in Argentina. Peron thanked the Justicialista coalition for its nomination, but said: "in view of the existing situation in the country, I find myself obliged to turn it down in favor of solutions that will permit the end of a military dictatorship that, with its errors, has brought the country to its present sad state."

The Justicialista party's convention defiantly renominated Peron Dec. 15, reportedly in a move to force political concessions from the government, which wanted the elections to take place but had in effect vetoed Peron's candidacy. However, Peron again rejected the nomination from Paraguay, giving his support to Hector Campora, his personal representative and the leader of the "political" wing of the Justicialistas.

Peron's final decision caused powerful labor union leaders to walk out of the convention early Dec. 16, charging that Campora and the party's professional politicians were greedy for political office and not forceful enough in prodding Peron to run. When the badly split convention reconvened later without the union leaders, Campora was nominated. His candidacy was then endorsed by the other groups in the Justicialista coalition, who secured the vice presidential nomination for one of their number, Popular Conservative party leader Vicente Solano Lima.

Campora was said to displease not only the Justicialista labor leaders—who represented much of the party's mass support and supplied most of its money—but also the military government, the New York Times reported Dec. 17. He was also ineligible to run under the same residency requirements that barred Peron, having traveled abroad since Aug. 25

without first seeking government permission.

Martinez sets presidential bid. Brig. Ezequiel Martinez resigned as planning and action secretary to the government Dec. 20 and accepted Dec. 21 the presidential nomination of the Federal Republican Alliance, a coalition of 11 parties in the interior of the country. He was replaced in the government Dec. 21 by Col. Juan Carranza Zavalia.

Widespread Unrest

The political activities preceding the 1973 election campaign were accompanied by serious labor unrest and dissent by various elements of Argentine society.

General strike cripples nation. Approximately five million workers from 110 unions remained away from their jobs Feb. 29 and March 1, closing down an estimated 85% of Argentina's industry, commerce and transportation. The 48-hour general strike had been called by the powerful General Confederation of Labor (CGT) Feb. 12 to protest the government's economic policies.

The shutdown, which had been declared illegal by President Alejandro Lanusse, affected factories, shops, banks, subways and trains. Government sources estimated it would cost the nation $104 million in lost production and wages.

Government troops guarded important installations throughout the country, and extra police details patrolled the heart of Buenos Aires. Although there was little violence, the London Times reported Feb. 29 that arsonists in Buenos Aires had set fire to more than a dozen buses and railway coaches.

According to the New York Times Feb. 29, labor leaders had called a national meeting for March 13 to decide on new protest measures. Alonso Correa, leader of the Cordoba lumber workers' union and a hard-line Peron-

ist, said there would be no solution to inflation and loss of purchasing power while Gen. Lanusse and "people who rob now in the name of the military" remained in power.

The government reportedly fixed maximum prices on bread, milk, butter and fish in the closing hours of the strike. Gen. Lanusse was on a state visit to Venezuela.

According to the British newsletter Latin America Feb. 18, the strike was voted by CGT moderates to counter growing support within the confederation for more active forms of protest including mass demonstrations and unannounced work stoppages. The vote among representatives against the more violent mesures was 65–53.

The current conflict over strike policy arose after the Lanusse government had rejected a CGT request for an immediate wage increase of 10%. Lanusse told union leaders Feb. 3 that the measures he introduced in December 1971, which included the suspension of collective bargaining, a 15% wage increase effective Jan. 1 and a further 10% rise in July, would remain in effect.

Although the January wage hike outstripped the cost of living increase by 3.7%, prices were expected to move ahead strongly throughout the first quarter, allowing real wages to decrease before the next wage increase in July.

The CGT had already ordered a general strike for March 10. In Cordoba, CGT unions had staged a 14-hour work stoppage Feb. 3, and the Metallurgical Workers' union, which participated in that stoppage, had held a similar strike Jan. 21.

Strikes & violence. The federal judge of Viedma ordered the release March 9 of five members of the city's food workers union, who had been arrested by military authorities for organizing a walkout during the Feb. 29–March 1 general strike.

Directors of the public employes union of the northeast province of Chaco decided March 17 to suspend for 10 days the daily six-hour work stoppages the union had recently carried out in support of demands for higher wages. The suspension was ordered to facilitate negotiations between the union and the government. Later March 17, a march by public employes on government offices in the city of Resistencia was broken up by police. The workers finally returned to the job March 21.

The director of a railroad workers' local was shot to death March 18 by unidentified gunmen as he and other union leaders went to make television addresses in La Plata.

Cement workers throughout Argentina staged a 24-hour work stoppage March 20.

Employes of the National Bank, the Development Bank and the National Postal Savings Bank in Buenos Aires staged a four-hour work stoppage March 20 to protest their failure to receive wage increases to which they were entitled by law Sept. 1, 1971 and Jan. 1.

Teachers protested against delays in their salary payments. Teachers in La Plata public schools refused to hold classes March 21 in a protest against repeated delays in their monthly pay checks. The striking teachers claimed they still had not received their February pay. Teachers in most public secondary schools in the northern province of Jujuy also suspended classes March 20–21 to demand February wages. They were joined by most public primary and secondary school teachers in the northeastern province of Santiago del Estero March 22.

Judicial employes in the northern province of Tucuman refused a government offer of wage hikes of 18% for low salaries and 12% for higher ones and began a 48-hour strike March 26.

Violence disrupts Mendoza. The western city of Mendoza was placed under a curfew April 4 after violent clashes between police and demonstrators protesting a 110% increase in electricity rates. The demonstrations coincided with a two-hour general strike which paralyzed the province of Mendoza. Air travel to and from Mendoza was suspended.

According to El Nacional of Caracas April 5, angered demonstrators stoned provincial government offices and businesses and burned buses and automobiles after police attempted to break up their march with tear gas and firehoses. The government in Buenos Aires declared a state of emergency and sent in army troops, which were able to restore order in Mendoza only after five hours of street battles.

Three people were killed, more than 100 injured and about 500 jailed April 5–7 in rioting in conjunction with daily CGT general strikes over the raised electricity rates.

Calm returned to the province only after President Lanusse went on nationwide television April 7 to announce the suspension of electricity payments for January-April and the creation of a special commission to overhaul the rate structure.

Workers at automobile plants in the central province of Cordoba held strikes in sympathy with the Mendoza protests April 5 as shootouts between police and snipers were reported in the provincial capital of Mendoza. The government blocked CGT funds the same day in an attempt to break the union's strikes, Le Monde reported April 7.

Rioting increased in Mendoza April 6 as demonstrators defying an army-imposed state of siege built barricades, set cars and buses on fire, and threw stones and Molotov cocktails at police and soldiers. In another attempt to break the strikes, the government ordered the arrest of several union leaders, including CGT regional director Carlos Fiorentini. Fiorentini and other detained union leaders were released April 9, when Fiorentini said the CGT was satisfied with the government's suspension of electricity payments.

A general strike paralyzed Mendoza April 7, leaving the city with low food and medical supplies, and sympathy strikes halted virtually all activities in Cordoba and in the western province of San Juan.

More than 2,000 soldiers in armored cars, riot police flown in from Buenos Aires and provincial policemen patrolled the streets of Mendoza April 7. A teacher was killed when she was caught in crossfire between army troops and snipers, and a student was shot to death when soldiers fired on youths stoning their truck.

Mendoza was calm April 8 as most citizens ignored a CGT call for another 24-hour strike. Troops continued to patrol the streets April 9, but the curfew imposed April 4 was lifted, and air and train service to the city, which had been suspended April 7, were resumed.

New Mendoza governor—Felix Enrique Gibbs assumed the governorship of the western province of Mendoza April 14. Gibbs' predecessor had been dismissed by President Lanusse.

'Hunger march' dispersed. At least 365 persons were arrested April 28 as about 5,000 police and an unspecified number of soldiers smothered an illegal "march against hunger" in downtown Buenos Aires. The demonstration had been organized by labor and student leftist organizations.

Fewer than 500 persons broke through police cordons to assemble a block from the presidential palace—the original destination of the march—but they were quickly dispersed by mounted police.

Cordoba general strike. The industrial city of Cordoba was paralyzed May 29 when workers left their jobs to commemorate the third anniversary of the city's May 1969 civil disturbances, which played a part in the downfall of President Juan Carlos Ongania.

Widespread disturbances. One person was killed and more than 500 were arrested June 22–30 as protests against the military government erupted into violence in several major cities.

The disturbances began June 22 in the northern provincial capital of Tucuman, where a strike for higher wages by teachers and civil servants led to riots in which more than 100 persons were arrested. Strikers and sympathetic students reportedly erected barricades in the center of the city, but were routed by police, who injured several students.

Rioting continued in Tucuman June 24–26 after a student died from injuries sustained in a clash with police. About 4,000 students took control of several city blocks near the local university, building barricades of trees and automobiles, but were again routed, this time by army troops and tanks.

The army occupied Tucuman June 27 as the city was gripped by a general strike, called by the General Labor Confederation (CGT) to protest government economic policies and repression. A CGT communique issued June 26 warned that if "indiscriminate repression" by the government did not cease, "neither the working class, nor the students, nor the people in general will be responsible for the chaos which could occur."

As the violence diminished in Tucuman, disturbances spread June 27 to Cordoba, Santa Fe, Salta and La Plata. Students and police clashed in Cordoba and Salta, while in Santa Fe about 1,500 students and workers demonstrated before provincial government buildings.

Troops and police massed in the streets of Buenos Aires and other main cities June 28 to prevent anti-government demonstrations marking the anniversary of the coup which brought the military to power in 1966. Further violence was reported from Tucuman, and Cordoba was the scene of another general strike.

Students occupied university buildings in Buenos Aires June 30, demanding the release of other students detained by police. Violence continued the same day in Tucuman and Cordoba, where at least 40 persons reportedly were arrested, and in Santa Fe, where troops and police clashed with striking workers.

CGT funds released—The Central Bank announced July 17 that CGT funds, blocked by government order July 7, were again available to the union.

Army occupies Malargue. The army July 3 occupied the Andean mining community of Malargue, in the province of Mendoza, amid a massive protest against the region's high rate of unemployment. The disturbance centered around the recent closing of the Santa Cruz manganese mine, which left 200 families without work.

The protest began July 2, when residents took control of Malargue, blocking access from the north and appointing five citizens to assume the functions of the municipal government. Municipal Intendent Jose Ranco resigned in sympathy with the protest, which he called "peaceful and symbolic," and police refused to take action against the insurgents.

Meanwhile, about 100 residents of Malargue arrived in the provincial capital of Mendoza after a 250-mile "hunger march" to dramatize their region's economic situation. Officials assured the marchers July 4 that their demands for more agriculture and industry in Malargue would be satisfied.

Most commercial activity stopped in Malargue July 3 as residents began a general strike to protest the army occupation. Shopowners reportedly refused to sell food to security officers, forcing the government to send in supplies from Mendoza, but no serious incidents were reported.

The National Development Bank agreed July 14 to furnish the credit necessary to reopen the Santa Cruz mine.

The announcement followed the appointment of Walter Alejandro Vaccari as Malargue's new municipal intendant July 13.

General Roca occupied. In a similar development July 4, troops occupied the town of General Roca, in the province of Rio Negro, after residents occupied the municipal government building and began to form a "provisional committee of government."

The protest reportedly grew out of a decision by the provincial governor, Gen. Roberto Requeijo, to establish a court in a neighboring town, allegedly discriminating against General Roca.

General Roca was virtually paralyzed July 6 after troops used tear gas to disperse a demonstration by residents against the administration of Gen. Requeijo.

Emergency measures were imposed in General Roca July 10–18 to quell continuing disturbances.

Protests reached a peak July 9 as citizens booed troops and forced the army to abandon its Independence Day parade. Townspeople later held their own celebration.

President Alejandro Lanusse declared General Roca an emergency zone July 10, naming Lt. Gen. Guillermo Anibal With as the military commander and supreme authority in the region. Gov. Requeijo arrived in Buenos Aires the same day to discuss the situation with Interior Minister Arturo Mor Roig and Lanusse.

Assuming command of General Roca July 11, Gen. With issued a series of decrees barring strikes, ordering prison sentences for persons disobeying military or security forces, and imposing press censorship. Most businesses resumed operations the same day, but the town newspaper struck to protest the censorship decree.

After a week of relative calm, the emergency measures were lifted July 18. Troops were withdrawn and a new municipal intendent, Col. Enrique Pellicetti, was installed. However, demonstrations against Gov. Requeijo resumed that night, with townspeople building bonfires and racing cars through the streets.

Thirty-two persons were arrested during protests July 19 and released the next day. About 2,500 persons demonstrated in front of the municipal building July 20, but no police action was reported.

Interior Undersecretary Guillermo Belgrano Rawson arrived in General Roca July 20 to discuss grievances with local members of the Law College, political parties and the chamber of commerce. Belgrano left July 22 after promising to study Gov. Requeijo's decision to establish a civil court outside General Roca, the action that had triggered the unrest.

Teachers strike. More than 300,000 teachers across the nation began a 48-hour strike July 5 for higher wages, revocation of the government's current educational reform proposals, and greater national budget allocations for education. Only 12.5% of the Argentine budget was assigned to education, while a United Nations Educational, Scientific and Cultural Organization convention recommended an allocation of at least 25%.

Newsmen protest police action. The Argentine Federation of Journalists charged

July 6 that newsmen in La Plata, Tucuman, Cordoba and other cities had been harassed by security forces while trying to report on the recent nationwide civil disturbances.

A communique from the federation's executive board noted that offices of the newspaper El Litoral in Corrientes had been attacked during the disturbances, presumably by local policemen. The board called for "severe measures" by the government to stop such attacks.

Doctors, dentists strike. More than 70,000 physicians, dentists and biochemists struck July 11–12 to protest a government plan to revamp Argentina's hospital system. The plan, embodied in a new public health law, included key changes in the rights of patients enrolled in government, labor union and private health plans to choose their own doctors. The Argentine Medical Confederation and the Dentists Association claimed the government had disregarded the professional rights of doctors and dentists.

In a second action, physicians, psychiatrists and biochemists across the nation held a 72-hour strike July 19–21, virtually paralyzing Argentina's hospitals and clinics. The stoppage, called by the Argentine Medical Confederation to protest new public health laws and demand greater government funding, was supported by shorter strikes among dentists, pharmacists and mental health workers.

Cordoba hit by strikes. Municipal workers and employes in Cordoba agreed Nov. 27 to suspend for 48 hours a strike begun Nov. 7 to demand payment of October wages and "a solution to the difficult economic situation" they faced. The move followed talks between union leaders and Col. Pedro Enrique Martinez, who was appointed military commander in the city Nov. 23 following the resignation of municipal intendant Ramon Crucet. Municipal workers and employes in the rest of Cordoba province began a 24-hour strike Nov. 28.

Teachers in Cordoba and Santiago del Estero provinces began a 48-hour strike Nov. 28. All but teachers in intermediate schools observed the stoppage. It followed a nationwide teachers' strike Nov. 23 demanding enactment of the 12% wage increase decreed by President Alejandro Lanusse in September.

Cordoba was virtually paralyzed Dec. 27 by a CGT-called general strike. Strikers protested high prices and a breakdown of cooperative contract negotiations. They demanded the lifting of the state of siege and the release of political prisoners and arrested CGT and student leaders.

Unpaid doctors and interns, nurses and health workers in Cordoba public hospitals began a 16-day strike Dec. 30, following an earlier strike Dec. 19–25. They demanded a free, efficient public hospital for the city; full employment for health professionals, 70% of whom were not being paid for their work; a "rational" state health policy and an increase and redistribution of the health budget.

CGT leader released—Agustin Tosco, the combative leader of Cordoba's light and power union and regional CGT, was released from prison Sept. 23 after being held for more than 17 months under the national state of siege. He immediately denied that his release had been secured by Jose Rucci, secretary general of the CGT, who was said to be working to ease the conflict between the union and the government, and to be a supporter of President Lanusse's new economic policies.

Tosco's release followed the reopening Sept. 19 of Cordoba's CGT offices, closed by the government Aug. 24 during demonstrations against the killing of 16 subversives at a Patagonian naval prison.

Violence, Terrorism & Countermeasures

Priest, businessman held. La Prensa of Buenos Aires reported Jan. 7 that naval authorities had abducted from their homes businessman Ricardo Beltran and the Rev. Albert Fernando Carbone, a member of the Third World Priests Movement, for questioning about an aborted Peronist plot to attack a coast guard post in the city of Zarate Jan. 3.

Beltran was reported active in Peronist circles and Carbone had previously been given a two-year suspended sentence in connection with the slaying of former President Pedro Aramburo by Peronist-oriented guerrillas in 1970.

Despite protests from Third World Movement priests that Carbone had no knowledge of military tactics, federal authorities were reported Jan. 11 to be holding the men custody in a Buenos Aires jail.

Report accuses police of torture. Lawyers and relatives of 30 persons held in Argentine jails compiled a 60-page report accusing police of torturing prisoners, according to the Miami Herald Jan. 14.

The report contained statements from the alleged victims. Most of the prisoners named in the document were linked by police to various guerrilla organizations.

Torture was systematically applied to suspected subversives by police and military authorities, the French newspaper Le Monde reported April 20. Buenos Aires lawyers had recently denounced police brutality toward six arrested women, two of whom were pregnant, Le Monde said.

Leftists rob bank. Fifteen members of the People's Revolutionary Army (ERP), a Trotskyite guerrilla group, took as much as $800,000 from the state-owned National Development Bank in Buenos Aires Jan. 30. It was called the biggest bank robbery in Argentina's history.

According to newspaper accounts, the guerrillas held 13 bank employes hostage for eight hours while they bored a hole in the bank's vault. A police report implicated two bank employes.

Notices distributed later in Buenos Aires bars said the money was "expropriated for the people's cause, and will be used to continue the revolutionary war."

Wave of terrorist attacks. A wave of political assassinations and kidnapings was sweeping Argentina, the New York Times reported March 22, 1972.

Participating in the terrorist campaign,

the Times noted, were Peronist urban commandos, who defied a recent plea from Gen. Juan Domingo Peron to his followers for a halt to violence.

Among incidents reported:

Four police bomb disposal experts were killed Jan. 14 when a bomb they were defusing exploded in the Buenos Aires home of former Justice Minister Jaime Perriaux. A communique issued later by the Armed Liberation Forces (FAL) said the group had left the bomb in Perriaux's home because he had introduced the death penalty and state of siege regulations during his administration (July 1970–mid-1971).

Police arrested 43 suspected subversives in Buenos Aires, Salta and Bahia Blanca Jan. 13 and 14, confiscating arms, munitions, wigs and masks, and discovering documents in which guerrilla attacks were allegedly planned.

Members of the terrorist Revolutionary Armed Forces (FAR) set off explosives in the Buenos Aires social building of the Argentina Association of Hereford Raisers Jan. 22, causing structural damage to the building.

Six leftist guerrillas in Tucuman, 665 miles northwest of Buenos Aires, commandeered a milk truck Feb. 7 and delivered its 1,000-gallon load of bottled milk to poor people in two shantytowns.

A leader of the New Force party was killed by members of the Peronist Montonero guerrilla organization March 18, the same day that Montoneros set fire to a New Force office in Buenos Aires.

At least 10 members of the Armed Forces of Liberation were reported March 19 to have blown up the clubhouse of the exclusive Buenos Aires San Jorge Polo Club with three bombs.

Alleged ERP terrorists attacked a police station in Rio Tala April 27, killing two officers and seriously wounding the San Pedro police commissioner.

Seven youths disarmed two guards and then blew up a coast guard installation about five miles from Buenos Aires, the Miami Herald reported May 2.

Terrorists set off explosives at the homes of several police officers in the northwestern city of Tucuman May 5. No one was reported injured.

The offices of five U.S. companies in Buenos Aires were bombed in apparent response to the U.S. escalation of the Vietnam war, the Washington Post reported May 12.

Sixteen bombings were reported in Buenos Aires, Cordoba, Rosario and Santa Fe June 9, on the 16th anniversary of an abortive Peronist military coup. Among the sites bombed were the offices of the Buenos Aires newspaper La Opinion and a steel plant near the capital.

A renewed outbreak of terrorist attacks in Buenos Aires, Rosario, La Plata, Salta, Sante Fe and several smaller communities was reported Aug. 20. The actions followed the explosion of 15 bombs in Cordoba Aug. 18.

Carlos Raul Capuano Martinez, sought for alleged involvement in the 1970 kidnapping and murder of ex-President Pedro Aramburu, was killed in a shootout with Buenos Aires police Aug. 17.

(A retired naval captain, Aldo Luis Molinari, had charged that Aramburu was killed not by Montonero guerrillas, as reported officially at the time, but by government agents, the London newsletter Latin America reported Aug. 4. Molinari said Aramburu had been plotting against President Juan Carlos Ongania, and the government, which fell 10 days after Aramburu's death, had accused the Montoneros as a diversion.)

Meanwhile, the wave of violence begun July 26, the anniversary of the death of Peron's wife Eva, continued. A policeman and a youth were reported shot to death in Buenos Aires July 28, and the explosion of more than 50 bombs in Buenos Aires and other cities was reported Aug. 4.

At least five persons were wounded and nine arrested Aug. 3 when a gunfight erupted between rival Peronist factions at Ezeiza International Airport in Buenos Aires.

Bombings mark Peronist anniversary— A series of bomb explosions occurred Oct. 17, the anniversary of Peron's release from prison in 1945 under the pressure of popular demonstrations. The blasts, which disrupted train services in Rosario and damaged buildings and installations throughout the country, followed the bombing Oct. 16 of the new U.S.-owned Sheraton Hotel in Buenos

Aires. A Canadian woman was killed in the blast and two other persons were injured.

The wife of a leading radical Peronist theoretician was seriously wounded Oct. 19 by a bomb set off in their Buenos Aires apartment. The Buenos Aires office of a lawyer who defended left-wing guerrillas was bombed the same day.

A guerrilla was shot to death in a gunfight with Buenos Aires police Oct. 18 following the explosion of a bomb at the home of the father of a Cabinet minister, according to police.

Police using tear gas broke up Peronist demonstrations in Buenos Aires and other cities Oct. 17.

An armed band blew up an exclusive social club in Santa Fe Oct. 13 after clearing the building. Bombings were reported Oct. 12 in Buenos Aires and other cities and at the farms of several military officers.

Bomb explosions Nov. 24 damaged several Cordoba buildings housing union offices. A Cordoba nightclub had been destroyed by a bomb Nov. 2.

A powerful bomb explosion damaged the San Miguel de Tucuman branch of the U.S.-owned International Business Machines Corp. Nov. 9.

Fifteen bombs exploded in Argentina Dec. 22, damaging buildings used by the armed forces, labor unions, political parties, banks and businesses, but causing no casualties. Bombs were set off at six businesses in Rosario early Dec. 20.

Fiat executive slain. Oberdan Sallustro, 56, president of Argentina's Italian-owned Fiat automotive industries, was kidnaped by ERP terrorists March 21, 1972 as he drove to work in Buenos Aires. He was found shot to death in a suburban house April 10.

The body was found after a police car searching for Sallustro discovered the ERP hideout. It was fired on by several guerrillas, and Sallustro was reportedly executed during the shootout that ensued. One of the guerrillas was captured.

According to the New York Times April 11, the ERP had sought a $1 million ransom for Sallustro and the release of 50 of the more than 500 political prisoners held in Argentina. Fiat had reportedly been willing to pay the ransom, but President Lanusse had barred any form of negotiations with the ERP, calling its members "common delinquents."

El Nacional of Caracas reported April 11 that Lanusse had also rejected a plea for negotiations with the ERP from Italian President Giovanni Leone. Lanusse had maintained that Sallustro's kidnaping was an internal Argentine matter.

After the government's refusal to allow negotiations, the ERP had announced that it would execute Sallustro "at the appropriate moment."

The army announced April 18 that it had captured the eight-member ERP team that had kidnaped and murdered Sallustro.

Eighteen other alleged ERP members, 15 of them women, were also arrested in connection with the case, and six other accomplices were said to be at large.

Two of the men arrested in the Sallustro case, Andres Ernesto Alsina Bea and Ignacio Ikonicoff, charged in the Montevideo weekly Marcha May 12 that they had been tortured in Buenos Aires jails.

(Alsina Bea, a journalist for the Buenos Aires newspaper La Opinion, said he was kicked severely and electric shock was applied to his genitals and mouth. Ikonicoff, a journalist for Inter Press, was also beaten and claimed other prisoners were burned with acid.)

(Three of the defendants were given life sentences March 16, 1973 for their roles in Sallustro's kidnap-murder, and seven received terms of one to 12 years. (A three-judge court agreed that two of the defendants had been tortured.)

General assassinated. Gen. Juan Carlos Sanchez, commander of the army's 2nd Corps, was machine-gunned to death April 10 as he rode to his office in the industrial city of Rosario, 150 miles north of Buenos Aires. Unidentified attackers also seriously wounded Sanchez' chauffer and accidentally killed a news vendor.

The People's Revolutionary Army (ERP) and the Revolutionary Armed Forces (FAR), two urban guerrilla organizations which had not worked together before, issued a joint communique

April 10 claiming responsibility for Sanchez' death and promising further assassinations. The communique said Sanchez had been killed in reprisal for his anti-guerrilla campaign.

(According to El Nacional of Caracas April 11, the 2nd Corps had pursued terrorists vigorously, extending military repression over groups not directly connected with urban guerrillas, such as progressive Roman Catholic priests. Soldiers under Sanchez' command had been accused of torturing persons they arrested, but authorities had dismissed the charges.)

The ERP-FAR document also denounced President Alejandro Lanusse for "threatening a fascist coup" and for promoting "an electoral farce" by declaring general elections for March 1973. Numerous sources said Lanusse's election plan and his recent negotiations with ex-President Peron had caused the latest wave of terrorist attacks in Argentina.

Lanusse flew to Rosario April 10, where he was joined by other members of the army high command in paying last respects to Sanchez. Lanusse ordered Rosario closed to all traffic, and the 2nd Corps called on civilians to help army officers capture the assassins.

Argentina's major political, labor and business leaders met with Lanusse in Buenos Aires later April 10, condemning guerrilla violence and asserting their support for the president.

The National Security Council, meeting late April 10, decreed that all trials for kidnaping, violating the public peace and attacking institutions would henceforth be transferred to military tribunals.

Authorities announced June 24 that Dr. Luis Alejandro Gaitini, 27, had been arrested in connection with Sanchez' assassination. Gaitini, an alleged member of FAR, reportedly confessed participation in Sanchez' murder and other terrorist activities.

Gaitani and two other defendants were sentenced to life imprisonment and two others to terms of nine and 11 years Feb. 9, 1973 for alleged participation in the affair.

Torture reports grow. More than 50 persons reportedly had been tortured at prisons and military installations during the past year, and accounts of political torture were growing in magazines and newspapers, according to the Miami Herald May 26.

The most publicized recent case of political torture involved Norma Morello, a Roman Catholic schoolteacher and rural organizer, who returned to her home in Goya May 14 after being held without charge for nearly six months. After her release, Miss Morello signed an affidavit saying she had been tortured for three days with electric devices, repeatedly threatened with rape, and denied sleep for 15 days while she was interrogated at a military installation outside Rosario.

Miss Morello said May 15 that she had been tortured because police wanted her to link the Catholic movement in Goya to Argentina's guerrilla movements. She said she had told her captors nothing.

Two other women, arrested in connection with a kidnaping, claimed they had been tortured by federal police with an electric needle, the Herald reported May 26. Police denied the charge.

The army issued instructions May 25 intended to prevent the mistreatment and torture of political prisoners. However, government sources admitted that authorities were virtually powerless to stop torture, since the names of torturers were not on the staff lists of any of the police security forces, the London Times reported May 26.

Lawyers march dispersed. Police armed with tear gas and fire hoses broke up a demonstration by several hundred lawyers in downtown Buenos Aires June 23. The march was part of a nationwide day of protest by about 25,000 lawyers against repressive laws and alleged police kidnaping and torture of attorneys and other political prisoners.

According to El Nacional of Caracas June 24, lawyer's organizations across Argentina held paramilitary organizations of right-wing policemen responsible for the disappearance in 1970 of attorney Nestor Martins, and the kidnaping and torture in May of lawyer Eduardo Jozami. The organizations demanded an end to such action against individual lawyers, the lifting of the state of siege and other repressive legislation.

Suspended sentences for publishers. Two publishers of leftist magazines, Casiana Ahumada and Osvaldo Vely, were given suspended sentences after a Buenos Aires court found them guilty of "defending violence," according to the Miami Herald June 14.

Ahumada, publisher of the Catholic weekly Christianity and Revolution, had been arrested in December 1971 after her magazine printed a communique from the Montoneros, an Argentine terrorist organization, and numerous articles defending Latin American priests who took up arms against their governments. Her case reportedly had aroused international sympathy, causing the Argentine government some embarrassment. She received a 15-month suspended sentence.

Vely, publisher of Liberation, received a suspended nine-month sentence.

The newsletter Latin America reported July 28 that a special government-named commission had begun reviewing all publications entering Argentina by mail or through customs in an effort to weed out those which might disturb "the country's tranquility and sovereignty."

Kidnaped businessmen ransomed. Three kidnaped businessmen were freed unharmed in Buenos Aires Sept. 6 after ransoms reportedly totaling $850,000 were paid to their captors, the Associated Press reported Sept. 7.

Jan J. Van de Panne, a Dutch citizen who headed the Philips Argentina electronics firm, was released by alleged Peronist Montonero guerrillas after his company paid them $500,000. He had been held since Sept. 5. Two Argentine businessmen—Adolfo Kaplun and Eduardo Falugue, both abducted Sept. 4—were freed after their families reportedly ransomed them for $150,000 and $250,000. Police arrested nine "common criminals" in connection with Kaplun's kidnaping, La Prensa of Buenos Aires reported Sept. 15.

A wealthy landowner, Eden Ronald Bongiovani of La Pampa province was reportedly kidnaped Sept. 6 and held for $200,000 ransom.

Aldo Benito Roggio, an engineer from Cordoba, was kidnaped Sept. 21 and released Sept. 22 after his family paid a reported ransom of $130,000-$170,000.

Enrico Barella, an Italian, was kidnaped in Buenos Aires Nov. 7 and released unharmed Nov. 10 after his family reportedly paid a $500,000 ransom.

Felix Azpiazu, a Spanish industrialist kidnaped Dec. 6, was freed unharmed Dec. 8 after his firm paid a reported $100,000 ransom.

Ronald Grove, managing director of Great Britain's Vestey industrial group in South America, was kidnaped in Buenos Aires Dec. 10 and released unharmed Dec. 19 after Vestey paid a reported $1 million ransom. His abductors belonged to the Trotskyist People's Revolutionary Army.

Vicente Russo, an executive for a Buenos Aires subsidiary of the International Telephone and Telegraph Corp., was kidnaped in the capital Dec. 27 and released unharmed Dec. 29. Company officials refused to comment on local newspapers reports that a ransom of $500,000-$1 million had been paid.

(Police in La Plata announced Feb. 21, 1973 that they had captured a seven-person FAR cell implicated in, among other crimes, the kidnapings of Ronald Grove and Enrico Barella. The group was said to be led by Francisco Urondo, a journalist and poet.)

Admiral assassinated. Rear Adm. Emilio R. Berisso, plans and strategy officer for the naval chief of staff, was shot to death near Buenos Aires Dec. 28 by presumed urban guerrillas. The assassins escaped. President Alejandro Lanusse appeared on nationwide television to warn that "nothing or no one" would thwart his government's plans to hold general elections in March 1973.

Berisso's position in the Navy reportedly linked him to the armed forces security network responsible for repression of the country's guerrilla groups.

The FAR (Revolutionary Armed Forces) later claimed credit for Berisso's death.

Death penalty lifted—President Lanusse Dec. 27 abolished the death penalty, reintroduced by a previous military government in 1970 following the assassination of former President Pedro Aramburu.

Trelew Prison Break & Killings

16 killed after prison break, hijack. Sixteen suspected guerrillas, including at least three women, were shot to death Aug. 22 while allegedly trying to escape from the prison at the naval air base near Trelew, in the southern province of Chubut. Three other alleged subversives were reportedly wounded.

According to police officials, all of the victims had been arrested Aug. 15 at the Trelew airport, where they had helped 10 other alleged terrorists hijack an Austral Airlines jet with 96 aboard.

The hijacking was carried out in conjunction with a mutiny at an army maximum security prison at Rawson, 15 miles from Trelew, during which a group of inmates escaped. Some escapees were reportedly among the hijackers, who commandeered the jet to Santiago, Chile, where they surrendered to police and requested political asylum.

Those killed included 12 members of the left-wing People's Revolutionary Army (ERP), one of the Revolutionary Armed Forces and two of the Peronist Montoneros. They had surrendered to military authorities after helping in the hijacking. Their deaths were widely assumed to be a retaliatory execution ordered by the government.

News of the killings at Trelew caused large demonstrations in several cities in which hundreds of persons were arrested. In the industrial city of Cordoba 600 protestors were arrested Aug. 22, and labor unions held a two-hour protest strike Aug. 23. Sixty students were detained overnight in La Plata, and students briefly took over six university buildings in Buenos Aires Aug. 22.

The protests were joined by Peronists, whose powerful Justicialista party condemned the killings Aug. 23 as "a new violation of human rights." The Justicialista supreme council sent a Peronist youth leader, Juan Licastro, to Trelew to investigate the killings, but he was immediately arrested by the army. The naval base was sealed off and authorities refused to give further information about the killings.

Lawyers for the slain guerrilla suspects Aug. 22 denounced their clients' deaths as "a virtual execution," charging it would have been impossible for them to try to escape because they were held in separate cells under heavy guard.

Former President Arturo Frondizi also joined in the outcry, charging Aug. 22 that "the government has shown itself absolutely incapable of preserving order. I pray to God that this bloodbath, which Argentines neither want nor deserve, will cease."

Trelew hijackers reach Cuba. The 10 Argentine guerrillas who hijacked an airliner from Trelew to Santiago were sent to Cuba by the Chilean government Aug. 25.

The Argentine government, which had demanded extradition of the guerrillas, angrily recalled its ambassador from Santiago Aug. 26 and delivered what it called a "very severe" protest to Chile Aug. 27.

In a nationwide radio and television message Aug. 25, Chilean President Salvador Allende said his government's decision to grant the guerrillas political asylum and then send them to Cuba was motivated by "profound humanity and morality" and followed "international conventions and principles and the dispositions of our internal laws." Allende added that Chile remained "deeply" committed to maintaining friendly relations with Argentina, which had been "strengthened with satisfactory results" by his administration.

Allende's decision not to return the guerrillas to Argentina was reportedly sealed by the fatal shooting of 16 of their comrades at Trelew's naval air base prison Aug. 22.

Upon arrival in Havana Aug. 26, the 10 guerrillas told newsmen that armed Marxist and Peronist groups in Argentina would step up their offensive against the government of President Alejandro Lanusse. ERP leader Roberto Mario

Santucho, whose wife was among the 16 killed at Trelew, accused Lanusse of direct responsibility for the "assassination" of his fellow guerrillas.

In Argentina, meanwhile, the government reportedly gave two conflicting versions of the Trelew killings, one on an "off the record" basis to newsmen, and an official version released Aug. 25. According to the London newsletter Latin America Sept. 1, journalists were originally told that the prisoners had escaped from their cells early Aug. 22 and after seizing the second-in-command of the base, Capt. Luis Sosa, were proceeding toward the armory when they were engaged in fierce combat by guards.

The later version, however, held that Sosa had ordered the prisoners out of their cells and was inspecting them in a narrow passage—some five feet wide—when he was seized by a guerrilla, who took his submachine gun and began shooting at the guards. The weakest part of the version, the newsletter noted, was that the guerrilla had missed his targets while Sosa alone had escaped unharmed from a fusillade which cut down 16 guerrillas and wounded three of their comrades.

The official version was denounced by a group of six lawyers, who told a press conference Sept. 8 that a statement calling it "completely false" had been sworn by the three surviving guerrillas, who were being held in a prison hospital in Buenos Aires.

Confusion over the actual events at Trelew was heightened Aug. 24 when the paramilitary police invaded Peronist headquarters in Buenos Aires, where the bodies of three of the guerrillas were lying, and arrested several hundred persons who had turned a wake into a demonstration against the government. The bodies were hurriedly buried by the military to avoid further public disturbances.

Security forces Aug. 28 broke into the offices of Primera Plana, a Peronist weekly, whose edition that day carried reports that the body of one of the guerrillas showed severe wounds from blows to the back of the head. However, authorities arrived too late to seize more than a few copies of the issue.

Protests continue—Protests against the Trelew killings mounted Aug. 23–

25 as students, workers and political leaders demonstrated and fought security forces in major cities. Authorities quelled the disturbances after making hundreds of arrests, and then carried out a series of raids in different cities Aug. 26–27, claiming arrest of numerous subversives and confiscation of quantities of arms and ammunition.

Students demonstrated Aug. 23 in Buenos Aires, Cordoba, Rosario, Santa Fe, Tucuman, La Plata, Corrientes and Bahia Blanca. Hundreds of students and labor and political leaders were reported arrested in the capital, where several bombings were reported. In Cordoba, home of at least seven of the Trelew victims, more than 700 students were arrested in separate demonstrations, and workers at auto and heavy industrial plants held a two-hour work stoppage.

Demonstrations continued Aug. 24 in Buenos Aires, Cordoba, Tucuman, Rosario, La Plata, Santiago del Estero and Santa Fe. The army took control of Cordoba, where it closed the local offices of the Peronist-dominated General Labor Confederation (CGT). Authorities charged the union had been "abetting subversives," and declared illegal a 14-hour CGT general strike called for the next day. CGT leaders called the government action "arbitrary and illegal."

The CGT strike was held as planned Aug. 25, crippling Cordoba. Banks, businesses and schools closed, and public transportation was halted. Security patrols circulated throughout the city while CGT leaders reportedly went into hiding.

Trelew victims describe 'massacre.' The three survivors of the recent killing of 16 subversives at the Trelew naval air base prison had given mutually consistent accounts describing the action as a "massacre" by prison guards, the Washington Post reported Sept. 24.

The statements, which differed widely from official accounts of the killings, were released by Maria Antonia Berger, Alberto M. Camps and Ricardo R. Haidar, all of whom were wounded in the incident. Due to a new censorship decree barring publication of statements by subversives, the accounts were reported in Argentina only by the English-language

Herald, a small Buenos Aires newspaper.

According to the survivors, they and their 16 comrades had been lined up outside their cells by naval guards and officers, who then shot them down with automatic weapons fire. Guards allegedly passed among the fallen afterwards to finish off survivors point blank.

Berger said she was shot through the chin by a guard after she fell into her cell, bleeding from three wounds. Before long, she continued, a medic entered and found her still alive, but left her on the floor for five hours. She said she was then taken by ambulance to a hospital, but was not treated until a naval medical team was flown in from another base four hours later. Camps and Haidar gave similar accounts of the shootings.

According to the Post, Interior Undersecretary Guillermo Belgrano Rawson claimed he was unaware of the accusations or of claims that editors were afraid to publish them. (The government Sept. 16 closed the Peronist weekly Primera Plana, which had published reports contradicting the official version of the killings at Trelew.)

Economic Developments

Foreign credits sought. Central Bank president Carlos Brignone flew to Washington Jan. 30 on the first leg of a trip to the U.S. and Europe in search of $1 billion in credits to restore confidence in the economy.

Brignone's goal, the New York Times reported Jan. 29, would consist of about $440 million from the International Monetary Fund (IMF), credits of $600 million from Western banks, and the purchase by foreign companies operating in Argentina of about $150 million in government bonds in place of profit remittances.

Argentina had to meet debt payments of $600 million by July 1973. Its foreign reserves, which had reached about $800 million in October 1970, were virtually wiped out by trade deficits and flight of capital. Reserves of only $150 million in gold remained.

After meeting Feb. 8 with representa-

Argentina: Military Expenditures[1] in Current Prices in Relation to Gross Domestic Product (GDP) and Fiscal Sector Expenditures, and Military Expenditures on a Constant Price Basis, 1967-72

Values in Millions of New Pesos[2] and U.S. Dollars

Year	GDP	Expenditures[3]		Military expenditures as:		Military expenditures on constant price basis[4] (1967 = 100)	
		Fiscal sector	Military	% of GDP	% of fiscal sector	Pesos	US$[5]
		—In current pesos—					
1967	59,120	8,436	1,463	2.5	16.8	1,463	418
1968	68,822	9,483	1,591	2.3	16.8	1,400	411
1969	80,422	10,205	1,795	2.2	17.6	1,506	430
1970	[6]96,571	11,984	1,925	2.0	16.1	1,357	388
1971	[6]138,029	15,266	2,608	1.9	17.1	1,370	392
1972	—	22,961	4,169	—	18.1	—	—

[1] Data are estimated on the basis of functional allocations for defense and allocations for social security expenditures for the armed forces.

[2] A new peso, equal to 100 old pesos, was introduced January 1, 1970. All national currency data in this table are expressed in new pesos.

[3] Budgetary data.

[4] Current prices converted to constant prices by using implicit deflators of the gross domestic product for 1967-69 and the consumer price index for 1970-71 from International Monetary Fund, *International Financial Statistics*, August 1972.

[5] Values in constant pesos converted at 350 old pesos (3.50 new pesos) to the U.S. dollar, the official rate at the end of 1967.

[6] Estimated on the basis of the reported rate of growth in the gross national product.

Sources: Data on GDP and implicit deflators as follows: 1967-69 from Banco Central de la Republica Argentina, *Suplemento de Boletin Estadistico No. 1*, January 1971; 1970-71 estimated on the basis of data in Agency for International Development, Division of Statistics and Reports, *Economic Data Book*, Argentina: Revision sheet, No. 306, April 1972.

Expenditure data from the annual budget laws (*Presupuesto General para el Ejercicio del Ano . . .*) and amendments.

From Latin American Military Expenditures 1967-1971 (U.S. Department of State)

tives of 15 U.S. banks, Brignone flew to London. The British newsletter Latin America reported Feb. 11 that Brignone had been assured IMF credits totaling $250 million. The newsletter added Feb. 18 that U.S. banks were willing to add to Argentina's credit if European banks would also participate.

The U.S. government, Latin America commented Jan. 28, would cooperate to assure the success of President Alejandro Lanusse's economic policy and thereby neutralize the Peronist movement.

In a related development, the newsletter reported Feb. 11 that Fiat would invest $90 million in Argentina during the next four years, mostly in automobile production.

Brignone returned to Buenos Aires Feb. 26 and announced March 2 that $960 million in loans were being negotiated.

Brignone and his credit-seeking aides then spent eight days (March 24–31) in Japan, where, the Miami Herald reported March 31, Japanese banks agreed to lend Argentina $30 million to consolidate its foreign exchange reserves.

The U.S. Export-Import Bank granted Argentina credit of $31 million to buy 80 locomotives from the General Motors Co. and components for other trains to be built in Argentina, the Miami Herald reported March 12. The Morgan Guaranty Co. also loaned the country $31 million to improve its railway system.

The Inter-American Development Bank agreed June 14 to lend Hierro Patagonico, a subsidiary of the Sierra Grande Mining Co., $32 million for equipment and construction.

Fraud uncovered. Police disclosed Feb. 17 that they had uncovered a massive fraud which cost the country nearly $8 million—equivalent to 5% of the trade deficit for 1971. Four directors of importing firms were reported under arrest in connection with the case.

According to the Washington Post Feb. 19, the alleged fraud took advantage of a concession in Argentina's financial laws which allowed importers of essential goods to buy U.S. dollars at the minimal parity of five pesos to the dollar.

Arms purchases increase. According to a Swedish study quoted in La Prensa of Buenos Aires Feb. 19, Latin American countries had made massive purchases of warplanes, submarines, tanks and missiles since 1968.

The study, to be published in June by the International Institute for Pacifist Research in Stockholm (SIPRI), stated that the principal buyers of war materials were Argentina, Brazil, Chile and Peru, although since 1970 Venezuela and Colombia also had made large purchases. The arms were supplied by the U.S., France, Great Britain, West Germany, Italy, the Netherlands, Australia, Sweden and Norway. Only Cuba bought military equipment from the U.S.S.R.

Although the study did not include the cost of the armaments, a 1971 SIPRI report estimated that from 1950 to 1970 Latin America bought arms at an average annual cost of $95 million, 85% of it spent by Argentina, Brazil, Chile, Cuba, Peru and Venezuela.

According to the study, Latin American governments had bought 478 military aircraft—from propeller-driven transport carriers to French Mirage and Soviet MiG-21 jet fighters—in 1968–71. Argentina, Brazil, Peru, Colombia and Venezuela together had purchased 77 Mirage III and Mirage V fighters, although only Peru had received the aircraft, the report said.

Argentina had bought 14 Mirages in 1970, with delivery scheduled sometime in 1972, the report stated.

Peso devalued in economic crisis. Amid one of the gravest economic crises of the century, the government devalued the peso by 9.2% Feb. 23 through a modification of exchange regulations for imports and exports.

According to the New York Times, the move, which followed the closing of the foreign exchange market Feb. 22, was taken to ease pressure on the peso, which had fallen to a low of 10.15 to the dollar on the official financial market.

Under the new regulations, importers and exporters had to change 43% of foreign payments and earnings at the financial rate and the remaining 57% at the lower commercial rate, which remained fixed at 5 to the dollar. After exchange transactions resumed Feb. 23, the peso closed at 9.60 to the dollar.

The government gave exporters of manufactured goods an incentive by allowing them to exchange 53% of their foreign earnings at the higher financial rate and 47% at the commercial rate.

Inflation unabated—Financial conditions had deteriorated dramatically in late 1971 and early 1972. The cost of living went up by 11.3% in January.

According to the National Institute of Census and Statistics (INDEC), wholesale prices rose by 48.1% during 1971, with an increase of 7.1% in December. INDEC statistics published in La Prensa of Buenos Aires Jan. 19 showed that the cost of agricultural and cattle products rose by 61.1% during the year, while other articles rose by 42%. The cost of imported products increased 50.3%.

Wage increases. Less than two months after pledging not to change his policy on wages, President Alejandro Lanusse April 26 ordered the 10% wage increase slated for July 1 moved up to May 1 and increased to 15%.

Lanusse reportedly made the decision over the objections of Finance Minister Cayetano Licciardo and Central Bank President Carlos Brignone, who contended the increase would merely contribute to Argentina's runaway inflation.

(The National Institute of Census and Statistics disclosed May 19 that wholesale prices had risen by 5.1% during April, and 30.7% since the beginning of the year, when Lanusse ordered a 15% wage increase. The price increase from April 1971 to April 1972 was 76%.)

The new wage policy was intended as a concession to organized labor and consumers, whose support Lanusse sought for his plan to hold general elections in March 1973, the New York Times reported May 14. However, the powerful General Confederation of Labor bitterly attacked the wage increase May 16, charging it had already been swallowed up by price increases.

Compensatory measures—The government May 15 announced a series of measures designed to help businessmen absorb the 15% wage increase.

Among the measures were abolition of the 1.5% tax on all bank loans, which went to the National Development Bank; a freezing of public service tariffs; and a promise that special credits would be available from the National Bank to companies which cooperated with the fight against inflation by holding down prices.

IMF suspends credit—The wage raise and a cancellation of electricity rate increases violated a stabilization agreement Argentina had reached with the International Monetary Fund (IMF) as the basis for a $119 million loan from the agency, the New York Times reported May 14. Consequently, the IMF removed Argentina's loan request from its agenda.

The IMF decision doomed Argentina's efforts to find $1 billion in foreign credit to ease its huge balance of payments deficit, the London newsletter Latin America reported May 5. Many potential creditors were unwilling to lend to Argentina unless the IMF did so.

The IMF June 14, however, approved its first credit tranche facility to Argentina for the equivalent of $119.4 million. This reversed its earlier denial of such a loan. The June 14 allotment brought to $362.8 million the IMF credits going to Argentina in 1972's first half to meet international debt payments.

Gold reserves up. High export earnings at the end of June brought Argentina's gold and foreign exchange reserves up to $172 million, the newsletter Latin America reported July 14.

Brignone resigns. The government announced July 25 that Central Bank President Carlos Brignone, a strong opponent of inflation-breeding government deficit spending, had resigned. He was replaced by Jorge Bermudez, head of the large state-owned National Bank.

According to the New York Times July 27, Brignone had been criticized for his inability to obtain significant foreign loans. Also, Brignone's tight money policies, often eroded by government spending, had caused a severe shortage of liquidity in the economy, and had not prevented inflation from reaching a record 37% during the first half of 1972.

(International Monetary Fund statistics cited in El Nacional of Caracas Aug. 5 showed Argentine inflation for the year ending May 31 was 56.5%, the highest in the world. The peso was devalued by another 3.54% July 21 through a modification of foreign exchange rules.)

Economic decisions—The government July 25 also announced these economic decisions, which Brignone opposed:

There would be no increases in utility rates, subway and commuter fares or costs for other public services, despite the government's record internal deficit and the current low point of foreign exchange reserves.

Payment of pension and welfare checks would be speeded. Some of the payments had been in arrears since November 1971 because of the shortgage of funds.

The minimum wage—about $40 a month—would be increased by about 25% within a few weeks.

Loans & financial problems. The U.S. Export-Import Bank agreed Sept. 4 to grant Argentina's Central Bank a direct $50 million credit, plus another $50 million in collateral on loans to be granted by "parties acceptable" to Eximbank. The credit was to finance U.S. purchases by Argentine state enterprises.

Granting of the credit followed approval Aug. 11 by the World Bank of an $84 million loan to finance modernization of Buenos Aires' suburban railway system. Contracts for the work were signed with a Japanese consortium headed by Marubeni Iida, it was reported Sept. 15.

Central Bank President Bermudez and representatives of 14 U.S. banks signed an agreement Oct. 6 for a $145 million loan from the banks to boost Argentina's foreign exchange reserves. Argentina signed other agreements Oct. 23–30 for $180 million credit from groups of

---

Argentina, Industrial Production of Selected Products, 1968-72
(metric tons unless otherwise indicated)

Product	1968	1969	1970	1971	1972
Air conditioners (units)	45,000	65,000	85,000	93,000	n.a.
Cellulose	n.a.	n.a.	115,574	146,042	160,370
Cement	4,222,867	4,346,868	4,769,591	5,553,332	5,398,000
Motor vehicles (units)	188,307	229,693	219,599	253,630	268,593
Paints	92,396	100,194	107,746	121,306	n.a.
Paper pulp	n.a.	n.a.	53,823	69,565	89,913
Pig iron	568,647	583,000	810,300	861,200	854,600
Plastics	129,308	156,521	101,700	182,171	n.a.
Refrigerators (units)	223,130	220,556	236,734	273,673	n.a.
Soaps	245,286	248,267	235,769	239,954	n.a.
Steel, cold-rolled	n.a.	n.a.	478,100	688,400	684,000
Steel, crude	1,573,100	1,690,100	1,823,400	1,912,900	2,105,500
Steel, hot-rolled	1,778,100	1,875,000	2,243,000	2,514,100	2,703,000
Sulfuric acid	162,531	201,325	205,688	222,585	264,554
Synthetic fibers	18,500	22,973	24,050	31,455	n.a.
Television sets (units)	168,000	181,236	193,623	216,445	n.a.
Tractors (units)	9,692	9,342	10,990	13,822	14,866

n.a.—not available.

Canadian and European banks, and Oct. 25 for a $31 million loan from a group of Japanese banks. Most of the European loans had been negotiated by former Central Bank President Carlos Brignone in February.

Signing of the European and Japanese loans followed the appointment Oct. 11 of Jorge Wehbe as finance minister, replacing Cayetano Licciardo, who resigned Oct. 8. Wehbe, an economy minister under former President Arturo Frondizi, was considered more attuned to President Alejandro Lanusse's recent economic policies, designed to win support for the projected March 1973 elections.

According to the London newsletter Latin America Oct. 27, Wehbe faced a budget deficit of more than $250 million for the first eight months of 1972, more than $100 million in unpaid bills and $50 million in unpaid salaries.

The official foreign debt had passed the $3.5 billion mark, it was reported Nov. 8.

Wage increases set. President Alejandro Lanusse Sept. 20 decreed across-the-board wage increases of 120 pesos a

Argentina, Production of Selected Crops, Crop Years, 1967-72
(in thousand metric tons)

Item	1967	1968	1969	1970	1971	1972
Apples	554	470	436	446	424	512
Barley	588	352	360	367	553	640
Beans and peas (dry)	27	64	91	58	76	70
Corn	6,560	6,860	9,440	9,360	9,930	9,800
Cotton	270	230	367	458	285	292
Cottonseed	148	228	294	270	167	172
Grapefruit	n.a.	112	131	128	143	140
Grapes	2,993	2,540	2,131	2,462	2,885	2,600
Lemons	n.a.	n.a.	194	202	198	186
Linseed	577	385	510	640	680	315
Oats	690	490	425	360	475	540
Olives	n.a.	41	66	31	62	36
Oranges	911[1]	1,038[2]	767[2]	864	990	819
Peaches	203	224	248	236	261	272
Peanuts	354	283	217	234	388	252
Pears	108	n.a.	n.a.	94	74	98
Potatoes	1,797	1,974	2,342	2,336	1,958	1,340
Rice	217	283	345	407	294	318
Rye	270	352	360	181	256	600
Sorghum	1,910	2,490	2,500	3,500	4,660	2,360
Soybeans	20	22	32	27	59	78
Sugar	811	872	913	970	908	991
Sunflower seed	940	876	940	1,140	830	828
Sweet potatoes	444	379	480	438	454	328
Tangerines	n.a.	n.a.	n.a.	227	265	233
Tea	n.a.	68	88	75	166	n.a.
Tobacco	63	62	54	66	61	65
Tomatoes	334	315	352	358	410	481
Wheat	7,320	7,400	7,020	4,920	5,400	8,100
Yerba mate	144	131	75	77	87	n.a.

n.a.—not available.

[1]Includes lemons, grapefruit, and tangerines.

[2]Includes tangerines.

month beginning Oct. 1. The increase worked out to about 12% for the lowest paid workers, less than the 15% demanded by the General Labor Confederation (CGT).

(According to the National Statistics and Census Institute Sept. 12, wholesale prices rose 2.3% in August, marking an increase of 54.9% since the beginning of 1972 and 74.8% since August 1971.)

Announcement of the wage increases followed a strike by Buenos Aires public transport workers Sept. 14-15, a stoppage by workers on oil tankers Sept. 14, and numerous other strikes in August. Nearly 300,000 teachers in all branches of education had struck Aug. 22-24 to demand higher salaries, increased retirement benefits, greater budgetary allocations for education and reversal of the government's educational reforms. Transport workers in Mar del Plata struck Aug. 30, and government and transport workers and teachers struck in Misiones Aug. 23-24. Municipal employes in the province of Buenos Aires staged short work stoppages Aug. 14.

Wages of judicial employes were raised by about 12% Oct. 19.

Meat shortage widespread. Argentina, Uruguay, Colombia, Chile, Bolivia, Peru and Venezuela faced bans, limitations or restrictions on meat consumption, and most other Latin American nations were making serious efforts to increase domestic production, according to El Nacional of Caracas Oct. 5. However, the meat shortage was a world problem, the newspaper noted.

In Argentina, where a partial ban on domestic consumption was in effect, meat exports had fallen from 668,000 tons in 1970 to 494,000 in 1971, due in part to a reduction in livestock. The ban and rising prices had cut domestic beef consumption from a record 220 pounds per person in 1956 to about 140 pounds in 1971.

Meat exports in January–October earned $543 million, 62% higher than the same period in 1971, but the 1972 volume was lower than the previous year's, the London newsletter Latin America reported Dec. 1.

Argentina's partial beef ban, limiting domestic sales to alternate weeks, was ex-

tended Dec. 28 to June 30, 1973.

In an effort to boost the fishing industry, the Agriculture Ministry would levy a 2% tax on cattle sales to subsidize construction of fishing vessels, it was reported Oct. 20. Foreign fishing vessels would be granted more extensive rights in Argentine waters, but their fee would be raised.

Copper deposits discovered. The Aguilar Mining Co. informed the Mining and Industries Ministry April 21 that it had discovered one of the world's largest copper deposits in the Pachon mining region of the western province of San Juan, near the Chilean border.

The deposit reportedly contained about 80 million tons of ore with 1% copper and another 60 million tons with .65% copper.

Other developments. Among other economic developments:

The Great Lakes Dredge & Dock Co. of Chicago announced June 12 that a consortium it sponsored had signed a $60 million contract with Argentina to dredge a segment of the Parana de Las Palmas River.

Argentina and China had signed an agreement under which China would buy 100,000 tons of Argentine corn, according to the Foreign Ministry June 16.

Frosts and abnormally low temperatures had caused severe crop damage in the provinces of Mendoza, San Juan and Neuquen, according to reports Oct. 10. Losses were estimated as high as $400 million, the bulk of them in Mendoza.

The government temporarily suspended wheat exports Dec. 9 to insure normal domestic supplies.

The minimum Buenos Aires bus fare was raised from 3¢ to 4¢ Oct. 24. Seventeen buses were burned in a coordinated attack on terminals in different parts of the city later that day. A government promise to increase the fare had helped prevent a transport workers strike called for Oct. 10.

The state oil concern YPF now had 65% of the Argentine oil market, compared with only 50% in 1970, it was reported Nov. 3. The principal foreign operators in the country, Shell /Argentina and Standard Oil of New Jersey, had suffered a corresponding drop in their share of the market.

The company set up by the armed forces to exploit the Sierra Grande iron ore deposits in Patagonia had signed two important contracts, Latin America reported Nov. 3. One, with the U.S. Bechtel Corp., was for construction of an 18-mile pipeline and the other, with an Argentine concern, for construction of a 108-mile aqueduct.

The government had come under criticism from nationalist circles for what they described as "excessively generous" incentives for investors under the new mining development law, Latin America reported Dec. 1. Government sources reportedly confirmed that Argentina sought U.S. capital withdrawn from Chile.

The Trade Ministry had fixed sugar production quotas for the next five years, which would rise from 362,000 tons in 1973 to 480,000 tons in 1978, the London newsletter Latin America reported Dec. 15. Export quotas would rise from 240,000 tons in 1973 to 400,000 tons in 1978.

Foreign Affairs

New extradition accord. Argentina and the U.S. signed a new extradition treaty Jan. 21, replacing the one which had been in force since 1896.

The agreement, signed in Washington by Argentine Ambassador Carlos Muniz and U.S. Secretary of State William P. Rogers, extended extradition penalties to crimes such as hijacking, terrorism, kidnaping, arson and endangering public health.

Lanusse on Latin tour. President Alejandro Lanusse flew to Quito Jan. 25, beginning a series of state visits to Ecuador, Colombia and Venezuela. The London newsletter Latin America said Feb. 4 that Lanusse's diplomatic initiative was designed to offer the region an alternative to Brazilian leadership.

Lanusse signed a joint agreement with Ecuadorian President Jose Maria Velasco Ibarra Jan. 27 expressing support for Latin American integration and political pluralism. Velasco Ibarra was overthrown in a military coup Feb. 15.

The Argentine president returned to Buenos Aires Jan. 27, stopping briefly in Lima to confer with Peruvian President Gen. Juan Velasco Alvarado.

Lanusse resumed his travels Feb. 23, flying to Bogota for talks with Colombian President Misael Pastrana Borrero. The two signed a joint agreement Feb. 26 which included a $10 million credit to Colombia for the purchase of capital goods from Argentina.

Lanusse flew to Caracas Feb. 27, where he conferred with Venezuelan President Rafael Caldera. He returned to Argentina March 1, shortly after signing an agreement with Caldera reaffirming support for democracy and Latin American unity.

Lanusse in Brazil—Lanusse resumed his tour of Latin American countries March 12 with a flight to Rio de Janeiro for a three-day state visit and conferences with Brazilian President Gen. Emilio Garrastazu Medici.

Before he returned to Argentina, Lanusse signed a joint communique with Medici March 15 calling for nonintervention, self-determination and peaceful resolution of conflicts. They agreed that world trade should be made more favorable to poor nations and that the world should not be divided into spheres of influence controlled by the major powers.

The Washington Post reported March 13 that before Lanusse's arrival the Brazilian government had leaked to the press the fact that the visit was an Argentine proposal accepted with little enthusiasm. La Prensa of Buenos Aires also noted March 10 that Brazilian officials were "shocked and irritated" that the Argentine embassy had divulged the schedule for Lanusse's activities in the country against their wishes.

According to numerous reports, meetings between Lanusse and Medici were "chilled" due to comments made by the Argentine president at a state banquet March 13. Lanusse reportedly surprised Brazilian officials by saying that "no state is so powerful as to forgo the others" and that Argentina "will not accept under any conditions a second-rate destiny," in apparent challenge to Brazil's aspirations to economic and political leadership in Latin America. Lanusse was also said to have mentioned two major Argentine-Brazilian disputes —over water rights and trade policy— further angering his hosts.

The London newsletter Latin America said March 10 that Lanusse was particularly concerned over Brazilian plans to build the world's largest hydroelectric power station at Sete Quedas on the Parana river. Argentina claimed the project would threaten the development of another vast hydroelectric complex on the river in Argentina, and make the lower Parana useless for navigation by reducing its level. Although Argentina had previously asked to be consulted before Brazil built any hydroelectric dams on rivers flowing into its territory, Brazilian officials said March 14 there would be no such consultation.

Lanusse was also said to be concerned over alleged discriminatory Brazilian trade policies which affected the $400 million annual flow of trade between the two countries.

Chile pact replaced. Argentina announced March 12 that it was withdrawing its adherence to a 1902 treaty with Chile under which the two countries agreed to settle by arbitration a long-standing dispute over the Beagle Channel and three small islands at the southern tip of South America. The treaty had been automatically renewed every 10 years.

Argentina would invoke an article in the treaty which allowed either nation to withdraw on six months' notice at the end of each 10-year period. Argentina said ways of resolving international disputes had evolved so much since 1902 that it was necessary to bring the treaty up to date.

Chile had recently invoked an article in the treaty to ask Queen Elizabeth II to arbitrate in a fresh effort to resolve the dispute.

President Alejandro Lanusse assured Chilean President Salvador Allende in a telephone call March 10 that Argentina would still accept British arbitration in the dispute. Allende said later that Lanusse sought "an instrument more suitable for modern techniques," and that Chile was in full agreement.

Chilean Foreign Minister Clodomiro Almeyda and Argentine Foreign Minister Luis de Pablo Pardo signed a 10-year arbitration agreement April 5 to replace the 1902 treaty. Under the new treaty, the two countries would take unresolvable differences to the International Court of Justice in The Hague. The new treaty would not, however, affect arbitration under the 1902 agreement of the current dispute over the three islands in the Beagle Channel.

In early December, the Argentine Foreign Ministry approved the new treaty, an action sealing the restoration of normal relations between the two countries (after a disruption caused by Chile's acceptance of Argentine guerrillas freed by the Trelew prison break).

River Plata development fund set. The fifth River Plata Basin Conference took place in Punta del Este, Uruguay Dec. 4-7, with the foreign ministers of Argentina, Brazil, Uruguay, Paraguay and Bolivia attending. The conference established a $20 million development fund and approved an Argentine resolution calling for consultation and exchange of information among nations on projects involving the use of common water resources.

The development fund, to be used preferentially for feasibility studies and other preliminary investigations, would be controlled equally by the five nations. Argentina and Brazil would each contribute one-third of the money, and the other three countries the final third. The larger countries would have three years to pay their quotas, and the smaller ones 10 years.

According to the London newsletter Latin America Dec. 15, the conference's proceedings ignored important issues such as development of the waters of the Parana river system, which equally and most directly concerned Argentina, Brazil and Paraguay. The three countries were involved in a long-standing dispute over joint Brazilian-Paraguayan plans for a huge hydroelectric project on the Parana.

According to present plans, the 1,100-megawatt project involved a dam at Sete Quedas, in Brazil near the Paraguayan and Argentine borders, and a power station at Itaipu, 93 miles downstream. The dam would create a lake 62 miles long only 62 miles from the Argentine border and might, according to Argentines, bring any of the following consequences:

Modification of the climate; modification of fish fauna; modification of silt characteristics; modification of the winding river course, impairing navigability; and a direct threat to the water supplies of six major cities, including Buenos Aires. Ecologists were said to fear parasites, industrial wastes and air pollution from factories set up near the dam, and even thermal pollution and nuclear radiation if Brazil carried out plans to develop nuclear power plants further up the Parana. The project would also limit the size of a dam Argentina could build further down the river at Corpus.

Brazilian Foreign Minister Mario Gibson Barbosa had announced Oct. 4 that a major conflict over the project had been resolved with agreement by Brazil to keep Argentina informed on all plans for the dam and power station. The agreement was signed by the two countries at United Nations headquarters in New York.

China ties established. The Foreign Ministry announced Feb. 19 that Argentina and China would "normalize" diplomatic relations on the basis of "mutual respect for the principles of sovereignty, territorial integrity, non-intervention in internal and external affairs, equality, and mutual benefit." A simultaneous declaration was made in Peking.

According to the agreement, China would recognize Argentina's jurisdiction over waters up to 200 miles from its coast, while Argentina would recognize the People's Republic of China as the only legal government of China. Argentina would not, however, be required to suspend all relations with the Nationalist Chinese government on Taiwan.

President Alejandro Lanusse had informed U.S. President Nixon of the development in a transatlantic telephone conversation Feb. 7.

Connally on tour. Former U.S. Treasury Secretary John B. Connally Jr., acting as a special emissary for President Nixon, visited six Latin American nations June 6–14 on the first leg of a world tour to discuss international trade and monetary matters and explain the import of Nixon's recent trips to China and to the Soviet Union.

He met with Argentine President Lanusse, Foreign Minister Luis M. de Pablo Pardo and top economic officials in Buenos Aires June 12. Connally reportedly told Lanusse that Washington was concerned about Argentine nationalistic tendencies on foreign investment and inflation.

Zaire, Guyana ties. The Foreign Ministry announced intentions to establish relations with Zaire Oct. 4 and with Guyana Oct. 6.

1973: Peron's Return to Power

Pre-Election Developments

After 18 years of an exile interrupted only in 1972 by his 28-day visit to Argentina, Juan D. Peron came home for good in 1973.

On his return, the former dictator was quickly reelected president, and the enthusiastic electorate indorsed Peron's selection of his third wife as vice president.

The election of the Perons was the second held for a president in 1973. After the departing military regime had barred Peron from the year's first presidential election, Hector J. Campora, Peron's candidate, won the first election and became president. Then, following Peron's return, Campora vacated the presidency to clear the way for Peron's election.

Election slates set. Nine political parties and coalitions filed lists of candidates for the March 11 elections before the official deadline Jan. 2. In addition to the president and vice president of Argentina, voters would select 69 senators, 243 parliamentary deputies, 595 mayors and 6,250 municipal councilmen.

The presidential candidates and their running-mates:

Popular Alliance—Oscar Alende and Horacio Sueldo.

Federalist Popular Alliance—Francisco Manrique and José Rafael Martinez Raymonda.

Federal Republican Alliance—Brig. (ret.) Ezequiel Martinez and Leopoldo Bravo.

Popular Left Front—Jorge Abelardo Ramos and José Silvetti.

Justicialista Liberation Front—Hector Campora and Vicente Solano Lima.

Integration and Development Movement (Desarrollistas)—Arturo Frondizi and Americo Garcia.

New Force—Julio Chamizo and Raúl Ondarts.

Socialist Workers party—Juan Carlos Coral and Nora Sciapone.

Radical Civic Union—Ricardo Balbin and Eduardo Gamond.

Democratic Socialist ticket approved— The national electoral judge Jan. 24 approved the presidential ticket of the Democratic Socialist party, which reportedly had missed the official deadline for completion of registration forms.

The Democratic Socialist ticket was headed by Americo Ghioldi and Rene Balestra.

Lanusse sees continued military power— President Alejandro Lanusse had asserted the armed forces intended to retain an active role in the government which emerged from the March elections, it was reported Jan. 3.

In a message read over the state radio station, Lanusse admitted the new government would not be a "genuine democracy," but rather "transitional," because "no party is in a position to act alone and because we should relearn the uses of democracy." Lanusse criticized "some naive people" (implicitly Peronists) who "are trying to cut out the armed forces without accepting that their participation has no other purpose than to guarantee respect for the people's choice."

(The joint chiefs of staff decided Jan. 4 to maintain the existing state of siege in view of "the resurgence of subversive and terrorist actions." Lanusse had said in November 1972 that he would lift the siege by the end of that year if conditions permitted.)

Military chiefs back elections—The armed forces commanders issued a statement after a meeting Jan. 24, pledging to continue the electoral process, with participation of "all those who obey the laws at present in force"; to guarantee the full effectiveness of all republican institutions, insuring an authentic democracy; to guarantee the independence and fixed tenure of the judiciary; to prevent any indiscriminate amnesties for those charged with or convicted of crimes of subversion; and to share power with the future elected government through the designation by the armed forces themselves of military members of the Cabinet.

A virtually identical statement was signed by nearly all army generals in active service following ex-President Peron's remark that the military would not easily give up power, the newsletter Latin America reported Feb. 16.

The navy issued a statement of its own that backed the elections but asserted that it would not accept the victory of those who sought to restore "the vices of past times." The air force declared its determination to "transfer power to the majority" in "a clean process without proscriptions."

Charges brought against Peron. The government began legal proceedings against ex-President Juan Peron Jan. 17, charging recent statements he made in Madrid were "instigations" to violence.

The charge stemmed from a news conference by Peron in Madrid Dec. 31, 1972, in which the ex-president denounced the "outrageous gorillas of the military dictatorship who scourge [Argentina]," and asserted "if I were 50 years younger, it wouldn't be hard to understand if I went around planting bombs and taking justice into my own hands."

Television and radio officials had said Jan. 14 that the government had ordered them not to broadcast Peron's political opinions. The official prohibition referred to "comments made abroad about the [March] elections by persons not involved in the electoral process." Peron had refused his Justicialista party's presidential nomination in December 1972 after the government disqualified his candidacy.

Peron excluded, FREJULI sued. The regime Feb. 6 barred Peron from returning before May 25 and began legal action to dissolve Peron's political coalition, the Justicialista Liberation Front (FREJULI). The action followed, among other developments, disclosure of an opinion poll taken by military intelligence which indicated FREJULI would win 53%–55% of the vote in the first round of the general elections March 11.

Peron was barred until after the new elected government took power (May 25, according to current plans) because of "new evidence concerning [his] conduct and intentions." Peron had sharply criticized the Argentine regime in an interview in the Rome newspaper Il Messagero Feb. 5, saying President Alejandro Lanusse "wants to continue the dictatorship . . . The military men who boast of power will not give up the reins so easily. They are beasts."

Peron warned that the Argentine people "could be incited to violence" if the armed forces canceled the March elections. Of FREJULI presidential candidate Hector Campora, whom Peron designated after the military barred his own candidacy, he said: "[Campora] is very loyal. Because of his loyalty, he will make an excellent president." Peron said he had abandoned his own presidential ambitions, but added: "I am still the strategist, the leader. A leader who is more Argentine than Peronist."

The government's suit against FREJULI was based on one of the coalition's electoral slogans, "Campora to the government, Peron to power," which the public prosecutor alleged violated the principle of representation set forth in Article 22 of the Constitution. FREJULI was also accused of violating articles 22 and 50 of decree-law 19,102, which governed the reconstitution of political parties under the current regime. The articles provided for suppression of any party which incited its followers to violence.

According to the London newsletter Latin America Feb. 9, the alleged incitement to violence related to the failure of Justicialista leadership to condemn acts of violence by urban guerrillas, whom they clearly respected; the chanting of proguerrilla slogans at FREJULI rallies; and the Peronist insistence on amnesty for political prisoners.

The suit against FREJULI was strongly opposed among civilians and within the government by Interior Minister Arturo Mor Roig, who threatened to resign if FREJULI were proscribed, and Gen. Alcides López Aufranc, chief of the general staff, Latin America reported Feb. 16. López Aufranc was reported Jan. 26 to be opposed to further military intervention in the electoral process, believing that only trouble had resulted from Lanusse's efforts to reach a workable contract with civilian politicians, and that if the military were to govern it should do so directly.

The government, meanwhile, reportedly controlled the information media to exclude Peronist propaganda as far as possible, prevented massive Peronist rallies and harassed Peronist leaders.

Peron, who continued to live in Madrid, visited Rumania Feb. 6–10 on invitation from the Rumanian Institute for Cultural Relations with Foreign Countries. He met Feb. 8 with President Nicolae Ceausescu, discussing Rumanian "relations with Argentina" and "problems of current international developments, action by peoples for peace, and national independence and well-being," according to the Rumanian press agency Agerpress.

Peron sees first-ballot victory. Ex-President Juan Peron predicted in an interview in the French newspaper Le Monde Feb. 26 that his Justicialista Liberation Front coalition (FREJULI) would win a majority of the votes in the first round of the general elections March 11, obviating the runoff balloting scheduled for March 25.

Peron noted, however, that "it is one thing to reach the government and another to take power. That is why I say, first the government, and a month later

power." The military regime was due to transfer power to an elected government May 25, but there were reports it would refuse to do so if the Peronists won the elections.

Peron's prediction was supported Feb. 25 by ex-President Arturo Frondizi, whose Integration and Development Movement was a member of FREJULI. Frondizi charged "para-official groups" were responsible for the incidents which frequently disrupted FREJULI meetings and rallies.

FREJULI presidential candidate Hector Campora Feb. 24 denounced the government for its "campaign of incitement and intimidation" against the coalition. His press secretary read a long list of government actions that Campora said "engendered violence." The actions included raids on regional Peronist headquarters and the homes of FREJULI candidates, false allegations against coalition leaders and candidates, and the arrest or detention of numerous Peronists, including 380 young FREJULI campaigners.

IDB sets Salto Grande power loan. The Inter-American Development Bank (IDB) had authorized an $80 million loan to help finance construction by Argentina and Uruguay of a 1,620,000 kilowatt hydroelectric power station at Salto Grande on the Uruguay River, it was reported Jan. 17.

The station would provide power for a 110,000 square mile market area in Uruguay and northeast Argentina with a population of 5.2 million. The total cost of its first stage was estimated at $432 million, of which the IDB loan would cover 18.5%, suppliers' credits 23.6%, and the Argentine and Uruguayan governments 57.9%.

The loan for the project, the largest ever granted by the IDB, was set in December 1972. The bank awarded a record $807 million in credits in 1972, of which $213 million went to Brazil, according to an IDB report Jan. 15.

Brazilian encroachment charged. A FREJULI senatorial candidate, Marcelo Sanchez, accused Brazil Jan. 17 of seeking "to install itself in a fringe of Argentine Antarctic territory." The Argentine press had expressed alarm in December 1972 at a projected Brazilian scientific expedition to the Antarctic, where Argentina, Chile and Great Britain claimed national sovereignty.

Sanchez also criticized the government for its stand on the hydroelectric power station Brazil would build at Itaipu on the Parana river, which flowed into Argentina. He said FREJULI presidential candidate Hector Campora had promised that if elected, one of his first acts would be to renounce the October 1972 Argentine-Brazilian accord on the projected power station.

Fishing bill signed. President Lanusse's signature of a bill banning foreign trawlers from fishing within 200 miles of the Argentine coast was reported Feb. 16. The signing followed Argentina's decision Jan. 19 not to ratify a 1967 agreement with Brazil which allowed both countries' vessels to fish in each other's territorial waters up to six miles from the coast without paying duty. Argentina had arrested four Brazilian fishing boats Jan. 13 and another one Jan. 15 for alledgedly violating Argentine territorial waters.

Foreign debts exceed $6 billion. Argentina's total public and private sector foreign debts, including interest owed, had reached $6.22 billion at the end of 1972, according to an unofficial computation cited Feb. 14 in the U.S. weekly Noticias, a news digest published by the National Foreign Trade Council. More than one-third of the sum reportedly fell due in 1973. In other economic developments:

The government had canceled plans for the private steel firm Propulsora to build a plant, financed by the Italian group Finsider, with a capacity of 1.36 million tons a year, Latin America reported Jan. 5. The decision was seen as a victory for the state concern Somisa, which reportedly wanted to exclude the private sector from Argentina's steel expansion plans before a new government took over in May.

It was reported Jan. 2 that the cost of living in Buenos Aires had risen by 64.1% in 1972. The London newsletter Latin America reported Jan. 12 that the Ar-

gentine cost of living had risen by 80% during 1972.

Public Works Minister Pedro Gordillo said Jan. 4 that government expenditures in public works and services would increase by 60% in 1973.

Unpaid doctors in Cordoba public hospitals voted Jan. 13 to extend until Jan. 18 the strike they began Dec. 30, 1972. Cordoba municipal workers and employes ended a two-day strike Jan. 10 after being paid their December 1972 wages.

The government had admitted that the national treasury's cash deficit had risen by 83.1% in 1972, it was reported Jan. 31.

Imports reached $1.87 billion in 1972, up only .5% over 1971 but considerably higher than the government had expected, it was reported Feb. 14. The year's trade balance closed with a $24 million deficit.

The chamber of Argentine exporters had fixed a 1973 export target of $2.3 billion, a rise of $500 million over 1972, the London newsletter Latin America reported Feb. 2. The newsletter said Feb. 23 that the government had effectively devalued the Argentine peso for manufactured goods exporters by 9%, to help them combat the results of inflation.

Finance Minister Jorge Wehbe had announced that "rigid controls" would be established to prevent unjustified price increases in 1973, it was reported Jan. 31. The National Statistics and Census Institute reported Feb. 6 that consumer prices had risen by 4.6% in January.

The Labor Ministry had announced the minimum legal wage and minimum amount of severance pay would soon be increased, it was reported Feb. 14. Collective wage bargaining reportedly had neared an end with the signing of 473 agreements before the official deadline Feb. 5. The government said that most of the 140 agreements still pending had been held up for formal motives, and would be signed soon. Most of the agreements signed in January included increases of 30%–35%, but many subsequent ones went above 40%. The highest increase, 55%, was granted to metal workers. Negotiations for the agreements were marked by strikes in numerous industries.

Terrorism continues. A nightclub in Rosario was destroyed early Jan. 4 by a bomb explosion set off by six persons claiming to be members of the Revolutionary Armed Forces (FAR). The FAR, of Peronist orientation, had claimed credit for the assassination Dec. 28, 1972 of Rear Adm. Emilio Berisso.

A band of terrorists attacked a small Buenos Aires police installation Jan. 1, wounding two officers and stealing a number of weapons.

Bomb explosions in Tucuman Jan. 11 damaged the homes of an industralist and a local leader of the General Labor Confederation

The young son of a television actress was kidnapped in a Buenos Aires suburb Jan. 18 and released Jan. 20 after his family paid a ransom equivalent to $310,-000.

A Buenos Aires businessman was kidnapped Jan. 19 and freed Jan. 21 after his family paid a ransom equivalent to $70,-000.

Terrorists in La Plata Feb. 16 set off bombs at the homes of a government official, a former governor of Buenos Aires province and a Peronist candidate for Congress. Similar explosions were reported in Santa Fe, Cordoba and Tucuman Jan. 26.

About 40 members of the left-wing People's Revolutionary Army (ERP) temporarily occupied a military installation in Cordoba Feb. 18, disarming 70 soldiers and officials and escaping with an army truck carrying arms and ammunition. Other ERP guerrillas simultaneously occupied a nearby police installation to prevent police from intercepting the commandeered truck, which the guerrillas later burned.

The president of a Buenos Aires soft drink bottling company was released by kidnappers Feb. 21 after being held for two weeks. A communique from his captors claimed a large ransom had been paid, but did not give the sum.

Police in La Plata announced Feb. 21 they had captured a seven-person FAR cell implicated in, among other crimes, the kidnappings of British businessman Ronald Grove and Italian industrialist Enrico Barella. The group was said to be led by Francisco Urondo, a journalist and poet.

Naum Kacowicz, a prominent Buenos Aires businessman, was kidnapped Feb. 16 and reported freed Feb. 21 after a record $1.5 million ransom was paid.

Fourteen detainees, including six accused of taking part in important kidnappings, escaped from a police installation in the Buenos Aires suburb of San Martin early Feb. 24.

Pinuccia Cella de Callegari, wife of a Zarate industrialist, was kidnapped March 19 and released three days later after payment of a $250,000 ransom.

Peronists assassinated. An aide to José Rucci, secretary general of the Peronist-dominated General Labor Confederation, was shot to death in Buenos Aires Feb. 14 by gunmen attempting to break up a FREJULI meeting. It was the fifth politically motivated slaying in four weeks.

Gunmen in the Buenos Aires suburb of Lanus Jan. 22 had killed Julian Moreno, a Metallurgical Workers Union official and FREJULI candidate for Lanus municipal intendant, and fatally wounded his chauffeur. The Revolutionary Armed Forces (FAR) accepted responsibility for the killings and for the earlier assassination of two other Peronists, Jose Alonso and Augusto Vandor. The FAR said its victims—members of the labor sector which, led by Rucci, had sought to cooperate with the government—were traitors to the Peronist movement.

Seven persons were wounded Feb. 18 when a gun battle broke out at a FREJULI meeting in Mar del Plata.

Policemen assassinated. Unidentified gunmen killed two policemen in separate attacks in the Buenos Aires suburbs of Lanus and San Justo Feb. 21 and 22. A third policeman and a civilian were wounded in the second attack.

In Cordoba, soldiers of the army's 3rd Corps continued extensive raids Feb. 23 in search of the People's Revolutionary Army (ERP) guerrillas who raided a local army installation Feb. 18. The raid, the most successful in the ERP's history, was said to have netted the guerrillas two anti-aircraft guns, 75 rifles, 60 pistols and machine pistols, two machine guns, and other equipment.

Many of the Cordoba raids were on the

homes of FREJULI leaders, even though the ERP was Trotskyite and not Peronist. The chief of the general staff, Gen. Alcides Lopez Aufranc, was reported Feb. 23 to have warned that guerrillas had "infiltrated" political groups, particularly FREJULI. He alleged that two members of the Revolutionary Armed Forces (FAR), a Peronist guerrilla group, were Congressional candidates in Buenos Aires province.

Prisoners mutiny. About 100 inmates at Buenos Aires' Caseros prison revolted Feb. 19, setting fire to parts of the jail in a demand for better food and living conditions, more humane treatment and an end to the alleged practice of taking inmates' blood for sale outside the prison. Armed police put down the mutiny, reportedly wounding a number of prisoners. No official account of the incident was released.

A month earlier, political prisoners in the Patagonian army prison at Rawson, the Buenos Aires prison ship Granaderos and the capital's Villa Devoto jail had gained public sympathy with a three-week hunger strike, begun before Christmas of 1972. According to the newsletter Latin America Jan. 19, their complaints against solitary confinement, censorship of mail and obstacles to visits were supported by a federal court ruling that the conditions in which they were held were inhuman.

Members of the Third World Priests Movement had charged in a press conference in Buenos Aires Jan. 10 that Argentine political prisoners were subjected to "inhuman treatment." Rev. Osvaldo Catena, a movement official who had been jailed for nine months, said he and all other prisoners had been "underfed and deprived of medical care." He estimated there were 1,200 political prisoners in Argentina, and asserted the families of many had not been informed that they had been arrested.

Prison doctor seized, then freed— Hugo Norberto D'Aquila, chief of psychiatric services at Buenos Aires' Villa Devoto prison, was kidnapped Jan. 11 by members of the Liberation Armed Forces (FAL) and released unharmed Jan. 13. The FAL said D'Aquila had been interrogated on conditions among political prisoners in Villa Devoto.

U.S. drug report disclosed. Washington columnist Jack Anderson reported Feb. 4 that a secret General Accounting Office (GAO) study in his possession showed narcotics smuggling into the U.S. through Latin America remained extensive despite U.S. efforts to eliminate it.

Several Latin American countries, Argentina only one them, were said to be involved. "Argentina has become a significant transit point for hard narcotics destined for the U.S.," the report said. "Cocaine is moved in from Bolivia in the form of coca paste and then is refined into cocaine in Argentina. The Argentine government . . . is acting against the traffickers [but] provincial police, whose jurisdiction is outside Buenos Aires, have virtually no narcotics capabilities."

Report on U.S. envoy scored. The U.S. embassy in Buenos Aires issued a statement Feb. 24 denouncing as "wholly without foundation" a Washington Post report that Ambassador John Davis Lodge was considered in diplomatic circles as an ineffectual curiosity. The report also said he had alienated U.S. embassy staff members.

The report, by Post correspondent Lewis H. Diuguid, was published Feb. 18. The embassy said it "ordinarily would not dignify with comment" an article of such "obvious inaccuracy and malicious intent," but noted that two Argentine newspapers had carried accounts of the story, which "questioned, by implication, the loyalty and integrity of [embassy] personnel."

The article said Lodge, 69, was best known among diplomats in Buenos Aires for "his boisterous after-dinner songfests and an apparent lack of interest in political discussion." It said Lodge rarely conferred with Argentine officials.

Lodge, appointed in 1969 by President Nixon, had formerly served under the late President Dwight D. Eisenhower as ambassador to Spain.

Lanusse in Spain. President Lanusse visited Spain Feb. 24–27, conferring with

Generalissimo Francisco Franco on bilateral and world affairs. A communique issued by the two leaders Feb. 27 pledged support for each other's national development programs and condemned internal and international "acts of violence and terrorism."

Peronists Win Elections

FREJULI sweeps elections. Ex-President Juan Perón's Justicialista Liberation Front (FREJULI) swept the first round of general elections March 11, virtually securing the presidency, a majority of provincial governorships and control of both houses of Congress.

The elections were the first relatively free ones since Perón won his second term in 1952, and the first of any kind since 1965. The armed forces had barred Peronists from full electoral participation since overthrowing Perón in 1955, and had barred Perón's presidential candidacy.

With most of the more than 12 million ballots counted March 13, Peron's hand-picked presidential candidate, Hector J. Campora, led with 49%, followed by Ricardo Balbin of the Radical party with 21.2%. Campora and his followers charged, however, that the military government had miscounted the ballots to keep him under the 50% plus one vote required for a first-ballot victory.

Despite Campora's failure to win a majority, President Alejandro Lanusse recognized Campora's victory in a nationwide television speech March 12, and Balbin reportedly said the same day that the Radicals would not oppose Campora in a second presidential vote.

Lanusse, whose willingness to turn over power to the Peronists had been in doubt, said March 12 that he and the armed forces together would see that "the popular mandate is carried out inexorably." He said his government would consult with Campora and his running mate, Vicente Solano Lima, to insure a smooth succession May 25.

Although a vote count on Congressional races was not available, FREJULI was assured control of both houses of the national legislature, El Nacional of Caracas reported March 15. FREJULI March 14 claimed 136 of the 243 seats in the Chamber of Deputies and an absolute majority in the 69-seat Senate. FREJULI was also credited with majorities in the provincial legislatures and most municipal governments, and at least seven provincial governorships.

The Buenos Aires newspaper La Opinion asserted March 13 that FREJULI's victory represented an overwhelming repudiation of the armed forces' interference in Argentine political life. The Washington Post noted the same day that the parties associated with the military regime had received less than 5% of the vote.

Peron struck a conciliatory note in messages from his exile home in Madrid March 12 and 13, urging unity among all parties and praising the armed forces for pledging to respect the election results. He said he would like to be present at Campora's inauguration May 25, but would not return to Argentina before then unless "things go wrong." The military regime had barred Peron from returning until after power was transferred to the elected government.

Perón had bitterly attacked the regime before the vote, warning his followers March 6 that "the military clique in power ... is trying to prostitute the elections as a means to thwart the people's will and prevent the victory of the majority." He charged "the groundwork has been laid for new juridical monstrosities," in apparent reference to a government suit to dissolve FREJULI, which was pending in the courts on election day. The suit was part of the government's general harassment of FREJULI, which included, during the last days of the campaign, crude attacks on the coalition on news programs broadcast over government-owned radio stations.

Campora too had attacked the government during the campaign, asserting he would accept no limitations from the armed forces on his administration's freedom, and praising the Peronist youth wing, which openly supported the Montoneros and other Peronist urban guerrilla groups. In response to military charges of Peronist links with revolutionaries, Campora had said: "the violence does not originate with us, it comes from above."

In an interview with the news agency LATIN March 10, Campora said his administration would institute "immediate and massive" wage increases and a series of "measures for economic reactivation" including nationalization of credit and foreign trade; cessation of imports that were or could be produced domestically; reactivation of "paralyzed" public works projects; promotion of industrial development throughout the country; new statutes to govern foreign investments, and reform of the agrarian and tax systems.

Campora also pledged full amnesty for political prisoners, and establishment of diplomatic relations with Cuba, North Korea and North Vietnam. Treaties signed "behind the backs of the people, such as the one in New York between Argentina and Brazil" (on the utilization of the Parana River system) would be repudiated, Campora asserted.

Campora victory declared official. The armed forces commanders March 30 declared Hector J. Campora president-elect of Argentina for a four-year term beginning May 25.

The announcement followed release of the official count for the March 11 elections, which gave 49.56% of the 11,920,925 votes cast to Campora and Vicente Solano Lima, his running-mate on the Justicialista Liberation Front (FREJULI) ticket. They were trailed by Ricardo Balbin and Eduardo Gamond of the Radical party, with 21.29%, Francisco Manrique and Rafael Martinez Raymonda of the Federalist Popular Alliance, with 14.9%, and Oscar Alende and Horacio Sueldo of the Revolutionary Popular Alliance, with 7.43%. The rest of the votes were divided among five other tickets.

The count left Campora short of the 50% plus one vote needed for a first-ballot victory, but the Radicals announced they would not participate in a presidential runoff election. Balbin reportedly had declined to run on grounds that a second round of voting would only further polarize Argentine politics. The Radicals said they would, however, participate in runoff elections for governorships and Senate seats. Runoffs in

13 provinces were scheduled for April 15.

The unusually slow vote count was attributed by the military government to a computer breakdown. Campora, however, had charged March 22 that the regime knew he had won over 50% of the vote and was "refusing to recognize its defeat." He warned there would be many military "maneuvers" and "provocations" to keep his Peronist coalition from power.

Campora also warned the military regime, which he refused to recognize as a legitimate government, against making any "decisions that compromise the elected government." The statement apparently referred to a number of recent military decrees, including a stipulation that the three branches of the armed forces be entitled to appoint their own commanders in chief.

Campora, Perón in Italy, Spain—Campora flew to Rome March 25 to meet with his political mentor, ex-President Juan Perón, and Italian and Roman Catholic Church officials. He accompanied Peron back to his home in Madrid March 31 and the two conferred with Generalissimo Francisco Franco before Campora returned to Argentina.

Campora said upon arrival in Buenos Aires April 1 that Perón would "continue to make contacts with European countries willing to collaborate with our government."

Perón had said March 23, on arriving in Italy from Spain, that he would not share power with Campora, but would remain "just a soldier in the ranks." He emphasized that he was "only the head of a political movement. The president-elect of the Argentine Republic is Dr. Campora." Of the FREJULI election slogan "Campora to the government, Peron to power," the ex-president said: "that is just a call devised by the boys. The government is in Campora's hands."

Perón had said in an interview with the Rio de Janeiro magazine Manchete March 21 that the armed forces would transfer power to Campora because "80%" of the officers supported FREJULI's victory. He asserted 20% of those officers were "intimately tied to the people," and the other 60% "are not with anybody, or, to put it better, are with the side that wins."

Campora met March 27 with Italian Premier Giulio Andreotti and later the same day with President Giovanni Leone. A brief communiqué issued after the Andreotti meeting reaffirmed Argentine-Italian friendship. Peron had made a brief "courtesy visit" to Andreotti shortly before Campora's arrival in Rome March 26.

Campora and his family were granted a private audience with Pope Paul VI at the Vatican March 29. The Vatican stressed that the conference did not touch on politics, but it was disclosed later that Campora had also met with two other Vatican officials, Msgr. Agostino Casaroli, the Vatican's "foreign minister," and Msgr. Giovanni Benelli, its deputy secretary of state. Peron was not allowed to accompany Campora at those meetings, having been excommunicated from the church in 1955 for persecuting Argentine bishops and priests.

Troops quell police revolt. Tanks and troops March 21 broke into the barricaded police headquarters in La Plata, capital of Buenos Aires province, to end an occupation by about 5,000 policemen demanding higher wages and better equipment.

At least four persons were killed in a brief gun battle after two tanks smashed the gates to the headquarters building. Rebel policemen with machine guns fired on troops from the roof of the building, and troops fought back with mortar bombs. The rebels were subsequently dislodged with tear gas, and 500 were detained for questioning.

The rebellion was connected with a series of actions by policemen in several provinces demanding better equipment and wage increases to at least $115 a month, the amount earned by federal policemen in Buenos Aires. The government had offered a 25% wage increase, considerably short of the policemen's demand.

Police strikes reportedly began in six provinces—Mendoza, San Juan, Tucuman, Santa Fe, Cordoba and Neuquen— soon after the March 11 elections. Policemen reportedly had wanted to strike at the beginning of March, but had waited in order not to jeopardize the elections, the first since 1965. The strikes eventually spread to Buenos Aires and Chubut provinces.

Policemen in Rosario (Santa Fe) reportedly occupied their headquarters March 13, remaining there until March 21, when the government called them to "civil defense service," placing them under military direction. The same measure was applied to striking policemen in the other provinces. Policemen had struck March 20 in Mendoza, Buenos Aires, Tucuman and Chubut, and the next day in those provinces plus Santa Fe and Neuquen. The strike in La Plata began March 20 and the occupation took place early March 21.

The armored attack on the La Plata police headquarters was ordered by Gen. Tomas Sanchez de Bustamante, who was suspected of seeking a major incident, according to the London newsletter Latin America March 30. Sanchez was said to have argued before the elections for proscription of the eventual winners, the Peronist Justicialista Liberation Front (FREJULI). The independent business daily El Cronista Comercial linked the La Plata attack with a plan by die-hard anti-Peronists to prevent the transfer of power to FREJULI, Latin America reported.

The government asserted March 22 that despite attempts by unidentified "political interests" to promote "anarchy and chaos," a civilian administration would take power May 25.

Wave of terrorism. More than 100,000 soldiers were reported mobilized April 12 to forestall possible guerrilla violence coinciding with the April 15 runoff elections. The move followed an increase in killings, bombings and kidnappings by terrorist groups in the wake of the first round of general elections March 11.

Most of the violence was attributed to the Trotskyist People's Revolutionary Army (ERP), which contended that election of a Peronist government would only delay an Argentine revolution. Some observers said ERP terrorism was designed to force the military to remain in power, while others speculated the guerrillas wanted important hostages to insure that President-elect Hector Campora kept his promise to release all political prisoners. The ERP was said to be again under the leadership of Roberto Santucho, who escaped from prison and fled to Chile and then Cuba in August 1972. He had reportedly returned to Argentina.

Peronist guerrillas were said to have halted most operations to insure that the armed forces transferred power to Campora May 25. However, the assassination of an army intelligence officer April 4 was laid to the Peronist Montonero group.

Campora said April 8 that the popular verdict in the March 11 elections rendered all terrorist activities "inadmissible." He had appealed earlier to guerrillas to "think and give us a sufficient truce so that we can prove whether or not we are on the path of liberation."

The military regime asserted April 4 that "nothing and no one will stop the process that climaxed with the March 11 election. The decision of the people will be respected at any price and the government will be delivered to the new authorities May 25."

Adm. Aleman kidnaped. Retired Rear Adm. Francisco Agustin Aleman, a former naval intelligence chief and merchant marine under-secretary, was kidnaped from his Buenos Aires apartment April 1, 1973 by three ERP terrorists, including his own nephew.

An ERP communique April 3 said Aleman was being held "as a prisoner of war" to further "the people's struggle for the liberation of all political and social prisoners."

Aleman's abductors painted a number of ERP slogans in his apartment, including "Popular Justice for Trelew."

Aleman was freed June 7.

Other terrorist developments—A powerful bomb explosion killed one person and injured others March 30 in the Buenos Aires building housing the naval commander's offices. The blast was one of four that day in the capital and Rosario. One Rosario explosion, apparently directed against Peronist leader Ruben Contesti, killed Contesti's mother.

Separate attacks against five policemen and assaults on three police headquarters, all attributed to the ERP, were reported by the Miami Herald March 28. ERP guerrillas March 25 temporarily occupied an atomic plant under construction in Atucha, 62 miles north of Buenos Aires, painting slogans on walls and stealing weapons from plant guards.

Gerardo Scalmazzi, Rosario branch manager of the First National Bank of Boston, was kidnapped March 28 and freed April 4 after the bank paid a ransom estimated at $750,000-$1 million.

Angel Fabiani, son of a Buenos Aires businessman, was abducted April 2 and freed April 5 after payment of a "large ransom," according to press reports.

The technical operations manager of Kodak Argentina S.A., a subsidiary of the U.S.-based Eastman Kodak Co., was kidnapped in Buenos Aires April 2 and freed unharmed April 7 after Kodak paid a $1.5 million ransom. The executive, Anthony R. DaCruz, reportedly was the first U.S. businessman kidnapped in Argentina. His abductors were identified as members of the Liberation Armed Forces.

The New York Times reported April 3, before DaCruz' release, that about 50 business executives had been kidnapped in Argentina during the past two years, and almost $5 million in ransom money had been paid for their release. Many observers asserted that a growing proportion of the kidnappings were the work of common criminals interested only in money rather than that of terrorists acting for political motives.

A shootout April 4 between Cordoba police and two men attempting to kidnap jeweler Marcos Kogan resulted in the deaths of Kogan and the abductors, La Prensa reported April 5.

The daughter of one of the nation's most powerful army commanders, Gen. Manuel A. Pomar, was kidnapped by presumed urban guerrillas April 5, according to military sources.

Alberto Faena, a Buenos Aires textile executive, was kidnapped by Liberation Armed Forces guerrillas April 6 and freed April 10 after payment of a reported $500,000 ransom.

Francis V. Brimicombe, a British tobacco company executive kidnapped April

8, was freed unharmed April 13 after his company paid a reported $1.5 million ransom.

Col. Iribarren Assassinated.
Col. Hector A. Iribarren, chief of intelligence of the army's 3rd Corps, headquartered in Cordoba, was shot to death April 4 by two gunmen who crashed their truck into his car. Iribarren, a key figure in anti-guerrilla efforts in the area, apparently was killed when he resisted an abduction attempt.

The murder was later blamed by authorities on the Montoneros, according to the Miami Herald April 8.

A number of ERP guerrillas attacked a small airfield outside Buenos Aires April 15 and destroyed two small aircraft, one belonging to the Argentine air force.

About 20 ERP "August 22" members took temporary control of the police station, post office and railway depot in the Buenos Aires suburban community of Ingeniero Maschwitz April 21. They set fire to the police station after taking arms, uniforms and documents from it. No casualties were reported.

The ERP April 26 seized Lt. Col. Jacobo Nasif, the third-ranking officer of the Cordoba frontier guard, which had been reorganized to combat guerrillas. Nasif's wife was told by an anonymous telephone caller that her husband would be questioned and then released unharmed. Nasif was freed June 5.

Santiago Soldati, son of a Swiss businessman, was kidnapped in Buenos Aires April 29 and freed unharmed May 4. The newspaper Cronica reported the next day that his family had paid a $1.5 million ransom.

Miguel Minossian, a Buenos Aires businessman, was kidnapped April 26.

Youths shouting Peronist slogans temporarily seized two railway stations in suburban Buenos Aires April 25, cutting telephone cables and robbing commuters.

FREJULI sweeps runoff vote.
President-elect Hector J. Campora's Justicialista Liberation Front (FREJULI) swept the second round of general elections April 15, taking nearly all the Senate seats and provincial governorships at stake.

More than seven million persons voted in the Federal District (Buenos Aires) and 14 provinces where candidates failed to win majorities in the first round of the elections March 11. FREJULI lost only the Senate seat in Buenos Aires and the governorships of Neuquen and Santiago del Estero, the latter two to Peronist dissidents.

A provisional count in the two rounds of elections gave FREJULI 20 of the 22 provincial governorships, 45 of the 69 Senate seats and 146 of the 243 seats in the Chamber of Deputies, La Prensa of Buenos Aires reported April 17. The major opposition group in the legislature would be the Radical Civic Union, which won 12 Senate and 51 Chamber seats.

Radical senatorial candidate Fernando de la Rua defeated FREJULI candidate Marcelo Sanchez Sorondo in the Buenos Aires race, giving the Radicals two of the three Senate seats from the Federal District. De la Rua reportedly was supported by anti-Peronist groups, the Communist party (which supported FREJULI in other runoff contests), and the Jewish community, which considered his opponent an anti-Semite. Sanchez Sorondo, of FREJULI's conservative nationalist sector, was only nominally backed by the coalition's left wing.

According to the Washington Post April 17, the defeat of FREJULI in the capital might be due to the recent wave of terrorism by left-wing guerrillas, which voters had come to associate with Peronism. Peronist guerrillas remained active despite a peace call by Campora. The most active terrorist group was the Trotskyist People's Revolutionary Army (ERP), which had informed Campora that it would continue to fight the armed forces and foreign corporations, the Post reported.

According to the London newsletter Latin America April 13, the continuation of Peronist terrorism was intended to ensure the release of political prisoners and institution of revolutionary changes by the new government, which could not easily disavow its guerrilla supporters.

ITT contract denounced. Public Works Minister Pedro Gordillo announced April 18 that he had asked the attorney general to begin annulment proceedings against two contracts signed by the state communications firm ENTel with a West German concern and a subsidiary of the U.S.-based International Telephone and Telegraph Corp. (ITT).

Gordillo and ENTel administrator Horacio Sidders told a press conference that the two companies, ITT's Standard Electric and an affiliate of Siemens AG, had overcharged the government $40 million under contracts for telephone equipment signed in 1969. The Standard contract totaled $135 million and the Siemens contract $65 million.

Sidders reportedly had denounced irregularities in the contracts in August 1972, but the government did not take action until a FREJULI senatorial candidate, Marcelo Sanchez Sorondo, publicized the charges in his campaign.

Trelew investigation vowed. A group of newly elected FREJULI legislators inspecting the army maximum security prison at Rawson, in southern Chubut Province, denounced the conditions in which political prisoners were kept and promised an investigation of the "massacre" of 16 prisoners at the nearby Trelew naval prison in August 1972.

The legislators said at a press conference April 20 that after the inauguration of the new government they would propose a law to free "all political, union and student prisoners."

Falklands talks resume. Argentine and British negotiators met in London April 27-28 to discuss the future of the Falkland (Malvinas) Islands, which were administered by Great Britain but claimed by Argentina. No communique was issued after the talks, the first in six months.

Great Britain April 27 reiterated its opposition to handing over administration of the islands to Argentina without prior approval by the Falklands' 2,000 inhabitants. The delegates later discussed ways of improving communications between the islands and the two countries.

In a related development reported May 4, the British ambassador in Madrid paid a courtesy visit to ex-President Juan Perón. The call was seen as a demonstration of British desire for a new relationship with the Peronist movement.

Adm. Quijada assassinated. Retired Rear Adm. Hermes Quijada was assassinated April 30, 1973.

Quijada was shot to death by two men disguised as policemen as he rode to work in Buenos Aires. His chauffeur, who was injured in the incident, fatally wounded one of the assailants, later identified as an ERP leader.

The ERP sent a communique to the press April 30 taking credit for the assassination. Quijada had chaired the joint chiefs of staff in August 1972, when 16 guerrillas were killed at the naval prison near Trelew.

Emergency declared. The military government declared a state of emergency in the Federal District and the five most populous provinces April 30 after Quijada's assassination.

The decree placed the armed forces in direct control of the capital and the provinces of Buenos Aires, Santa Fe, Cordoba, Mendoza and Tucuman. It said assailants of military or police personnel would be prosecuted in special military courts and sentenced to death, without the right of appeal. It also decreed the death penalty for persons making, selling or possessing unauthorized arms, ammunition or explosives.

Military commanders took control of the capital and provinces May 1, and subsequently decreed other severe measures.

President Alejandro Lanusse cabled President-elect Hector Campora soon after Quijada's murder, urging Campora to return from Madrid, where he was conferring with his political mentor, ex-President Juan Peron. Campora complied, returning to Buenos Aires May 2.

Campora met May 3 with Lanusse and the other armed forces commanders, navy Rear Adm. Carlos Coda and air force Brig. Carlos Alberto Rey. No details of the three-hour meeting were released, but

Coda said afterwards that it had been "very positive." Campora later issued a statement saying his government would assume office as scheduled May 25 and the armed forces would subsequently remain "subordinate to the national authorities."

Campora's statement referred only indirectly to recent guerrilla actions, expressing "deep concern that national pacification be achieved" with the "normalization of the country" after he assumed the presidency. Campora previously had refused to condemn Argentina's five guerrilla groups, seeking the continued support of the Peronists among them and of the Peronist youth movement, which supported the guerrillas. However, he was reported May 4 to have assured the commanders he would not tolerate guerrilla attacks on the armed forces after May 25.

The assassinations of Quijada and of army Col. Hector Iribarren and the kidnapping of retired rear Adm. Francisco Aleman reportedly alarmed the armed forces and led the navy to press for the declaration of a state of emergency. Lanusse was booed and insulted by angry naval officers at a wake for Quijada May 1. Ex-President Arturo Frondizi, whose political movement joined the Peronist coalition for the March general elections, was pushed to the ground by naval officers when he attempted to attend the wake.

The navy was said to be the most hostile of the armed forces branches to the transfer of power to Peronists. (In a move to reduce this and other military opposition, Peronist officials April 29 announced the resignation of Rodolfo Galimberti, leader of the movement's youth wing. Galimberti had alarmed the military by announcing Peronist youths would form a "people's militia" to protect the new government.)

Congress meets. The two houses of Congress held their first joint constituent session May 3, distributing posts, forming working committees and setting legislative schedules. Members of the Peronist Justicialista Liberation Front (FREJULI) were elected to all the major posts.

FREJULI Sen. Alejandro Diaz Bialet was elected provisional Senate president, and two copartisans, Sens. José Antonio Allende and Americo Garcia, were chosen first and second vice presidents, respectively. Raul Lastiri of FREJULI was elected president of the Chamber of Deputies, and Salvador Busacca and Isidro Odena of the coalition were chosen first and second vice presidents.

The Radical Civic Union, with the largest representation in Congress after FREJULI, reportedly was bitter that the Peronists had denied it any major legislative post.

Emergency lifted. The government May 19 ended the state of emergency in effect since May 1 in most of Argentina. Martial law was lifted in the Federal District and the provinces of Buenos Aires, Cordoba and Santa Fe. It had been lifted earlier in Mendoza and Tucuman following a decrease in guerrilla violence.

President Alejandro Lanusse said after announcing the action May 18 that "no guerrilla is capable of stopping our progress toward national unity to transform our Argentina into a modern and free society." He asserted the armed forces were "genuinely proud" that the March elections took place and that civilian rule would be restored May 25 with the inauguration of President-elect Hector J. Campora and his Peronist government.

Campora had moved during the previous two weeks to reach a consensus with almost all important national groups, the New York Times reported May 17. His statements reportedly were intended to quiet fears of his government among military officers, business associations, wealthy farmers and ranchers, and Roman Catholic Church officials.

Campora said at a Buenos Aires press conference May 8 that "the government and the governed should abandon party and sectarian attitudes" after May 25 and "accept a real political and social truce."

The president-elect proposed a five-point "national reconstruction agreement" for all political and civilian groups. Its points included Argentine participation in Latin American integration programs; respect for the multi-party agreements reached before the March elections; a truce between labor unions and business management; a pledge of respect for the national Constitution; and military participation in national life strictly as provided in the Constitution.

Roman Catholic bishops said after meeting with Campora that there was a feeling of "real hope and enthusiastic community effort" toward the new government, it was reported May 17. Church relations with Peronists had been strained since Peronists burned a number of churches in the 1950s.

The Rural Society, representing the wealthiest cattle ranchers and wheat farmers, also issued a statement supporting Campora. The nation's largest business association supported Campora's recent statements and issued a joint call with the Peronist-dominated General Labor Confederation (CGT) for a moderate economic program providing wage increases and a temporary freeze on prices.

Terrorism continues. Incidents of terrorism continued both during the 19-day state-of-emergency period and after it was lifted May 19, 1973.

Armed men in Buenos Aires May 1 kidnapped the son of the Swiss chairman of the Italo-Argentine Electric Co. After payment of $1.5 million, the youth was released May 4.

The Buenos Aires businessman Jose Marinasky, who had been kidnapped May 14 but who was freed May 18, was an uncle of Mario Raul Klachko, sought in connection with the 1972 kidnap-murder of Fiat executive Oberdan Sallustro. Klachko's wife, Giomar Schmidt, who had been accused of killing Sallustro, had been acquitted of all charges, La Prensa of Buenos Aires reported May 16.

About 20 guerrillas attacked a police radio station near Buenos Aires May 20, leaving one officer dead and three wounded. Some of the attackers also were reported wounded.

Dirk Kloosterman, secretary general of the powerful Mechanics Union, was killed by gunmen in La Plata May 22. He was identified with conservative Peronist labor leaders who had been under attack by left-wingers in and out of the Peronist movement.

In another shooting reported the same day, two Argentine executives employed by the Ford Motor Co.'s Buenos Aires subsidiary were wounded by unidentified gunmen in an unsuccessful kidnap attempt. One of the injured executives, Luis Giovanelli, died of his wounds June 25.

A bomb explosion May 21 destroyed a police installation in Mar del Plata. A communique to a local newspaper attributed responsibility to the Peronist Armed Forces.

Oscar Castells, president of the Coca-Cola Bottling plant in Cordoba, was kidnapped May 22. After payment of $100,000 ransom, he was released June 4.

The ERP released Argentine business executive Aaron Beilinson June 3, after 10 days' captivity, in payment for $1 million ransom. At a press conference, Beilinson read a statement in which the ERP pledged to use the money to "help finance the revolutionary struggle."

Ford grants ERP demands. The Argentine affiliate of the Ford Motor Co. agreed May 23 to distribute $1 million worth of medical equipment, food and educational materials to prevent further attacks on its employes by guerrillas of the ERP's August 22 column.

Ford Argentina May 28 began payment of $400,000 to be shared equally by two hospitals in Buenos Aires and Catamarca. A company spokesman said construction of ambulances for use in various provinces had begun in Ford factories, and $200,000 had been allocated for dried milk to be distributed in shantytowns around the capital. A further $300,000 would be spent on supplies for needy schools in the Buenos Aires area.

The ERP had sent Ford and the press communiques May 22 claiming responsibility for a machinegun attack earlier that day on two Ford executives, and warning of further attacks if Ford did not provide $1 million in welfare donations. The notes said the Ford employes, Luis Giovanelli and Noemi Baruj de Da Rin, had been wounded when Giovanelli resisted a kidnap attempt.

Edgar R. Molina, Ford's vice president

for Asian, Pacific and Latin American operations, said at the company's U.S. headquarters May 23 that Ford believed "we have no choice but to meet the demands." The company began negotiating with the guerrillas the same day on ways to distribute the money. A Ford spokesman in Argentina said the military government did not participate in the talks.

Economic developments. The cost of living rose by 8.6% in March, for a total increase of 22.2% since Jan. 1 and 76.5% since April 1, 1972, according to statistics from the National Statistics and Census Institute reported April 6.

The price of cattle on the hoof rose by 20% in February, helping reduce meat exports by the same amount and stimulating inflation, it was reported April 6. Beef prices had risen by 40% since Jan. 1.

Bus and subway fares rose by 25% and railway fares by 33% April 1, following a 20% rise in the price of gasoline March 28. In announcing the rises March 27, the government criticized President-elect Campora for not initiating consultations "on this delicate matter."

The Canadian government and an Italian engineering firm were awarded a $220 million contract to build Argentina's first nuclear power plant, it was reported March 21. A Canadian government firm, Atomic Energy of Canada Ltd., would receive about $100 million to design and supply the nuclear reactor, while Italy's Societa Italimpianti per Azioni would get about $120 million to design and build the plant. The two firms outbid two U. S. concerns and a West German firm.

Italy's Fiat Motor Co. denied rumors that by investing heavily in a new plant in Brazil, it planned to decrease its investments in Argentina, it was reported March 30. A company spokesman said Fiat expected to double its export earnings in Argentina in 1973, and to proceed with plans to invest $90 million in the country over the next few years.

Airline strike—Aerolineas Argentinas, the state airline, was paralyzed May 15–19 when terminal workers and flight attendants struck for higher wages.

In earlier strikes:
Primary and secondary school teachers across the country struck April 17–18 and 25–26 for higher wages and benefits and other demands.

Railway service was paralyzed April 10 as workers struck to protest administrative reforms, promotions and other measures decreed by the military administrators of the state railway firm. The Railway Workers Union said such measures should be left to civilians who would administer the railways after May 25.

Mrs. Perón in China. Isabel Martinez de Perón, wife of ex-President Juan Perón, arrived in Peking May 9 to prepare for Perón's projected visit to China. She was honored May 13 at a reception given by Premier Chou En-lai, and flew to Shanghai May 17 for a brief visit before returning to her home in Madrid.

Campora Becomes President

Campora inaugurated. Hector Jose Campora assumed the presidency of Argentina May 25, ending seven years of military rule and returning Peronists to power after 17 years of political proscription.

Hundreds of thousands of citizens marched in the streets of Buenos Aires, hailing ex-President Juan Perón and heaping abuse on the outgoing regime of Gen. Alejandro Lanusse. About 20 persons were reported injured in clashes between demonstrators and security forces after youths stoned the cars of several military officials on their way to the inaugural ceremony.

Vicente Solano Lima was inaugurated as vice president and eight Cabinet officials were sworn in. Civilian provincial and municipal authorities also took office.

In a three-hour inaugural speech before Congress, Campora outlined a nationalist and moderately leftist program for his four years in office, calling for a revitalization of the nation's economy, for public health, welfare and education projects, for economic benefits for workers and for relations with "all countries in the world."

He defended the record of Perón's government (1946–55) and promised to restore full rights to the ex-president, including his old rank of army general. Campora also pledged to revive the Eva Peron Foundation—the charity organization run by Perón's second wife, the late Eva Duarte—and turn it over to the ex-president's current wife, Isabel Martinez.

(Perón did not attend the inaugural ceremonies, remaining at his home in Madrid in order not to "distract attention" from Campora.)

Campora denounced the military officers who ousted Perón in 1955 and those who ruled Argentina directly or indirectly since then. He charged post-Peronist governments had sold out to foreign banks and multinational corporations, allowing Argentina to fall from 15th to 26th in the ranking of nations by wealth. In an apparent reference to the nation's guerrilla groups, Campora praised Argentine youth for "fighting [government] violence with violence."

Campora also pledged to support an amnesty bill introduced in Congress calling for release of political prisoners. He announced an executive pardon for all political prisoners later in the day, and signed the amnesty bill May 27.

Campora said he would send to Congress legislation to nationalize the banking system and establish state control over the meat and cereal trades. He asserted a reorganization of the country's financial system was necessary to turn the banks into "true public services, so the national savings can be managed by the state and allocated to the areas and sectors of highest priority."

The new president said his government would seek close relations with all nations, moving closest to "the countries of the Third World and particularly those of Latin America." He praised the six-nation Andean Group, offering it "intimate ties with Argentina," and stressed the need to revitalize the stagnant Latin American Free Trade Association.

Finally, Campora reminded the armed forces that he was now their commander in chief, and that their role, as strictly defined by the Constitution, was to "defend sovereignty" and assure "the fulfillment of the people's will."

Campora announced a major shake-up in the armed forces later in the day, naming new commanders in all three branches. The new leaders were Gen. Jorge Raul Carcagno of the army, Vice Adm. Carlos Alvarez of the navy, and Brig. Hector Luis Fautario of the air force. Carcagno pledged May 29 to support the new government as long as it abided by the Constitution.

(In promoting Carcagno, the army's youngest divisional commander, Campora forced the resignation of older generals who had helped oust Peron and had dominated the government in recent years. Observers noted that Argentine officers usually lost their influence in the armed forces soon after retirement.)

Following his inaugural address, Campora flew by helicopter to the presidential palace, where he received the baton of office from Lanusse. Dozens of foreign delegations attended the ceremony, and two presidents, Salvador Allende of Chile and Osvaldo Dorticos of Cuba, stood behind Campora throughout. U.S. Secretary of State William P. Rogers, who attended the inaugural ceremony in Congress, was kept from attending the investiture by his security men, who felt the motorcade ride to the palace might be dangerous.

After his investiture, Campora swore in eight members of his Cabinet, most considered to be moderate Peronists. The key Interior Ministry went to Esteban Righi, a professor of law and nephew of Campora. Juan C. Puig, another law professor, was named foreign minister and Jose Gelbard, founder and leader of the General Economic Confederation, which represented small and medium businessmen, was named finance minister.

The other ministers were union leader Ricardo Otero (labor), Jorge Taiana (education), Jose Lopez Rega (welfare), Antonio J. Benitez (justice), and Angel Robledo (defense). Ministers were yet to be named for the portfolios of agriculture and livestock, industry and commerce, and works and public services, all of which were temporarily managed by Gelbard.

Lanusse, whose retirement from the armed forces and public life was effective with Campora's investiture, had made his farewell address on nationwide radio and television May 24. He wished the new government success, and expressed "eternal gratitude to the men and women of my country in the name of a government which they did not elect but which gave them the possibility of electing."

Lanusse was insulted by spectators as he left the presidential palace after the investiture. Inside, he had been praised by Campora and Allende for restoring civilian rule in Argentina.

Political prisoners freed—Campora declared an immediate amnesty for political prisoners late May 25, after some 50,000 Peronists threatened to break down the gates of Buenos Aires' Villa Devoto prison, and prisoners belonging to the People's Revolutionary Army (ERP) occupied prison offices.

Prisoners began leaving the jail soon after the decree was announced, but the demonstration continued, resulting in clashes in which two persons were killed and about 65 arrested. Most of those arrested were detained only briefly.

At least 375 prisoners from different jails were released early May 26, and some counts put the total at more than 500. Those released included guerrillas jailed in connection with the killings of Fiat executive Oberdan Sallustro, ex-President Pedro Aramburu, and army Gen. Juan Carlos Sánchez.

An amnesty bill for political prisoners was passed by Congress May 27 and signed by Campora the same day. The president also signed legislation dissolving the military regime's special "anti-subversive" courts and repealing the ban on the Argentine Communist party.

(About 60 political prisoners were reported freed after the military regime lifted the state of siege May 23. The measure, in effect since June 30, 1969, had allowed the chief executive to order arrests without formal charges and to close information media.)

The ERP issued a statement May 27 asserting that despite the amnesty for political prisoners, it would continue to attack businesses and the armed forces. It also criticized Campora and some of his key conservative labor union supporters, charging they "did not vacillate in openly supporting the military dictatorship" before May 25 and now sought a "national unity between the army oppressors and the oppressed, between exploitative businessmen and the exploited workers, between the oligarchs who own the fields and the ranches and the dispossessed peons."

Nasif, Aleman freed. The Trotskyite People's Revolutionary Army (ERP) released its major hostages, Lt. Col. Jacobo Nasif and retired Rear Adm. Francisco Aleman.

Nasif, a regional police commander in Cordoba, was freed June 5 after 40 days in captivity. An ERP communiqué said he had been released only after the guerrillas determined that recently pardoned political prisoners were in good health.

Aleman, held 68 days, was freed June 7 after he admitted wrongdoing by the navy in the August 1972 killing of 16 imprisoned revolutionaries at the naval air base prison near Trelew, Chubut Province. Aleman said in a statement released by the ERP, that the killings "were a sad affair," and that the version presented by his captors indicated the navy's role in them was "ignominious." He also asserted the recently supplanted military government was a dictatorship that tortured political prisoners.

Terrorism condemned. By May 1973 many previously uncommitted political figures had started to oppose the terrorism so prevalent in Argentina

Terrorism was also assailed by many Peronists. Former President Juan Peron condemned guerrilla "provocations" in a statement published May 31. President Hector Campora met June 14 with 20 recently pardoned guerrilla leaders, and told them he wanted peace in Argentina by June 20, when Peron was scheduled to return from Spain.

The Peronist youth movement also attacked the ERP, with one group vowing to kill 10 guerrillas "for every Peronist that falls."

The ERP, for its part, vowed to fight on against "all injustice and postponements, against the exploitation of the worker, against all suffering by the people," until capitalism was "definitely eliminated" and "workers' power" established. In a statement May 29, the guerrillas attacked the government's attempts to reach a "national accord," and called on "progressive and revolutionary Peronist and non-Peronist" groups to join them in attacking "imperialist firms and the army oppressors."

The ERP and the major Peronist guerrilla groups—the Montoneros and the Revolutionary Armed Forces—held clandestine conferences with selected newsmen June 8. The Peronists issued a statement afterwards vowing a continued battle against "the military imperialist clique" but also pledging to destroy any guerrilla group that opposed the Campora government.

Newsmen reportedly met four ERP leaders, including Roberto Santucho. Santucho said "the causes of social exploitation and the political-economic dependency of the country have not disappeared or even been touched by the new government," but he pledged that the ERP would not attack the government or the police "if they do not repress the people."

The ERP leaders reportedly denied their organization had kidnapped a British businessman, Charles Agnew Lockwood, held since June 6 for a reported $2 million ransom. They also denied responsibility for the blackmail threats against Ford Argentina and subsidiaries of the U.S. firms Otis Elevator Co. and General Motors.

(According to the London newsletter Latin America June 8, the ERP was suffering from internal problems. There was an open split between the ERP majority and the August 22 column, with the latter reportedly supporting the government and criticizing continued guerrilla activities as rigid and sectarian.)

Otis' Argentine subsidiary flew 13 foreign executives and their families to Brazil May 31, after receiving a telephone call from a professed ERP member who threatened to kill an Otis executive unless the company granted its workers 100% wage increases and distributed $500,000 in food, medical supplies and clothing to hospitals and slum residents. Otis refused to

meet the demands, and expressed doubt the caller actually belonged to the ERP.

General Motors Argentina received a call June 1 threatening ERP reprisals unless it rehired 1,000 employes dismissed over the past two years. The company refused to comply.

Peronist clashes. Moderate and left-wing Peronist factions clashed throughout Argentina in early June, occupying government offices, hospitals and radio stations in an attempt to prevent each other from assuming positions of power.

The most serious clash reportedly occurred June 7 in Buenos Aires, where Peronist youths and sympathetic employes seized a Culture Ministry building to prevent the new undersecretary, Ignacio Anzoategui, a former rightist, from taking office.

The day before, a right-wing Peronist group called the National Liberating Alliance had occupied the National Commission for Scientific and Technical Investigations and said it would "prevent by any means" the appointment to the commission of left-wing Peronists.

In Cordoba, Mendoza and Mar del Plata, Peronists of various tendencies occupied government radio stations, in some cases changing the stations' names and modifying their programs, it was reported June 8.

In Buenos Aires, Peronist youths seized the building of Radio Municipal, which broadcast classical music and cultural programs, and said the station would end its "sophisticated" programming and devote itself "to the service of popular culture."

University takeover. The government took control of the 19 national universities May 30, appointing to each an official "intervenor," or special trustee who would have ultimate power in all administrative and ideological questions.

The action, ordered to put the schools "at the service of the people," followed growing disorders on the campuses because of financial problems, political strikes by students, and disputes between teachers and administrators. Several universities and large sections of the University of Buenos Aires recently had been seized by employes and students demanding that the government take them over.

In announcing the takeover, Education Minister Jorge Taiana said there would be reforms of "the objectives, content and teaching methods with participation of all university groups." He gave no details of the reforms.

Taiana asserted the "crisis that Argentine universities are undergoing reflects the economic and political dependence the country is suffering in the cultural sphere," in apparent reference to complaints by nationalist and left-wing students against what they called foreign, often U.S. methodological and statistical approaches to sociological and political subjects.

Students also complained of the lack of "relevance" in their courses. Medical students protested they had no opportunity to see live patients, and architectural students said they were offered no practical projects.

The intervenor of the University of the South in Bahia Blanca, Victor Benamo, had been jailed twice for political activities, it was reported June 1. The anti-Peronist Review of the River Plate charged "his qualifications are a series of entries and exits from most of the prisons of the country since 1958, most recently because of presumed links with the guerrillas," it was reported June 22. The new dean of law and social science at the University of Buenos Aires, Mario Kestelboim, had defended captured guerrillas, it was reported June 22.

Peronist students reportedly had been split between factions favoring a government takeover and others supporting the tradition of university autonomy. However, the takeover drew no strong protests from students, unlike the military takeover of the universities in 1966.

Labor-management pact. President Hector Campora June 8 announced an agreement between Peronist labor and management groups designed to revive the economy and give wage earners a greater share of the national income.

The two-year pact was negotiated in close collaboration with the government, and was expected to be the basis for the government's economic policies, including determination of wage levels for all Argentine workers. The Peronist-dominated Congress was expected to approve the pact's recommendations.

The agreement was worked out by the General Labor Confederation (CGT), the largest labor federation, and the General Economic Confederation (CGE), a Peronist management group representing small and medium enterprises. The CGE was not as representative of business interests as the CGT was of labor, but was expected to be the main voice for private enterprise in dealing with Campora's government.

The pact imposed austerity on both labor and management, providing for moderate wage and pension increases as well as a price freeze and some price rollbacks where justified. [See below] Like other government economic plans in recent years, it sought to arrest inflation by holding wage increases below the rise in the cost of living.

Salaries were raised across the board by about $20 monthly, and the minimum monthly wage was increased to $100. Family allowances were raised by 40%, and pensions by 28%. A labor-management price and wage commission was proposed, and a more equitable tax system was promised.

The plan also outlined government objectives in housing, education, employment, and small and medium industry. It recommended that the rates of state utilities be increased to reduce the huge losses at which they operated. It also pledged nationalization of the cattle and grain export trades—the country's major sources of foreign revenue—and regulation of foreign investments.

Campora hailed the pact before Congress as providing the basis for "the national reconstruction" promised by his government. He charged the outgoing military government had left the economy in a shambles.

The president promised that within four years, the wage earners' share of the national income would return to the levels achieved under ex-President Juan Peron. According to Peronist statistics, wage earners received 50% of the national income in 1955, the last year of Peron's rule, while they currently received only 36%.

If these statistics were true (they were disputed), the percentage was likely to fall still further during the two-year period of the pact, the Washington Post reported June 10. The pact recommended only a 20% wage hike, following a 37% hike for the first half of 1972 under the outgoing government, while inflation was reported running at 75%–80% annually.

Campora defended the pact's economic conservatism, asserting it conformed to what he called Peronist socialism. "It is not a Utopian socialism," he said. "It rejects dogmatic international socialism and asserts that the essence of its doctrine is genuinely national, popular and Christian."

CGT President José Rucci said the salary increases were less important than "the fact that we have returned to a policy destined to increase salaries."

The plan was denounced as "a complete fraud" by Agustin Tosco, head of the Cordoba light and power union and one of the country's major left-wing labor leaders. "Workers are being offered less than even the military government would have given them," Tosco charged.

Prices frozen—The government June 9 froze consumer prices and imposed price ceilings on 20 basic food items, including milk, bread and butter. It also intervened in six major private markets in Buenos Aires, and said it would continue the beef rationing in effect in the nation's restaurants.

Cattle and beef price ceilings had been imposed June 1. Ranchers had initially withheld cattle from the market, but yielded when government agents threatened compulsory purchase.

The National Meat Board announced June 16 that the government would set beef export quotas.

Banks to return to local control—The government June 15 advised the foreign owners of seven Argentine banks that Congress would pass a law expropriating their stock in the banks.

Alfredo Gómez Morales, president of the Central Bank, said the owners would be compensated. He asserted President Campora would not incorporate the banks into the state banking system but would allow them to continue operating privately.

The banks had all come under foreign control since 1966. Their owners included U.S., Spanish and West German interests.

Foreign investment curbs proposed—The government June 12 proposed laws that would curb foreign involvement in the economy by limiting investments and restricting bank deposits.

Cuba recognized. Campora met May 28 with Cuban President Dorticos, and announced afterwards that Argentina and Cuba had established diplomatic relations. Dorticos hailed the resumption of ties between the two nations as "a gesture of sovereignty and independence."

Campora had met May 27 with Chilean President Allende, who, like Dorticos, had repeatedly been hailed in large street demonstrations by leftists and Peronists. Allende gave a farewell speech the same day on behalf of foreign diplomats who attended Campora's inaugural, supporting Latin American unity on the basis of nationalism, "ideological pluralism" and a desire for independence from U.S. policies.

North Korean, East German ties. The government established diplomatic relations with North Korea June 1 and East Germany June 26.

U.S. jet fighter sales authorized. President Richard M. Nixon, in a break with previous U.S. policy, had authorized the sale of F-5E supersonic jet fighter planes to Chile, Argentina, Brazil, Colombia and Venezuela, it was announced June 5.

Secretary of State William P. Rogers made the disclosure while testifying before the House Foreign Affairs Committee. He said the U.S. "should no longer attempt to determine for the Latin Americans what their reasonable military needs should be."

Peron Returns

Shootouts greet Perón's return. At least 20 persons were killed and 300 wounded near Ezeiza international airport June 20, when rival Peronist groups exchanged gunfire in a crowd of nearly two million people awaiting the arrival of ex-President Juan Perón.

Perón, who returned from exile in Spain accompanied by President Hector Campora, was forced to land at the Moron military air base and to cancel a scheduled address to the crowd. He was taken directly to his home in the Buenos Aires suburb of Vicente Lopez.

Machinegun and handgun fire broke out shortly before Peron's plane landed, and continued sporadically into the evening. Several reporters said the initial fire came from snipers in woods near the stage from which Perón was to speak. Neither troops nor police were near the scene, since security had been entrusted to armed members of the Peronist youth wing.

According to the Washington Post June 22, much of the fire was exchanged between rival factions of Peronist youths, who had been bitterly divided over which would direct security operations. The groups, one "socialist" and the other "nationalist," began by shouting slogans at each other and then resorted to gunfire, the Post reported.

According to another report, the shooting erupted when young left-wing Peronists tried to mount the stage to place guerrilla banners in full view of the crowd. They were blocked by conservative trade unionists, who had played a key role in organizing Perón's homecoming. A trade unionist reportedly fired a warning shot into the air, and then volleys were unleashed from both sides.

Snipers and gunmen reportedly stalked each other and terrorized thousands of bystanders for more than an hour, and indiscriminate shooting continued even after ambulances began removing the dead and wounded, according to the report.

Government sources reported June 22 that moderate Peronists, including many congressmen, were demanding the resignation of Interior Minister Esteban Righi, who entrusted security to the Peronist youths. Righi was involved in a serious dispute with the federal police, having accused it of collaborating with the outgoing military government and ordered numerous changes in police procedures. He had also abolished the police intelligence squad and ordered its records destroyed.

The left-wing Peronist Youth (JP) June 22 accused right-wing Peronists and U.S. Central Intelligence Agency infiltrators of provoking the Ezeiza shootouts. It alleged that retired Lt. Col. Jorge Osinde, who organized the homecoming, had directed an "ambush" by "three hundred armed mercenaries" to keep Peron from speaking.

The JP asserted Osinde's men opened fire when one of its columns tried to join the crowd near the stage. It also charged unnamed persons had tried to remove wounded JP members from hospitals, and had tortured others at Ezeiza's international hotel.

Another group, the Peronist Working Youth, also blamed Osinde and other homecoming organizers for the bloodshed. "The committee organizing [the celebration] had been taken over by those who, having been traitors for a long time, had opposed Perón's order designating Campora as the [Peronist] presidential candidate," the group charged.

Perón urges unity—Perón deplored the shootouts and called for national unity in a radio and television speech June 21.

"We have a revolution to carry out, but for it to work it must be a peaceful reconstruction that does not cost the life of a single Argentine," Perón asserted. "We cannot continue destroying, faced with a destiny full of pitfalls and dangers." The nation was living through a "post-civil war" period, Perón asserted.

"Each Argentine, whatever he thinks and feels, has the inalienable right to live in peace and security," Perón continued. "Whoever violates that principle, . . . no matter what side he is on, will be a common enemy that we must fight without pause."

Peron also made overtures to the military, stating: "If in the armed forces, each citizen, from soldier to general, is prepared to die in the defense of national sovereignty and the established constitutional order, sooner or later he will join the people, which will await him with open arms as one awaits a brother returning to the united home of the Argentines."

Perón's speech was greeted favorably in the next few days by moderate and conservative Peronists and even formerly die-hard anti-Peronists, it was reported June 26.

Francisco Manrique, a center-right presidential candidate in the March elections, said the speech was "a good starting point, serene and realistic." Ex-President Roberto Levingston, who headed the military regime in 1970–71, reportedly welcomed Peron's call for national unity.

Ricardo Balbin, who ran second behind Campora in the elections, June 22 applauded Perón's emphasis on consolidating the peace and assuring legal and constitutional order, which he said had been the main goals of his (Balbin's) campaign. Perón and Balbin met for an hour in Congress June 24.

Campora, who sat silently behind Perón throughout his speech, said June 23 that the speech would be "a constant fountain of inspiration for the task of the government of the people."

There had been numerous reports of strained relations between Campora and Perón during Campora's visit to Spain June 15–19. Peron had not attended the elaborate receptions held for Campora by the Spanish government, and had forced Campora to come to his residence each time they met. Perón's aides said he was "indisposed" due to a digestive ailment, but most sources reported Perón's motives were political.

Some reports suggested Perón was angry with Campora for being unable to restore civil peace in Argentina after his investiture.

In a tough radio and television address June 25, Campora assailed divisive elements within Peronism and "ideological groups outside the law," warning that his government would "exercise its authority to assure orderly change." He called for an end to all guerrilla activity, and issued new instructions to police to clamp down on possession of firearms and explosives.

ERP scores government—The People's Revolutionary Army (ERP) charged at a news conference June 27 that the government was responsible for the Ezeiza killings and that Campora was defrauding the people who elected him.

Roberto Santucho, the guerrilla group's leader, told 22 selected newsmen that fascist gangs organized by "the Social Welfare Ministry under the immediate supervision of the torturer Osinde" had carried out the "unexpected and ferocious attack against revolutionary Peronists" near the airport. He claimed at least 25 persons were killed.

Santucho denounced Campora's June 25 speech as "provocation." He said the president's orders, "added to the economic and political plans of the government, signify a betrayal of the popular will, of the mandate received." He said the government should be modeled after Cuba's socialism, but stressed that Cuba had given the ERP only moral support.

Santucho denied the ERP was Trotskyite, as was commonly assumed. He asserted: "The ERP is Socialist, with a broad program attracting comrades of distinct tendencies—Marxists, Peronists, Catholics, but no Trotskyites."

The guerrilla leader noted that two factions had split off from the ERP but were still using that name. One of them, the ERP-August 22, appeared to have seceded because of the majority faction's intransigence regarding Peronism. Santucho said that group was very small.

Santucho asserted the ERP had been incorrectly held responsible for several recent kidnappings and extortions. He admitted his group had carried out kidnappings since Campora's investiture, but would not say which of four cases involving foreigners were ERP operations. He also acknowledged recent ERP invasions of factories.

Three foreign executives had been kidnapped recently, and a fourth, British financier Charles Lockwood, continued to be held for a reported ransom demand of $2 million.

John Thompson, president of the Argentine affiliate of the Firestone Tire & Rubber Co., was kidnapped June 18 in what appeared to be a guerrilla operation. Ten armed men intercepted his car after it left the Firestone plant in a Buenos Aires suburb. A $1 million ransom demand was reported by newspapers June 21.

Hans K. Gebhardt, a West German technical manager of a women's apparel manufacturer, was seized by armed men June 19. Mario Baratella, an Italian banker, was reported kidnapped June 25 and held for a reported $2 million ransom.

Six persons were kidnapped in Cordoba June 26, less than 24 hours after Campora's speech.

In a related development June 25, Ford executive Luis Giovanelli died of wounds sustained in a kidnap attempt May 22.

Congressman slain—Ernesto Armesto, a Peronist congressman, was killed by an unidentified gunman June 25.

Rightists accused in Ezeiza killings— A special government commission investigating the Ezeiza shootouts received overwhelming evidence that the violence was initiated by right-wing Peronists, it was reported June 29.

Leonardo Favio, a movie actor and director who witnessed the bloodshed, said at a press conference June 24 that the shooting was begun by thugs hired by leaders of the General Labor Confederation (CGT) and by retired Lt. Col. Jorge Osinde, who organized Peron's homecoming rally. Favio added that he had seen prisoners taken by the thugs beaten and tortured at the airport's international hotel.

Favio's testimony reversing his previous contention that the left-wing Peronist Youth (JP) began the violence—corroborated reports by the JP, Argentine journalists and some congressmen.

The investigating commission, appointed by President Campora, included Vice President Solano Lima, Foreign Minister Puig, and Education Minister Jorge Taiana.

Kidnappings continue. John R. Thompson, president of the Argentine affiliate of the Firestone Tire & Rubber Co., was kidnapped June 18, 1973, then released July 5. The ERP confirmed July 10 that it had abducted Thompson and that his firm had paid a record $3 million "revolutionary tax" for his release.

It was reported that bargaining for Thompson's release had taken place openly at the Presidents Hotel in downtown Buenos Aires. An undisguised ERP negotiator was said to have haggled with Firestone officials there before the ransom figure was agreed on. The ransom, in bundles of 500-peso notes, was reported

to have filled an armored car provided by the ERP.

At least 16 major kidnappings were reported in different parts of the country June 27–Aug. 7, and other abductees were ransomed. Hans Gebhardt, a businessman kidnapped June 19, was ransomed for $80,000 July 2. Mario Baratella, an Italian banker seized June 25, was reported ransomed July 5. Raúl Bornancini, assistant manager of First National City Bank of New York in Cordoba, was abducted July 2 and reported released July 13.

The government took a number of steps to end the kidnapping wave, including establishment of a special kidnapping unit in the federal police July 2. All permits to carry arms were revoked July 3 by Interior Minister Esteban Righi, who charged violence was being promoted by "sectors of the privileged oligarchy obedient to imperialist designs."

Two ERP members were arrested in Cordoba June 30, and another was seized July 7. The arrests were the first of guerrillas since the amnesty of political prisoners May 25.

Campora Vacates Presidency

Campora resigns. President Hector Campora and Vice President Vicente Solano Lima resigned July 13 to enable Juan Perón to regain the presidency through new elections.

Raúl Lastiri, Chamber of Deputies president and a conservative Peronist, was sworn in as interim president. He was required by the Constitution to call new elections within 30 days.

The Cabinet also resigned, but Lastiri retained all but two ministers, both identified with the left wing of the Peronist movement. Interior Minister Esteban Righi was replaced by Benito Llambi and Foreign Minister Juan Carlos Puig by Alberto Vignes. Both new ministers were considered conservatives.

In a nationally broadcast speech explaining his resignation, Campora said: "I have always had very clear in my consciousness the conviction that my election was for no other reason than to restore to Gen. Perón the mandate that was taken from him unjustly" in a military coup in 1955.

In an emotional broadcast later July 13, Perón hinted he would run for the presidency, asserting: "If God gives me health ... I will spend the last efforts of my life fulfilling my mission." He vowed to fight for all Argentines and to respect the Constitution "to the letter."

Perón praised Campora's seven-week term of office for its "excellent execution," but said Campora had promised him before the March elections to resign "so that the people could truthfully and genuinely elect the candidate they wanted."

The sudden resignations caused widespread confusion. Some Peronist politicians ascribed the developments to Campora's alleged inability to carry out Perón's policies and to forge a stable government. One close aide to Peron, Hector Villalon, called the administration "anarchic and nepotistic."

Other Peronist spokesmen cited Campora's apparent inability to deal with the broad splits within the Peronist movement, which encompassed right-wing, left-wing and moderate political tendencies.

Since his return from Spain June 20, Perón reportedly had ignored his movement's internal conflicts and concentrated on building bridges with his traditional enemies—the armed forces and opposition parties.

The army commander, Gen. Jorge Carcagno, issued an order to all army commands July 14 to respect the transfer of power, "as long as it takes place within the limits of the national Constitution." Perón, restored to his old rank of army lieutenant general June 12, had met with Carcagno and the navy and air force commanders during the previous week.

A spokesman for the Radical Civic Union, the main opposition party, said July 15 that the party would support Perón in the elections. There was a reported understanding that Radical leader Ricardo Balbin, who ran second to Campora in March, would be Peron's vice presidential candidate.

The principal opposition to Perón's scheme came from left-wing Peronists, who feared the new government would be more conservative than Campora's. A communique from left-wing Peronist groups July 16 warned that a "handful of traitors within the Peronist movement," including Lastiri and Social Welfare Minister José Lopez Rega, sought to take advantage of Campora's resignation to provoke "bloody aggression against the working class."

The groups called for a leftist government program including "socialization of the means of production, popular participation in all government decisions, and a rupture with and attack on imperialism and its agents, thus solidifying [Argentina] with the peoples of the Third World."

Fearing that the removal of Righi and Puig was a prelude to a widespread purge, students and teachers briefly occupied the University of Buenos Aires July 15 in support of the left-wing administrators appointed by Campora. University rector Rodolfo Puiggros asserted they acted "to defend the university."

Socialist and Communist youths had joined left-wing Peronists in occupying the university's law, philosophy and medical faculties July 13 to protest what some of them called "this right-wing coup."

Cordoba labor strife. More than 10,000 automobile mechanics and light and power workers struck in Cordoba July 17 to protest increased attacks by right-wing Peronists on left-wing labor union leaders.

Armed rightists had briefly seized the headquarters of the automobile mechanics' union and the local CGT office late July 16. They also attacked the headquarters of the light and power union, reportedly blowing open the front door with a bomb and firing on the building with machine guns, rifles and hand guns. Union leaders inside returned the fire, fighting off the rightists until police arrived. No injuries were reported.

Agustin Tosco, the light and power union leader and Argentina's most important left-wing unionist, charged July 17 that the rightist gunmen were "paid assassins" of national CGT leader José Rucci, a conservative Peronist.

Rucci had declared all CGT regional offices "vacant" July 1 in an attempt to purge left-wing regional leaders. Cordoba, where Marxists and left-wing Peronists had gained control of the city government and many unions, was considered the major target of the action.

Elections set; Perón, wife nominated. The provisional government July 20 scheduled presidential elections for Sept. 23 and the transfer of power to a new chief executive Oct. 12. The Justicialista party, the largest in the nation, Aug. 4 unanimously voted its presidential and vice presidential nominations, respectively, to Juan Perón and his wife, Isabel Martinez.

Perón said Aug. 5 that he would decide whether to accept the nomination "after consulting with the doctors" about his health. He said his wife would make her decision independently.

Many political observers in all parties assumed Mrs. Perón's nomination was "symbolic," and she would step down in favor of Radical party leader Ricardo Balbin, favored by the armed forces and, according to most reports, by Peron himself. However, Mrs. Perón and Balbin denied such a change would occur.

The government asserted "everyone" would be able to vote, including Communists, and no presidential candidates would be barred. The only person to challenge Perón thus far was former Social Welfare Minister Francisco Manrique, who ran third in the March presidential elections. He announced his candidacy Aug. 3.

Manrique called the resignations of President Hector Campora and Vice President Vicente Solano Lima a "degrading spectacle" staged by "those who wish to inherit [Perón's] power or his myth."

Perón had been under pressure from the left-wing Peronist Youth (JP) to name Campora as his running mate, to assure radical representation in his increasingly conservative circle of advisers. Social Welfare Minister José López Rega, called a "counterrevolutionary" by left-wing Peronists, was the major backer of Mrs. Perón for the vice presidential nomination.

Perón had avoided the JP since returning to Argentina in June, but met with four of its representatives July 21, after 30,000 youths demonstrated in front of his private residence. The JP reaffirmed its support for Perón after the meeting but rejected his suggestion that López Rega act as a liaison between them.

Perón's subsequent actions appeared to confirm reports that he was dissociating himself from his left-wing followers. He excluded radicals from the new executive committee of the Superior Council of the Justicialista Movement, appointed July 29, and condemned young "hotheads" in a speech the next day.

The new Justicialista committee effectively replaced party Secretary General Juan Abal Medina, considered close to the JP. It consisted of Jose Rucci, representing party unionists; Humberto Martiarena, politicians; Silvana Roth, women; and Julio Yessi, youth. The JP professed not to know Yessi, a member of López Rega's personal staff. The Superior Council as a whole represented the least combative sectors of Peronism, according to the London newsletter Latin America Aug. 3.

Perón's speech July 30, to the General Labor Confederation (CGT) leadership, attacked "hotheads" in his party who "think that things move too slowly and that nothing is being accomplished because people are not killed." Perón also criticized right-wing Peronists, calling for a middle course "between these two pernicious extremes," but press sources noted he was joined on the platform by conservative labor and political leaders who had been denounced by the JP.

The JP had urged July 17 that provisional President Raúl Lastiri call elections for the earliest possible date, fearing the longer he was in office the more solidly right-wing Peronists would become entrenched in power. Lastiri was considered conservative and loyal to Perón.

Lastiri warned in a televised speech July 31 that his government would be inflexible with groups which "seek through violence to prevent or twist the unequivocal popular will." He said special groups would be created in the federal and provincial police forces to coordinate anti-guerrilla activities, and steps would be taken to prevent publication of guerrilla statements in newspapers.

Newspapers recently had printed communiques attacking Lastiri's government from the Montoneros and the Revolutionary Armed Forces, two Peronist guerrilla groups, and from the Marxist People's Revolutionary Army (ERP), the nation's strongest guerrilla organization.

Meanwhile, conflicts between conservative and radical Peronists continued in Buenos Aires, Cordoba, Mendoza and Tucuman, where the provincial governors either actively supported or did not oppose the advance of radical Peronists, according to the newsletter Latin America July 27. In Buenos Aires, Deputy Gov. Victor Calabro, a supporter of CGT leader Rucci, had actively sought the removal of Gov. Oscar Bidegain, who had appointed JP members to key provincial posts. Peron reportedly mediated between the two sides.

In Cordoba, 13 unions formed the Cordoba Combative Labor Movement July 31 to emphasize their independence from the conservative national CGT leadership. One person had been killed and three wounded in the Cordoba city of San Francisco July 30, in disturbances growing out of a strike by the regional CGT to protest the failure of workers at an occupied noodle plant to receive recent wages and bonuses.

Meanwhile, Perón, the only person considered capable of uniting the disparate Peronist movement, was the subject of wildly varying rumors of failing health. Reports described him as suffering from influenza, pneumonia, a mild heart attack or cancer of the prostate. However, Latin America commented July 27 that a sick man could not have kept the busy political schedule Perón had maintained since returning to Argentina.

Perón, wife to run for office. Ex-President Juan Perón and his wife, Isabel Martinez, Aug. 11 accepted the presidential and vice presidential nominations of Perón's Justicialista movement.

Ricardo Balbin, leader of the opposition Radical Civic Union (UCR), accepted the Radical presidential nomination the same day. His running mate would be Sen. Fernando de la Rua. Balbin ran a distant second in the March presidential vote, and lost to Peron the last time he ran against him—in the 1951 presidential elections.

A third candidate, Francisco Manrique, Aug. 12 accepted the presidential nomination of the Federalist Popular Alliance, a coalition of seven small provincial

parties. His running mate would be Rafael Martinez Raymonda, with whom he ran third in the March elections.

Peron said he had postponed his acceptance for "medical reasons," but leading politicians suggested he had wanted to test reaction among Peronists, the armed forces and the opposition to the nomination of his wife. The left-wing Peronist Youth had continued to oppose Mrs. Perón's candidacy, favoring ex-President Hector Campora instead, but no other groups had raised strong objections.

Hopes for a Perón-Balbin coalition ticket, favored by the two candidates and the armed forces, apparently were ended by strong opposition within the UCR. Two important Radical leaders, Raúl Alfonsin and ex-President Arturo Illia, and the party's important Cordoba branch had been reported opposed to a coalition July 27.

Perón officially accepted the Justicialista presidential nomination at that party's convention Aug. 18, pledging to run "an austere and responsible administration that will end 18 years of improvisation and waste." His wife, Isabel, the Justicialista vice presidential nominee, repeated that she would not step down in favor of another candidate.

The Socialist Workers party became the fourth and last group to offer a presidential ticket by the official deadline Aug. 25. Its presidential nominee was Juan Carlos Coral, who lost in the March presidential election. His running mate was Francisco Jose Paez.

Agustin Tosco, the Cordoba left-wing labor leader, had declined the Socialist Workers presidential nomination Aug. 16, in apparent response to appeals from the Cordoba labor movement and left-wing Peronists.

Communists back Perón. The Argentine Communist party, recently restored to legal status, voted Aug. 23 to support ex-President Perón in the September presidential election. Party sources stressed their support for Peron's goals of "national liberation" and an independent foreign policy.

Expulsion of U.S. diplomat asked. The Chamber of Deputies unanimously recommended Aug. 1 that President Lastiri expel Max V. Krebs, U.S. charge d'affaires, for interfering in internal Argentine affairs by expressing misgivings about certain economic bills before Congress.

The Senate also condemned Krebs Aug. 3, but did not ask his expulsion. A Senate resolution said it was up to Lastiri to "see if the time has not come to declare [Krebs] persona non grata."

The newspaper Cronica had published July 31 leaked memoranda from Krebs to the Finance Ministry warning that certain draft legislation would have "an unjust effect on the legitimate interests of foreign investors" in Argentina. The legislation, approved by the Chamber Aug. 2, would renationalize a number of banks purchased by foreign interests since 1966; limit foreign investment in a number of areas including exploitation of natural resources; limit access by foreign firms to local and international credit; and limit to 12.5% the profits sent abroad by foreign companies.

Cronica also quoted Finance Minister José Gelbard as characterizing the memoranda as "veiled threats" and "improper intrusion in the internal affairs of our country."

Cronica's report touched off an immediate controversy, with legislators and the Peronist General Labor Confederation calling for Krebs' expulsion. Ex-President Juan Perón took a detached attitude, however, asserting Aug. 2: "It is of no importance to me. [Krebs] is a disrespectful character who directed himself disrespectfully to the government, and it was logical that the government had to silence him."

The U.S. State Department expressed its regret over the affair Aug. 2.

Political sources quoted by the New York Times Aug. 3 said Krebs had written the memoranda in late July at the request of Lastiri, to whom he had verbally expressed his reservations over the draft legislation. Lastiri gave the documents to Gelbard, who returned them to Krebs with the protest quoted by Cronica. Krebs apologized for his action to Foreign Minister Alberto Vignes, who summoned him July 26, and the incident appeared ended. However, the government subsequently leaked the documents.

The Krebs controversy contrasted with the current good relations between Buenos Aires and Washington. The New York Times had quoted top U.S. State Department officials July 29 as saying they had come to view Peron, an old enemy, as the best hope for stability and economic progress in Argentina.

Among other foreign developments:

■ The government told Brazil it was renouncing the agreement reached by the two countries in New York in September 1972 over use of Parana River waters, it was reported July 13. Argentina objected that the text of the pact "permits and stimulates differences of opinion."

■ Provisional President Raúl Lastiri and his Cabinet visited the Argentine air base on Seymour Island in the Antarctic Aug. 10, to emphasize Argentine claims to sovereignty over a wedge the size of Alaska in the area, stretching to the South Pole. Great Britain and Chile claimed much of the same territory.

■ Talks between Argentina and Great Britain over the Falkland Islands had broken down again after Carlos Ortiz de Rosas, Argentina's ambassador to the U.S., accused Britain of "virtually paralyzing" negotiations, it was reported Aug. 24. Argentina charged Britain sought to confine the talks to air and sea communications with the mainland and to avoid serious discussion of a transfer of sovereignty over the islands from Britain to Argentina.

Foreign news agencies restricted. A government decree Aug. 20 forbade foreign news agencies to supply Argentine newspapers with domestic news, and directed the nation's mass media to devote 50% of their news coverage to Argentina.

The measure, dated Aug. 16 and effective upon publication in the government's official bulletin, meant that only the government press agency, Telam, would be able to provide Argentine news to the dozens of small and medium-sized newspapers that could not afford their own correspondents outside their immediate locales.

The foreign news agencies affected by the decree were the Associated Press (AP) and United Press International (UPI). Based in the U.S., both used mainly Argentine correspondents for domestic news. They and other foreign agencies would still be allowed to provide international news to Argentine publications.

The decree also required news publications and radio and television broadcasts to give priority first to news of Argentina, then news of Latin America, and finally news of the rest of the world. However, it did not say how these priorities should be carried out, or how the government planned to enforce the 50% requirement on domestic news.

The presidential press secretary said the decree was issued because the government "must preserve the fidelity and consistency of news and information, controlling their veracity and adjudicating responsibility to those who diffuse them."

The Argentine Association of Newspaper Publishers warned Aug. 22 that the decree could have "grave consequences" and requested an "urgent" meeting with provisional President Raul Lastiri.

Cuba credits granted. The government Aug. 24 granted Cuba $200 million in credits to purchase trucks, tractors, agricultural machinery and other items manufactured in Argentina.

The credits had been announced Aug. 6 by Finance Minister José Gelbard, who had said Argentina would follow an independent international economic policy, trading with all countries of the world. "Our popular government does not and will not admit pressure from anyone, either from inside or outside, from the left or from the right," he had asserted. "We will have a policy for Argentina."

Ex-President Juan Perón had devoted most of his energies recently to developing an independent foreign policy, the London newsletter Latin America reported Aug. 17. Peron was reported moving Argentina closer not only to Cuba, but to Peru (with its "third position" between capitalism and communism) and the Arab nations.

Gen. Jorge Carcagno, the army commander, recently had visited Lima, where he had conferred with his Peruvian counterpart, Gen. Edgardo Mercado Jarrin, in what he later called highly productive

talks. Perón recently had conferred with Ibrahim Ibjad, director of Libya's information services, who subsequently praised Perón's leadership of the Third World.

Clashes mark Trelew anniversary. Some 2,000 youths battled riot police in downtown Buenos Aires late Aug. 22, after a rally to commemorate the first anniversary of the killing of 16 guerrillas at the Trelew naval air base prison.

The rally, with an initial attendance of about 8,000, was ending when some youths hurled fire bombs and fired guns. Police moved in, and in the ensuing battle 12 persons were injured and 98 arrested.

The demonstrators, violating a government ban on street rallies, also protested the government's failure to reopen an investigation of the Trelew killings. In another part of the capital, some 50,000 Peronist youths gathered in a stadium to mark the anniversary, but also pledged their support for the government.

The Peronist rally demonstrated the continued allegiance to ex-President Peron of the left-wing Peronist Youth (JP), claiming 200,000 members, despite Perón's repeated criticism of the JP and his approval of the creation of several right-wing Peronist youth groups. Members of the JP and three Peronist guerrilla groups said at the rally that they supported Perón in the Sept. 23 elections despite his selection of his wife as his running mate. Mrs. Perón was close to Social Welfare Minister José López Rega, the subject of numerous obscene chants at the rally.

Tucuman police chief slain. The ERP appeared to be responsible for the machinegun killing Aug. 5 of the Tucuman police chief, Hugo Tamagnini, accused by the guerrillas of torturing political prisoners. Before dying, Tamagnini reportedly identified one of his slayers as ERP member Carlos Santillan. An ERP communique later claimed responsibility for the murder, according to press reports.

Lockwood ransomed. British financier Charles A. Lockwood was ransomed July 29 as the wave of kidnappings and extortion continued.

Lockwood was released in good health in Buenos Aires after being held for 53 days. He conceded press reports of $2 million ransom were "pretty close." He added that he did not know to which organization his abductors belonged. The Trotskyist People's Revolutionary Army (ERP) had alternately claimed and denied responsibility.

At least 10 major kidnappings were reported in the press July 21–Aug. 7, four of them in Cordoba. Provincial Gov. Ricardo Obregon met Aug. 9 with local business representatives to discuss means of preventing further abductions and extortion. Business sources in Cordoba reported Aug. 12 that some 100 executives had moved away recently to avoid becoming victims.

The Interior Ministry claimed to have "cleared up" 27 kidnapping and extortion cases, identifying 83 suspects, and to have recovered $4.5 million in ransom money since Provisional President Lastiri ordered a crackdown on abductions July 31, it was reported Aug 10. More than 100 kidnappings had been reported since the beginning of 1973.

The ERP, which continued its severe criticism of the government, kidnapped an ex-policeman in Rosario July 18 and released him unharmed July 23 after questioning him about "torture and repression of the people" under the recently supplanted military government, and specifically about the kidnapping and murder of a young Peronist activist, attributed by the guerrillas to police officers.

The U.S.-based Coca-Cola Export Corp. began removing its executives and their families to Uruguay and Brazil Aug. 11, after professed ERP guerrillas demanded that the firm pay $1 million to specified charities or face attacks on its executives.

ERP outlawed. The People's Revolutionary Army (ERP), the nation's strongest guerrilla group, was outlawed by provisional President Raul Lastiri Sept. 24, 1973.

A group of asserted ERP guerrillas had captured a military supply center in Buenos Aires early Sept. 6 and held it under police and army siege for five hours, killing one officer before surrendering. Police said 11 guerrillas had been arrested at the scene and others detained elsewhere.

Professed members of the ERP's breakaway August 22 column Sept. 9 kidnapped a director of the Buenos Aires newspaper Clarin and held him until Sept. 11, after Clarin published documents by the guerrillas urging support for the Peron-Peron ticket in the Sept. 23 elections and sharply criticizing Lastiri and Social Welfare Minister Lopez Rega. An unidentified armed group threw firebombs and shot into Clarin's offices later.

Rucci slain, other terrorism. Secretary General Jose Rucci of the Peronist-dominated General Labor Confederation (GCT) was assassinated Sept. 25.

Rucci, his driver and a bodyguard were cut down by unidentified gunmen as Rucci left the house of a relative in western Buenos Aires. The government blamed the ERP for the attack, but there was also speculation it might be the work of left-wing Peronists, who had bitterly opposed Rucci's conservative union leadership. The ERP Sept. 27 denied having killed Rucci.

The CGT began a 30-hour general strike to protest the murder at 6 p.m. Sept. 25, virtually paralyzing the country. Lastiri appeared on television afterward to warn that the government would meet "violence with violence, whether from the right or left." Labor unions, professional organizations and political groups across the country denounced Rucci's killing Sept. 26.

A left-wing Peronist, Enrique Grimberg of the JP, was murdered Sept. 26, causing fear of open warfare between conservative and radical Peronists. Thousands of workers at Rucci's funeral the same day clamored for "vengeance" against "Yankees and Marxists."

Marcelino Mancilla, leader of the Mar del Plata CGT and an orthodox Peronist, had been murdered Aug. 27, apparently by guerrillas of the FAR. Members of the JP at Mancilla's funeral the next day led chants against Peronist guerrillas, and floral offerings were refused from left-wing Peronist officials such as Buenos Aires Province Gov. Oscar Bidegain.

A group of professed ERP guerrillas had seized a military supply center in Buenos Aires early Sept. 6 and held it under police and army siege for five hours, killing one officer before surrendering. Police said 11 guerrillas had been arrested at the scene and others detained elsewhere. Lastiri called an "urgent" Cabinet meeting the same day to consider the attack, and the government later pledged to throw "the full weight of the law" against guerrilla groups.

Professed members of the ERP's breakaway August 22 column Sept. 9 kidnapped a director of the Buenos Aires newspaper Clarin and held him until Sept. 11, after Clarin published documents by the guerrillas urging support for the Peron-Peron ticket in the Sept. 23 elections and sharply criticizing Lastiri and Social Welfare Minister López Rega. An unidentified armed group threw firebombs and shot into Clarin's offices later Sept. 11. Several newspaper employes and attackers were reported injured.

Headquarters of the Socialist Workers party in Mar del Plata were damaged Sept. 30 by a bomb explosion.

Other terrorism—Spokesmen for two U.S.-based airlines, Pan American World Airways and Braniff International, said Oct. 1 the companies had been threatened with reprisals unless they each paid extortionists, identified by police as ERP members, the equivalent of $1 million. The companies, which claimed to have received numerous such threats recently, said they had adopted stricter security measures.

David Heywood, an executive of Nobleza Tabacos, a subsidiary of the British-American Tobacco Co., was kidnapped Sept. 21 and freed by police Oct. 20. Police said they arrested four of the abductors, all "common criminals," and recovered more than $280,000 in ransom money.

Bomb explosions in Cordoba Oct. 9 caused considerable damage to the offices of two U.S.-based companies, Firestone Tire & Rubber Co. and Coca-Cola Co., and a West German concern, Mercedes-Benz.

Peron Elected President

Perón, wife elected. Ex-President Juan Perón and his third wife, Maria Estela (Isabel) Martinez, were elected president and vice president of Argentina Sept. 23.

The Peróns, running on the Justicialista Liberation Front ticket, crushed their nearest rivals, Ricardo Balbin and Fernando de la Rua of the Radical Civic Union. Final results reported Sept. 25 gave the Peróns 61.8% of the more than 12 million votes cast, to 24.3% for Balbin and de la Rua. The two remaining tickets —Francisco Manrique-Rafael Martinez Raymonda of the Federalist Popular Alliance, and Juan Carlos Coral-Francisco José Paez of the Socialist Workers party—trailed.

Hundreds of thousands of Peronists celebrated their victory in the streets of Buenos Aires after the voting Sept. 23 and again Sept. 24. An official Peronist statement called the election result "a national definition: to win liberation from all foreign interests and to construct, according to the Peronist motto, a nation that is socially just, economically free and politically sovereign."

Perón, just short of his 78th birthday, had campaigned little, sending his wife on provincial campaign tours. He admitted Sept. 14 that he suffered from a "pericardiac problem " and had been advised by his doctor to "spend three months without excitement."

Perón vowed in a radio and television address Sept. 21 that if elected, he would seek the help of "qualified [persons] of all significant political parties" to govern. He pledged to use "emergency" measures to combat any violence that might persist after the election.

Perón attributed recent political and criminal violence in Argentina partly to "a political and economic disturbance" in which he saw "the foreign influence of imperialism, which has never stopped working against freely elected governments." He asserted "the revolution we long to carry out will be for Argentines."

An estimated 300,000 Peronists had held a rally to support Perón in Buenos Aires Aug. 31, during a 14-hour strike called by the Peronist-dominated General Labor Confederation (CGT), the nation's largest labor group. The largest single contingent at the rally was a 25,000-member group organized by the left-wing Peronist Youth (JP), which had repeatedly criticized the CGT leadership as too conservative.

Perón had improved his relations with the JP and other left-wing Peronists during the campaign. He met Sept. 8 with leaders of the JP, the Peronist Working Youth, the Peronist University Youth, and two Peronist guerrilla groups, the Montoneros and the Revolutionary Armed Forces (FAR). Most of the youth leaders called the meeting "very positive," and reaffirmed their support for the ex-president. Peron had also sent one of his most conservative aides, Social Welfare Minister Jose Lopez Rega, on a tour of foreign nations to placate left-wing Peronists.

Military & middle-class aid sought— Peron had made a number of moves before the inauguration to secure support for his government from the armed forces and middle classes and to avoid the combined opposition that toppled the left-wing Chilean government of the late President Salvador Allende.

He pledged Oct. 4, before the General Economic Confederation, a management organization, that the new government would not alter Argentina's general economic orientation. He met Oct. 6 with the three armed forces commanders, provisional President Lastiri and the defense and economy ministers. And in an unprecedented move, the Peróns were escorted to Congress for the inaugural Oct. 12 by the military commanders.

In another apparent bid for middle class and military support, Perón Sept. 29 issued strict instructions to Justicialistas to eliminate "Marxism and Marxists" from the movement and from provincial governments it controlled. He ordered all groups in the movement to officially declare themselves against Marxism, and demanded the expulsion of any group refusing to participate in the "war" against the philosophy.

The orders appeared to threaten the left-wing Peronist Youth, but the London newsletter Latin America noted Oct. 12 that Perón was less opposed to socialism than to the rifts within his movement, caused in part by antagonism between Marxists and non-Marxists, and to the Marxist idea of class struggle, which opposed Perón's call for a "class alliance" to solve Argentina's social and economic problems.

(The ambiguities of Perón's position, Latin America reported, were illustrated in his support for Buenos Aires University Rector Rodolfo Puiggros, a Marxist intellectual. Puiggros had been forced to resign Oct. 1 by Education Minister Jorge Taiana, who attempted to replace him with a conservative, Alberto Banfi. Students, fearing Perón had ordered the change as part of a purge of leftists, occupied the university and prevented Banfi from taking office. Perón subsequently expressed his continued confidence in Puiggros, and Taiana admitted the decision to replace the rector had been provisional President Lastiri's. Finally, a political ally of Puiggros, Ernesto Villanueva, was appointed rector, Latin America reported.)

In still another move to insure government control over the military, Perón had secured issuance of a decree by Lastiri modifying the structure of the armed forces, Latin America reported Oct. 12. The autonomous high command of each of the three services was abolished and replaced by a general staff within the Defense Ministry.

Perón, wife inaugurated. Juan Domingo Perón and his wife, Maria Estela (Isabel) Martinez, were inaugurated president and vice president of Argentina Oct. 12, more than 18 years after Perón was overthrown by the armed forces and sent into exile.

Perón, wearing his army general's uniform for the first time since his ouster, took the oath for his third term of office in the main hall of Congress in Buenos Aires, before some 500 legislators and guests including three ex-presidents. His wife became the first woman vice president in Latin American history.

The administration of the oaths was preceded by an address by the interim Senate president, José Antonio Allende, who called the Peróns' overwhelming victory in the Sept. 23 elections "testimony of the vocation of the Argentine people" for peace, "national reconstruction, restoration of the institutions, [and] establishment of a modern democracy with an organic sense and a [true] social accent."

Following the inaugural ceremony, the Peróns were taken under extreme security measures to the presidential palace, where interim President Raúl Lastiri gave Perón the baton and sash of office and Perón swore in his Cabinet, the same eight officials who served in Lastiri's three-month government.

Perón then briefly addressed a crowd of some 100,000 cheering persons from the palace balcony. He vowed to serve the Argentine people "to the last breath," and asked them to help by "maintaining peace, unity and solidarity, each fulfilling the mission he will receive to [further] the greatness of the fatherland and the happiness of the people."

In a special appeal to Argentine youth, Perón expressed his "deep affection" for young people and urged them to "work and train themselves, for [they]will be the authors of the destiny we dream of." Perón's Justicialista movement had long been split between its largely leftist youth wing and older party conservatives.

Finally, Perón pledged to keep in close contact with the people and to follow "the old Peronist custom" of appearing on the same balcony each May 1 "to ask the people if they are satisfied with the government's performance."

Inaugural celebrations took place without incident, partly because of the severe security measures and partly because of an agreement by the feuding Peronist factions to overlook their differences for the day. The only trouble occurred when unknown persons spiked orangeade being sold outside the palace with a nausea-inducing chemical, causing scores in the crowd to fall ill.

Executive units created. President Peron issued a decree Oct. 17 establishing two new executive units, the Technical Secretariat and the General Secretariat, to assist him in his presidential duties and coordinate government activities, respectively. The second and more important unit was turned over to ex-Vice President Vicente Solano Lima.

Solano Lima would be assisted by four subordinate secretaries for politics, military affairs, trade unions and youth. His task, according to the London newsletter Latin America Oct. 26, was to hold together Perón's complex civilian movement and insure the loyalty of the armed forces.

The political secretary had a wide mandate to "assist the president . . . in everything related to internal political activity . . . , promoting concord and unity in pursuit of the essential goal of reconstruction and national liberation." The trade union and youth secretaries would attempt to restructure the unions and prevent further conflict between the radical youth and conservative labor wings of Peron's movement.

Finance Minister José Gelbard, recently named economy minister, would work within this new political framework, but would retain great freedom in directing economic policy, Latin America reported. His first tasks reportedly were with the development of basic industry, planning power supplies, and dispersal of the population.

Peronist leader assassinated. Constantino Razzetti, a Peronist leader in Rosario, was shot to death Oct. 14, presumably by right-wing Peronists.

Razzetti, a biochemist and vice president of the Rosario municipal bank, reportedly had been close to ex-President Hector Campora and leaders of the left-wing Peronist Youth (JP). He was killed soon after delivering a speech at a Peronist luncheon severely criticizing the conservative Peronist labor bureaucracy.

The leader of that bureaucracy, José Rucci, had been assassinated three weeks earlier, possibly by left-wing Peronists. The government initially had blamed the outlawed People's Revolutionary Army (ERP) for the killing. The guerrilla group, denying responsibility Sept. 27, issued a communique that asserted: "ERP policy is not to execute union bureaucrats, because they are not the monopolies or the army oppressors."

(Buenos Aires television station Channel 9 had been closed by authorities Sept. 28–29 and the newspaper El Mundo had been closed Sept. 28–Oct. 1 for reporting the ERP communique.)

Another conservative Peronist, Julian Julio, leader of a bus drivers' union in Mar del Plata, had been killed by unidentified gunmen Oct. 9.

In another apparently political murder, José Domingo Colombo, political and union news editor of the San Nicolas (Buenos Aires Province) newspaper El Norte, was shot to death by gunmen who invaded the paper's offices Oct. 3. El Norte's director said fliers distributed in the city a few days earlier quoted the JP as charging the newspaper employed "Communists and Trotskyists."

There was other political violence Oct. 4–22, including several attacks on radical Peronists. Jorge Lellis, a JP leader in Rosario, narrowly escaped assassination Oct. 4 when gunmen in a passing vehicle fired on him. In Cordoba the same day, two construction union members were reported wounded when gunmen fired on local headquarters of the General Labor Confederation, dominated by left-wing Peronists.

In Buenos Aires, offices of the JP magazine Militancia were severely damaged by a bomb explosion Oct. 9. JP headquarters in Formosa were fired on Oct 17, with no injuries reported. And in Mendoza, a bomb explosion Oct. 22 nearly destroyed the offices of provincial Gov. Alberto Martinez Baca, who had been criticized by conservative Peronists for not ridding his administration of radical Peronists.

Despite these developments, the JP was attempting to cooperate with President Peron and the union bureaucracy was taking a conciliatory line toward the leftists, the London newsletter Latin America reported Oct. 19. The most active JP sections reportedly had been working with the armed forces in a program to repair flood damage in Buenos Aires Province, a pilot project which might be repeated in all parts of the country.

However, at least one blow to the JP by Peronist leaders was reported Oct. 19. The Superior Council of the Justicialista Movement, dominated by conservatives, ruled that only duly authorized organizations could operate as branches of the movement. The decision reportedly was aimed at the hundreds of political halls opened by various left-wing Peronist groups, particularly the JP.

Leftist Peronists killed. Three more left-wing Peronists were assassinated as conservative Peronists, aided by their own terrorist groups, continued to try to purge the Justicialista movement of "Marxist infiltrators."

Pablo M. Fredes, a leftist leader of the Transport Workers Union, was taken from his Buenos Aires home Oct. 30 and shot to death by unidentified gunmen. Bus drivers struck briefly the next day to protest the assassination.

Antonio J. Deleroni, a leftist lawyer, and his wife, Nelida Arana de Deleroni, were killed in Buenos Aires Nov. 27 by a gunman later identified as a member of a right-wing Peronist youth group and former bodyguard for the Social Welfare Ministry. Lawyers' groups in the capital protested the killing Nov. 29.

Ruben Fortuny, a radical former police chief of Salta Province, was shot to death Nov. 29 by a former police officer whom he reportedly had fired for torturing political prisoners during the supplanted military government.

A member of the left-wing Peronist Youth (JP) was stripped and beaten by right-wing Peronists Nov. 2, and a leftist member of the Transport Workers Union was kidnapped and tortured Nov. 21. Following the first incident, leaders of the JP obtained an audience with Interior Minister Benito Llambi and Federal Police Chief Miguel Antonio Iniguez to protest the right-wing campaign against Peronist leftists, which included not only murders and torture but almost daily bombings of leftist offices.

The National Council of Peronist Youth, representing the JP, the Peronist

Working Youth (JTP) and the Peronist University Youth, issued a statement Oct. 25 denouncing rightist bands which "kill, kidnap and ambush Peronists." It blamed right-wing violence on Peronists who "betrayed Peronism, doubted the return of the general and exchanged views with [ex-President Alejandro] Lanusse."

The rightist campaign had been denounced Oct. 17 by the Argentine Communist party, which had supported President Peron in the September elections. It charged the Peronist right sought to separate Peron from his popular base, and demanded an end to repressive legislation and police action. (A bomb exploded outside a Communist office in Buenos Aires Nov. 21.)

Roberto Quieto, a leader of the Montoneros, a Peronist guerrilla group, protested the rightist campaign Nov. 2 at a meeting with ex-Vice President Vicente Solano Lima, who remained close to Peron despite resigning his office in July. The Montoneros issued a statement Nov. 6 pledging to fight "corrupt leaders and their bands of hired assassins."

As Quieto met with Solano Lima, some 20,000 JTP members rallied in a Buenos Aires stadium to protest the campaign and a projected labor union law which they and other leftists charged would benefit the conservative union leadership. The law would further centralize labor leadership and extend from two to four years the term of office for union officials.

The combative Cordoba Light and Power Union, led by the leftist Agustin Tosco, was disaffiliated by the Argentine Federation of Light and Power Workers Nov. 8 for allegedly trying to separate the federation from the national organized labor movement.

In a related development, Sen. Hipolito Solari Yrigoyen, a member of the Radical party, was wounded Nov. 1 when a bomb exploded in his automobile. Solari had represented combative labor unions and political prisoners accused of guerrilla activities.

In another development Nov. 7, army Col. Florencio Crespo was kidnapped in La Plata. The Cuban news agency Prensa Latina reported the ERP took credit for the abduction and accused Crespo of "collaborating with the U.S." and contributing to Argentine repression. Crespo reportedly had recently returned from an antiguerrilla training course in the U.S.

Campora named Mexico envoy. Ex-President Hector Campora, whose resignation in July enabled Perón to regain the presidency, was named ambassador to Mexico Nov. 9. He arrived in Mexico Dec. 2.

Campora had been under attack from conservative Peronists, who demanded his expulsion from the Justicialista movement for supporting radical Peronists during his brief rule. However, Perón publicly reaffirmed his confidence in Campora before naming him ambassador.

U.S. executive murdered. John A. Swint, general manager of a Cordoba subsidiary of Ford Motor Argentina, was assassinated Nov. 22. The Peronist Armed Forces (FAP), one of several terrorist groups supporting President Juan Perón, later took credit.

Swint and two bodyguards were killed in an ambush in suburban Cordoba by about 15 gunmen. A third bodyguard was seriously wounded. Eyewitnesses said there was no attempt to kidnap the U.S. executive.

The FAP claimed credit for the assassination in a communique to newspapers Nov. 28, and warned Ford headquarters in Buenos Aires that day that it planned to "knock off" other foreign executives and their families "one by one," and to blow up the main Ford plant in suburban Buenos Aires. Ford reportedly moved some 25 U.S. executives and their families out of the country Nov. 28–29.

The government promised the alarmed foreign community Nov. 30 that it would take all necessary measures to protect the lives of foreigners, and Interior Minister Benito Llambi offered armed government bodyguards to foreign executives Dec. 3.

Ford announced Dec. 6 that it would bring back the executives it evacuated after the Swint assassination. The announcement followed a meeting Dec. 4 between Ford executives and President

Peron, who promised protection for Ford personnel and installations.

Border patrol troops armed with machine guns and automatic rifles began guarding Ford's plant in suburban Buenos Aires Dec. 5.

Meanwhile, kidnappings of foreign executives continued. David B. Wilkie Jr., president of Amoco Argentina, a subsidiary of Standard Oil Co. of Indiana, was kidnapped in suburban Buenos Aires Oct. 23 and ransomed by his company Nov. 11. The company said the payment was "well below" the $1 million reportedly demanded by the kidnappers.

Nyborg Andersen, regional manager of the Bank of London and South America, a subsidiary of Lloyds Bank of London, was kidnapped in Buenos Aires Nov. 17. The abductors reportedly belonged to the Marxist People's Revolutionary Army (ERP) and demanded $1.2 million ransom.

Swissair said Nov. 29 that its Latin American director Kurt Schmid, abducted in Buenos Aires Oct. 22, was freed Nov. 28 and immediately left the country. The airline refused to say whether it had paid a ransom.

Victor Samuelson, manager of the Esso Argentina oil refinery at Campana, north of Buenos Aires, was kidnapped Dec. 6. He was the fourth U.S. businessman abducted in Argentina in 1973.

An ERP communique Dec. 8 said Samuelson would be "submitted to trial" on unspecified charges. A subsequent message Dec. 11 demanded a $10 million ransom. Reuters reported Dec. 12 that Esso, an affiliate of Exxon Corp., had agreed to pay the ransom.

The $10 million was demanded in food, clothing and construction materials to be distributed in poor neighborhoods across Argentina "as a partial reimbursement to the Argentine people for the copious riches extracted from our country by [Esso] in long years of imperialist exploitation."

Yves Boisset, factory director of the Peugeot auto plant outside Buenos Aires, was kidnapped Dec. 28. An American businessman, Charles Hayes, was also abducted in December.

The U.S.-owned Cities Service Oil Co. Dec. 13 evacuated three executives and their dependents from Argentina to prevent their possible kidnapping or assassination. The U.S.-based IBM World Trade Corp., Chrysler Corp. and St. Joseph's Mining Co. were reported Dec. 15 to have removed their executives from Argentina.

Two Rosario policemen were wounded Dec. 7 when they were ambushed by ERP members. The guerrillas were not captured.

Peronist attacks continue. Violence among Peronists continued Dec. 13 as bomb and gunfire attacks were reported against two Justicialista party offices in Buenos Aires, headquarters of the left-wing Peronist Youth (JP) in Santa Fe, and the homes of two leaders of the Metallurgical Workers Union in Cordoba.

The Santa Fe attack was perpetrated by the self-styled "Jose Ignacio Rucci" commandos, a right-wing Peronist group named in honor of the assassinated leader of the General Labor Confederation.

The Communist party, which previously had denounced the campaign to purge leftists from the Justicialista movement, charged Dec. 12 that recent violence in Argentina was part of a plan to precipitate "a coup d'état like Chile's." (A Communist office in Buenos Aires was bombed Dec. 15, but no injuries were reported.)

Army, navy chiefs quit. The commanders of the army and navy resigned following disputes with the government over promotions within their services. Observers linked the disputes to attempts by President Juan Perón to eliminate opponents of his Justicialista movement from the high military commands.

The Defense Ministry announced Dec. 18 that army commander Lt. Gen. Jorge Carcagno had resigned and been replaced by Gen. Leandro Anaya. Carcagno's resignation was attributed to the refusal by the Senate Dec. 13 to approve the promotion to brigadier general of four of 13 colonels suggested by the army commander.

The Senate had said it would withhold confirmation of the four until it received "new information" on them. Sources quoted by the news agency LATIN said three of the colonels—Juan Carlos Duret, Julio Cesar Etchegoyen and Juan Carlos Colombo—previously had been hostile to Peronism, and the fourth, Juan Jaime Cesio, chief of the army staff's political division, was close to left-wing Peronist youth groups. A fifth colonel, Eduardo Matta, reportedly had been dropped from Carcagno's list following government opposition to his promotion.

The four colonels subsequently had asked to be retired, leading Carcagno to consider submitting his own resignation, it was reported Dec. 17.

The navy commander, Adm. Carlos Alvarez, had resigned Dec. 6 and been replaced by Rear Adm. Emilio Massera. Alvarez reportedly had sought to have Massera, a fleet commander, sent to Washington, D.C. as a representative to the Inter-American Defense Board, despite opposition from Peron, Defense Minister Angel Robledo and high navy officers.

Massera's promotion reportedly forced the resignations of one vice admiral and seven rear admirals, effecting a thorough change in the navy leadership. The navy previously had been considered the armed service most hostile to Peron.

The Buenos Aires newspaper La Nacion asserted Dec. 16 that the disputes between the government and the military commanders involved "nothing less" than an effort by the government to insure its survival should Peron die or become incapacitated. Observers had said before that the armed forces might take power to prevent the succession of Vice President Maria Estela Martinez de Perón, who was considered inexperienced politically.

The magazine El Descamisado, organ of the leftist Peronist youth wing, had said in its last issue, reported Dec. 12, that the government was maneuvering to "eliminate . . . the sectors that could plot against the institutional process. More clearly, the sectors that could carry out a coup."

Economic plan set. President Juan Perón Dec. 21 announced a three-year plan designed to double the nation's economic growth rate and increase by a third the income of each family.

The scheme, called the Triennial Plan for Reconstruction and National Liberation, called for investment of $10 million in public works and housing projects and an expansion of exports from the current $2 billion to $5.8 billion by 1977. It would raise the gross national product by a record 7.8%, compared with the current growth rate of 4%.

The plan included construction of three hydroelectric plants at a cost of $2.5 billion, and an annual increase of 8.8% in electric power consumption. The plan also called for a sharp expansion in steel, petrochemical, oil, natural gas and coal production.

Perón told a nationwide radio and television audience that the plan was aimed at bringing Argentina to an "economic take-off" point and "recovering economic independence by demolishing foreign financial, technological and commercial control" over the economy.

Press sources noted that since coming to power in May, Peronist economists led by Economy Minister José Gelbard had succeeded in virtually halting inflation and in reducing unemployment from 6.6% to 4.5% of the work force.

IDB loan—Gelbard had announced Dec. 17 that the Inter-American Development Bank would grant Argentina loans totaling $665 million in 1974, to be used in small and medium industry, agriculture and rural development, capital goods exports, and urban infrastructure plans.

In other economic developments:

China and Argentina signed an agreement Dec. 14 under which China would buy three million tons of Argentine wheat and maize over the next three years. It was the first grain agreement between the two countries since 1966.

The Italian-owned Fiat-Concord Co. of Argentina signed a pact to export $100 million worth of vehicles to Cuba, it was reported Dec. 30. The U.S.-owned General Motors Corp. had agreed earlier in December to sell 1,500 tractors to Cuba as part of an Argentine credit package to Cuba.

Marine disaster. Two Argentine ships collided Oct. 28 in the narrow Punta Indio channel; 24 persons were missing and believed drowned.

1974: Peron's Death & Aftermath

Violence Precedes Peron's Death

Juan D. Peron died of natural causes July 1, 1974 and was succeeded by his widow, Maria Estela Peron, as president of Argentina. Peron's death was preceded by more than four years of terrorism and of internecine violence among his followers. The violence paused only briefly after Peron died.

Terrorism curbs approved. The Chamber of Deputies passed President Juan Peron's controversial anti-terrorism bill Jan. 25, less than a week after a bloody attack on an army tank garrison by guerrillas of the left-wing People's Revolutionary Army (ERP).

The bill, reforming the Argentine penal code, was approved 128–62, over the opposition of virtually all non-Peronist legislators and members of the leftist Peronist Youth (JP). Eight JP deputies resigned Jan. 24 rather than vote on the bill, which they said "could be turned against the Peronist people."

Police arrested some 70 opponents of the bill attempting to march on the Chamber during the all-night debate that preceded the vote.

The bill virtually doubled prison sentences for convicted kidnappers, conspirators and armed extremists, and turned over internal security functions to the federal police rather than local law enforcement officers. It also outlawed "illicit" political associations and "incitement to violence," but defined the terms ambiguously.

Similar measures had been repealed by the Chamber in mid-1973, before the ERP stepped up its attacks on the armed forces and foreign businessmen and before intra-Peronist violence accelerated.

Garrison attacked, governor forced out— Peron and the right wing of his movement had demanded swift approval of the bill after 60–70 ERP members attacked an army tank garrison at Azul, 170 miles south of Buenos Aires, the night of Jan. 19–20. The guerrillas occupied the garrison and fought a seven-hour gun battle with troops, leaving two guerrillas, a soldier, the base commander and his wife dead. The terrorists escaped with a hostage, Lt. Col. Jorge Ibarzabal.

Peron appeared on nationwide television after the attack, wearing his army general's uniform, and called on the armed forces, police, labor unions and his Justicialista Party to unite "to annihilate as soon as possible this criminal terrorism." He accused left-wing Peronists of being "complacent" about terrorism, and indirectly criticized Buenos Aires Province Gov. Oscar Bidegain, a left-wing Peronist, by asserting terrorists were "operating in the province with the indifference of its authorities."

A majority of Peronist senators and deputies demanded Bidegain's resignation

late Jan. 21, and the governor acceded
Jan. 23. He was replaced Jan. 26 by the
vice governor, Victorio Calabro.

Police and soldiers carried out
widespread raids in search of the Azul attackers and announced the arrest of 13
suspects Jan. 23, including several persons
allegedly wounded at the garrison. The
left-wing Buenos Aires newspaper El
Mundo printed an alleged letter from
Ibarzabal Jan. 24 in which the colonel
called himself a "prisoner of war" of the
ERP.

(Authorities had occupied El Mundo's
plant Jan. 21, apparently to prevent the
publication of ERP communiques. The
paper had resumed publication the next
day. An explosion Jan. 7 had seriously
damaged the Buenos Aires printing works
that produced El Mundo and the
semiofficial Peronist organ Mayoria.)

Presumed rightists Jan. 23 killed a
Communist Party member distributing
pamphlets calling for a march on
Congress to oppose the anti-terrorism
bill. The Liberation Armed Forces guerrilla group sent a communique to the
press the same day threatening to carry
out "people's justice" against any deputy
who voted for the bill.

Leftists attacked. Alejandro Giovenco, a leader of the left-wing Peronist
Youth, was wounded in Buenos Aires Jan.
2 in an ambush by unknown persons
presumed to be right-wing Peronists. In a
related incident Jan. 4, a Buenos Aires
office of the Justicialista Movement was
damaged by a bomb thrown by unknown
persons.

Nineteen separate bombings of offices
and homes of leftists were reported early
Jan. 26. Police said bombs exploded in
Buenos Aires at seven JP offices, the office
of a JP-dominated union, and a cafe fre-
quented by leftists; a woman was seriously
injured by the last explosion. Other bombs
exploded at the homes of leftist militants
in suburban Buenos Aires and Rosario
and at offices of the Communist Party and
the Young Socialist Movement in Bahia
Blanca.

Meanwhile, intra-Peronist murders
continued with the assassination of JP
member Jorge Gallardo in Buenos Aires
Feb. 6. A right-wing Peronist, Alejandro
Giovenco of the Peronist Youth of the Ar-

gentine Republic (JPRA), was killed Feb.
18 when a bomb exploded in his briefcase.

Left-wing Peronists seized—The campaign by right-wing Peronists to purge
leftists from the Justicialista movement
continued in the rest of the country in
February with the arrest of dozens of
members of the leftist Peronist Youth
(JP), Peronist Working Youth (JTP),
Peronist University Youth (JUP) and
Peronist guerrilla groups.

An estimated 30-40 persons were seized
in Buenos Aires Feb. 12 in connection with
an alleged plot by leftist Peronists and
Uruguayan Tupamaro guerrillas to
assassinate President Peron, Vice President Maria Estela Martinez de Peron
and Uruguayan President Juan Maria
Bordaberry during Bordaberry's brief
visit to the capital that day.

(Bordaberry and the Perons witnessed
the ratification of the River Plate treaty
between their countries and signing of an
accord recognizing the juridical capacity
of a mixed commission to oversee
construction and operation of the Ar-
gentine-Uruguayan hydroelectric complex at Salto Grande on the Uruguay
River.)

Federal police said Carlos Alberto
Caride, a founder of the Peronist Revolutionary Armed Forces guerrilla group and
associate of deposed Buenos Aires
Province Gov. Oscar Bidegain, and six
presumed Tupamaros had been arrested
as they allegedly proceeded to the planned
assassination spot. Later reports said
some 30 Uruguayan nationals had been
arrested. Police added that the assassination plot was part of a more extensive
plan by left-wing Peronists to assassinate
or kidnap public officials and attack state
oil and gas installations, discovered Feb.
10 when a number of leftist Peronists were
captured in a gun battle with police in Mar
del Plata.

Left-wing Peronist leaders denounced
the plot allegations Feb. 12-14, asserting
they had previously warned government
officials that police officers were fabri-
cating assassination plots to separate
them from Peron. The London newsletter
Latin America suggested Feb. 22 that the
alleged plot was a "frame-up" of Caride.

(Caride was freed April 1 by a federal
judge who ruled that the government had

presented insufficient evidence against him.)

Police raids and dozens of arrests in Buenos Aires were reported Feb. 14 and 15. A lawyer for Mario Firmenich, a Montoneros guerrilla leader, charged Feb. 14 that Firmenich had disappeared and demanded to know if and why he had been arrested.

Another Montoneros leader, Roberto Quieto, was arrested in Rosario Feb. 19 on charges of "usurping authority and adulterating public documents."

(Quieto was released March 8 and Firmenich March 16.)

Two days later, federal police raided JTP headquarters in Buenos Aires and arrested more than 30 persons. The raid was directed by the three top police leaders, who reportedly had joined the Peronist right wing in its crusade against the left. Another 17 JTP members were later arrested in Moron, Buenos Aires Province, according to La Prensa of Buenos Aires Feb. 27.

JTP leader Jose Rosenberg had been held and reportedly abused in Mar del Plata Feb. 16–17, along with JUP member Norberto Trucchi. Leaders of the JP in La Plata charged Feb. 23 that police had arrested three JP members but had refused to acknowledge it.

Other unrest—The Montoneros had returned to action in January, after remaining inactive since the Peronists returned to power May 25, 1973, it was reported Feb. 1. They had occupied and seized documents from the registrar's office in the town of Carlos Paz, Cordoba Province, among other activities.

At least four persons were killed and 15 wounded Feb. 22 in a gun battle and rioting in the southern town of Comodoro Rivadavia. The violence began when some 500 workers from the left-wing "official" branch of the local petroleum workers' union marched to reclaim their headquarters from a group of right-wingers who had occupied it since Feb. 20 to protest alleged Marxist infiltration of the union leadership. The protesters were being guarded by police when the shooting broke out.

Some 60 members of the right-wing JPRA attacked the editorial offices of the Buenos Aires leftist newspaper El Mundo early Feb. 23, firing on the building and beating a reporter. Police later intervened and reportedly arrested 17 newspaper employes. All were subsequently released except Ana Maria Guzzetti, a reporter who had angered President Peron at a recent news conference.

(Peron had asked that Guzzetti be tried for slander after she asked him if the government planned action to "deter the fascist escalation and wave of crimes committed by parapolice groups."

(The Association of Argentine Journalistic Entities Jan. 31 had denounced alleged attacks on press freedom including "threats, intimidations and confiscation of [newspaper] editions." It called on the government to respect the press and its role in a democratic society.)

A powerful bomb was thrown at the entrance of the building of the Buenos Aires leftist Peronist newspaper Noticias March 9. Three persons in the building next door were injured.

A bomb was thrown at Buenos Aires headquarters of the national Metallurgical Workers Union the same night, after elections for the union leadership. Members opposed to the conservative leadership had charged they were prevented from running opposition slates. The official candidate for adjunct secretary general of the union was Labor Minister Ricardo Otero.

Bomb explosions in Buenos Aires April 19 later damaged several shops near the printing company that published political magazines of the Peronist right and left. Ten days earlier, members of the Peronist Armed Forces guerrilla group had taken credit for attacks on 12 buses in Mar del Plata to protest an increase in bus fares.

More than 20 bombs exploded in Buenos Aires May 29–30, most at automobile dealers, according to the Miami Herald June 1. At least 10 bombings were reported the same days in Cordoba, presumably in commemoration of the fifth anniversary of the Cordoba worker and student rebellion which helped bring down Gen. Juan Carlos Ongania, then the nation's military dictator.

A bomb had blown up the Buenos Aires headquarters of the General Labor Confederation May 28. Other explosions had damaged a department store and two branches of the Bank of Commerce in the capital May 25.

Peronists assassinated. Intra-Peronist violence continued.

Rogelio Coria, former secretary general of the national Construction Workers Union, was shot to death in Buenos Aires March 22. According to the French newspaper Le Monde March 24, Coria was among "the most corrupt elements" of the right wing of the Peronist labor movement and had opposed the return of President Juan Peron to Argentina and the designation of Hector Campora as Peronist presidential candidate in December 1972. He had recently returned to Argentina from his residence in Paraguay.

Luis A. David, a supporter of Peron and head of the right-wing Nationalist Liberation Alliance, had been found shot to death March 21 near San Nicolas (Buenos Aires Province). The adjunct secretary of the San Nicolas Construction Workers Union, Roberto Jose Kusner, had been shot dead the day before.

Another right-wing Peronist, Miguel Angel Castrofini, of the Nueva Argentina university faction, was assassinated March 8.

Juan Manuel Abal Medina, ex-secretary of the National Justicialista Movement and an organizer of radical Peronist youth groups, was wounded in the arm in an assassination attempt in Buenos Aires March 23. Presumed rightists fired on him from a passing car and threw two grenades into the apartment building into which he retreated.

Unknown gunmen fired on the home of Tucuman City Councilwoman Lucialda Cerca March 25. Cerca belonged to the government's Justicialista Liberation Front (FREJULI).

Police dismantled a bomb April 3 outside the San Fernando (Buenos Aires Province) home of Deputy Miguel Angel Davico, also a FREJULI member.

Antonio Magaldi, secretary general of the regional General Labor Confederation in San Nicolas (Buenos Aires Province), was shot to death April 4. The next day a leftist Peronist organizer, Fernando Quinteros, was dragged from his Buenos Aires home and shot dead by two men claiming to be policemen.

Quinteros, who worked in shantytowns around the capital, had opposed Social Welfare Minister Jose Lopez Rega's program for slum dwellers, which he claimed made their situation worse than before.

Police had killed a slum dweller March 25 in a demonstration against Lopez Rega's policies by some 300 persons. The Peronist Montoneros guerrilla group later blamed the social welfare minister for the killing and said the "crime must be paid for sooner or later," the London newsletter Latin America reported April 5. This was the first implicit death threat by the Montoneros against anyone so close to President Peron.

Maria Liliana Ivanoff of the leftist Peronist Youth (JP) was kidnapped and shot to death by presumed Peronist rightists outside Buenos Aires April 26. Carlos Mugica, a leader of the Third World Priests Movement with close ties to the JP, was gunned down as he left his church in the capital May 11.

The government news agency TELAM charged May 14 that Mugica had been killed by the Peronist Montoneros guerrilla group, presumably for his recent appeals to leftists to moderate their attacks on the orthodox Peronist leadership and remain loyal to President Peron. However, the London newsletter Latin America noted May 17 that Mugica had first gained prominence by defending two dead Montoneros, and that the guerrillas never killed a person for making appeals such as Mugica's.

JP leader Carlos Castelacci was killed May 10 in a gun battle with other leftist Peronists over possession of one of the JP's Buenos Aires offices.

Three young members of the Socialist Workers Party were kidnapped from a meeting in suburban Buenos Aires May 30 and later found shot to death. The unidentified abductors, who were armed with machine guns, also kidnapped, beat and later released three other party members, all women.

It was announced by authorities in Buenos Aires June 11 that Remo Crotta, head of the paper industry union, and Francisco Oscar Martinez, of the Peronist Youth organization in La Plata, had been found dead. Both had been reported kidnapped earlier.

May Day violence. Right- and left-wing Peronists battled in the streets of Buenos Aires May 1, after President Juan Peron delivered his traditional May Day address to 100,000 supporters and bitterly attacked the Peronist left.

Bands of leftists and rightists fought with staves and fists, causing several injuries but no reported deaths.

Peron extolled the conservative trade unions, which dominated his political movement, saying: "I want this first meeting of ours on Labor Day to be an act of homage to those organizations and their wise leaders." He eulogized conservative unionists who had recently been assassinated, and warned that "the voice of punishment has not yet sounded" for their murderers.

Peron denounced leaders of the leftist Peronist youth organizations, calling them "beardless infiltrators" and "mercenaries of foreign forces." When leftists interrupted his speech with chants for a more radical government, Peron angrily called them "idiots."

More than 20,000 leftists attended the rally. One of their leaders, Juan Carlos Anon, had charged April 23 that the government had been arresting leftists to prevent them from attending. Police had announced the arrest of seven Peronist Montoneros guerrillas April 23 on charges of illegal possession of arms and explosives.

New security unit. The rally had been preceded by other Peronist violence and by non-Peronist guerrilla violence, which had influenced the government to appoint a new National Security Council to re-establish civil peace. The council, created April 19 by Defense Minister Angel Robledo and Interior Minister Benito Llambi, consisted of members of the state and federal police and the three branches of the armed forces.

The government May 28 created a special industrial police force to guard Argentine and foreign factories against guerrilla attacks.

ERP, Latin guerrillas unite. Leaders of the left-wing People's Revolutionary Army (ERP) had said at a clandestine press conference near Buenos Aires Feb. 14 that they would step up their attacks on the Argentine military and form a "common front" with leftist guerrillas of Chile, Bolivia and Uruguay.

One of the leaders, who identified himself as Enrique Gorriaran, said: "We consider that to halt or diminish the fight against the oppressor army would allow it to reorganize and to pass over to the offensive." He asserted the recent ERP attack on the army's Azul garrison in Buenos Aires Province had proved to be a "political success" because it further separated leftists from the "bourgeois reformer" President Peron.

Another of the leaders, identified as Domingo Mena, said the ERP and the Revolutionary Left Movement of Chile, the National Liberation Army of Bolivia and the Tupamaro guerrillas of Uruguay were "prepared to do combat under a joint command." A joint declaration by the four groups pledged to overthrow "imperialist-capitalist reaction, to annihilate counterrevolutionary armies, expel Yankee and European imperialism from Latin American soil, country by country, and initiate the construction of socialism in each of our countries . . ."

The ERP June 12 made public documents asserting that it had distributed $5 million among the other members of the Latin American guerrilla "Revolutionary Coordination Board," the coordinating organization set up by the Argentinian, Bolivian, Uruguayan and Chilean terrorist groups. The ERP documents, signed by Mario Roberto Santucho, reported that the money was part of the Samuelson ransom. The ERP said the guerrillas were using the money to finance "a new stage of military development," the establishment of rural guerrilla movements to mobilize and organize the masses and complement the operations of the existing guerrilla units.

Terrorist kidnappers active. Douglas Roberts, administrative director of Pepsi-Cola S.A., local affiliate of the U.S. firm PepsiCo, was abducted in suburban Buenos Aires Jan. 4. Roberts was freed Feb. 2 after the payment of an undisclosed sum. The police announced later that they had arrested three of the abductors and recovered part of the ransom.

Some 6,000 workers at the Peugeot automobile factory outside Buenos Aires staged a two-hour strike Jan. 4 to protest the kidnapping Dec. 28, 1973 of the factory director, Yves Boisset. Boisset's release was announced by Peugeot March 18. French sources in Buenos Aires said the abductors had demanded $4 million in ransom.

The ERP announced the release of Julio Baraldo, director of the local affiliate of Italy's Bereta arms factory, in exchange for an undetermined quantity of arms, it was reported Jan. 19.

U.S. engineer Charles Hayes was freed Jan. 31 after a month in captivity, when his A. G. McKee construction company reportedly paid a $1 million ransom.

Enrique (Henry) Nyborg Andersen, Danish regional manager of the Bank of London & South America, kidnapped in Buenos Aires Nov. 17, 1973, was released Feb. 19, 1974 after payment of a ransom estimated at $1,145,000.

Mario Reduto, a retired naval petty officer kidnapped Feb. 22, was found dead in a garbage dump in Zarate (Buenos Aires Province) March 14. The ERP admitted "executing" Reduto, whom it had accused of heading a parapolice group which allegedly attacked and tortured leftists.

Members of the ERP Feb. 23 kidnapped Antonio Vallocchia, an executive of Swift & Company in Rosario, whom they held responsible for the "unjustified dismissal of 42 workers demanding decent salaries." Swift said Feb. 26 that it would reinstate the 42 employes and pay them for the days they were out of work, in accordance with ERP demands.

The French-based Peugeot auto firm announced March 18 that its Argentina production manager, Yves Boisset, had been released by kidnappers who had held him since Dec. 28, 1973. French sources in Buenos Aires said the abductors had demanded a $4 million ransom. Jose Chohelo, a Peugeot representative in the capital, was kidnapped June 3 and ransomed for $200,000 June 11.

The personnel manager at the Fiat-Concord automobile plant in Cordoba, Roberto Francisco Klecher, was shot to death on a downtown street April 4. The Peronist Armed Forces later claimed credit.

ERP members in Buenos Aires kidnapped a retired army officer March 29 and released him unharmed the same day. The former officer, Lt. Col. Jorge Alberto Rivero, was the prosecutor in a court martial against an army private who allegedly collaborated in an unsuccessful attempt by the ERP to occupy the headquarters of the Argentine Medical Corps in September 1973. Rivero said the guerrillas questioned him about the case for 45 minutes.

The ERP May 15 freed army Col. Florencio Crespo, whom it had kidnapped in November 1973. Crespo told newsmen he had been treated "very well" by his captors but had been released for "health reasons."

Gregorio Manoukian, president of the Tanti chain of supermarkets, was killed in a kidnap attempt in Buenos Aires June 7. Jose Chohelo, a Peugeot representative in the capital, had been kidnapped June 3 and ransomed for $200,000 June 11.

Samuelson ransom paid. Esso Argentina paid a record sum to the People's Revolutionary Army (ERP) to ransom its refinery manager, Victor Samuelson, but the guerrillas waited for 1½ months before releasing him.

The Exxon Corp. affiliate announced March 13 it had paid $14.2 million for Samuelson, kidnapped by the ERP in December 1973. The guerrillas had also demanded that a communique they issued on the kidnapping be printed by 12 newspapers in Buenos Aires and some 30 in the provinces, but all but three papers in the capital declined in fear of reprisals from the government.

The left-wing El Mundo published the message on its front page March 13. The government closed the paper the next day and ordered criminal proceedings against its publishers and editors for "trying to encourage the propagation of subversive action." (But the Superior Court of Justice May 3 annulled the decree against El Mundo.)

(Newspapers were officially forbidden to publish ERP messages or even mention the guerrilla group's name, but this was frequently violated. The conservative opposition newspaper La Prensa reported the group's activities and printed its name almost daily.)

The ERP communique said Esso had agreed originally to pay $4.2 million in supplies to victims of recent floods in Argentina, plus $10 million in cash as "indemnization" for "the superprofits that Esso has obtained in the country, thanks to the exploitation of its workers." However, the message stated, "existing obstacles" had made distribution of the supplies unfeasible, so the entire $14.2 million had been paid in cash.

Esso repatriated its remaining U.S. executives March 14–15 to avert any new kidnappings. Fear of abduction or murder had caused more than 500 U.S. business executives to leave Argentina during the past few months, the Miami Herald reported March 22. The estimated 300 U.S. businessmen who remained in the country reportedly headed small concerns.

The ERP freed Samuelson April 29.

An ERP communique to Buenos Aires newspapers said Samuelson had been released at the home of the pediatrician who had treated his children before they and Samuelson's wife left Argentina in January. The statement guaranteed the safety of other ERP captives, but it warned: "There will be no truce for exploiting firms and the oppressor army."

Samuelson's release had been delayed while his captors changed the huge ransom from U.S. dollars into other currencies or other dollars, so the serial numbers could not be traced, according to Argentine financial sources cited in press reports April 27.

The June 4 issue of the ERP's official publication, Red Star, said the guerrillas would spend $7 million of the ransom to finance "armed struggle in Chile, Argentina, Bolivia and Uruguay."

U.S. aide wounded, kidnapped. Guerrillas of the left-wing People's Revolutionary Army (ERP) April 12 wounded and briefly kidnapped Alfred A. Laun III, director of the U.S. Information Service in Cordoba. Laun was the first U.S. diplomat kidnapped in Argentina.

The guerrillas invaded Laun's home outside Cordoba in the morning and wounded him in the head, abdomen and shoulder when he resisted abduction. They released him that evening, apparently for fear he would die in captivity.

Laun underwent surgery in a Cordoba clinic, and was reported "out of danger" April 15.

Shortly after the kidnapping, the ERP sent a message to a Cordoba radio station claiming credit for the abduction. The guerrillas said Laun would be "interrogated on counterrevolutionary activities in Vietnam, Santo Domingo, Brazil and Bolivia, and for his active participation as a liaison in the fascist military coup against our brother people in Chile. He will also be interrogated on his ties with the Central Intelligence Agency."

The Argentine Chamber of Deputies called April 21 for an investigation of the possibility that Laun had "carried out extradiplomatic activities for some special organization of his country, such as the" CIA. The police had found a high-powered transmitter in Laun's home.

The U.S. embassy in Buenos Aires denied Laun had ever worked for or with the CIA, or served in Brazil or Bolivia. It also denied he had participated in any activities connected with Chile. Laun previously had served in the Dominican Republic, South Vietnam and Thailand.

(Claudio Alberto Luduena, sought in the brief kidnapping and wounding of Laun, was killed in Cordoba April 28 as he attempted unsuccessfully to kidnap Antonio Minetti, a business executive.)

Other terrorism. Among other developments involving terrorists:

Unknown terrorists attacked a police station in Rosario Jan. 16, seriously wounding one officer before setting fire to the building.

Police raided an ERP hideout in Rosario March 6 and arrested Oscar Ciarlotti, who allegedly participated in the 1973 kidnapping of his uncle, retired Rear Adm. Francisco Aleman.

ERP members stole firearms in attacks staged on police stations in Ciudadela (Buenos Aires Province) March 8, Resistencia (Chaco Province) March 15 and Melincue (Santa Fe Province) March 23. The guerrillas killed a police officer in the Resistencia raid and freed two imprisoned comrades in the Melincue attack.

Police in Santa Fe reported smashing an ERP cell April 10, arresting two alleged guerrillas and seizing arms and explosives. The day before, an armed group had attacked headquarters of an army engineers battalion in Santa Fe, killing one soldier and wounding another.

A tourist bus garage and a branch of the United Bank of Holland were bombed by terrorists in Buenos Aires April 19. The next day some 30 alleged ERP members occupied the neighborhood of Villanueva in Campana, outside the capital and held a five-hour gun battle with police. Three policemen were seriously wounded and seven guerrillas captured in the action.

More than 100 persons were arrested in Campana April 22–23 as police conducted raids to find ERP hideouts.

ERP members shot and killed Jorge Quiroga, a former judge of the disbanded anti-subversive court, in downtown Buenos Aires April 28. Quiroga had interrogated and sent to prison the 16 ERP and Peronist guerrillas who were killed by authorities at the Trelew naval air base prison in August 1972.

Buenos Aires police claimed May 6 that the ERP was also responsible for the murder of Manuel R. Garcia, a moderate Peronist labor leader, outside the capital May 4. However, the ERP did not normally attack Peronists of any tendency.

ERP members April 30 occupied a highway police post outside the city of Tafi, and escaped with the station's transmitter equipment. The same day, police in Cordoba arrested Juan Martin Guevara, brother of the late guerrilla leader Ernesto "Che" Guevara, who allegedly was carrying false identification papers and copies of ERP publications.

Bombs exploded simultaneously May 5 at the Buenos Aires offices of five Ford automobile dealers and at the American Club. Another bomb was set off at the branch of the Bank of London and South America, causing property damage.

Two policemen were killed and a third was wounded May 6 in a shootout with presumed leftist guerrillas in San Justo, outside Buenos Aires.

Guerrilla hunt fails. Hundreds of persons were arrested in Tucuman Province May 18–21 as federal police mounted a major campaign against the left-wing People's Revolutionary Army (ERP). But the Tucuman drive ended in failure May 25.

The action followed further violence by the ERP and by members of the opposing Peronist political factions and a warning by President Juan Peron that Argentina faced civil war. Peron was quoted May 16 as saying that because of "revolutionary infantilism," Argentina might have "reached a situation of unavoidable confrontation."

Police backed by army helicopters seized more than 150 persons in a mountainous area of Tucuman May 18. About 100 were later released when they were found to have no connections with the ERP, according to unofficial sources.

Announcing the abandonment of the anti-ERP drive May 25, security forces said bad weather had enabled the guerrillas to escape encirclement.

The task force of more than 1,000 policemen and soldiers reportedly captured only 27 alleged guerrillas, none of them major ERP leaders. The failure of the anti-guerrilla effort was dramatized May 31 when more than 40 ERP members briefly occupied the town of Acheral, which had served as a center of operations for the campaign.

At a parade celebrating Army Day May 29, the army commander, Gen. Leandro Anaya, spoke out strongly against guerrilla violence and said the army would "contribute decisively to prevent the aggressor from achieving his final objective: the seizure of power and the dissolution of our institutions."

Security command formed. Bombings, assassinations and kidnappings continued in Buenos Aires and other cities, leading President Juan Peron to set up a new committee to command all security operations. The committee, reported June 7, consisted of Peron, the ministers of defense, interior and justice, and the three armed forces commanders. Its orders would be carried out by a new security secretariat headed by Brig. Gen. Alberto Caceres, the frontier police chief who had served as federal police chief under the supplanted military dictatorship.

Peron warned June 17 that if violence continued, the government "must answer with a repression that is also a little more violent and stronger."

Socialists arrested—Police in Rosario raided a meeting of the Socialist Youths Union May 19, arresting 51 persons and allegedly seizing weapons.

Press crackdown. The magazine El Descamisado, the most widely read and authoritative organ of the left-wing Peronist Youth movement (JP), was closed by order of the Interior Ministry April 8. The magazine Militancia, which also reflected JP opinion, was closed the next day.

El Descamisado had repeatedly attacked conservative trade unionists, the government's anti-inflationary wage-price freeze, and virtually every major official around President Juan Peron. In recent issues it had commended the assassination of right-wing union leaders and had called the March shooting of former Construction Workers Union leader Rogelio Coria a case of "popular justice."

A March issue of El Descamisado reportedly had embarrassed Peron by citing 1969 statements implying he had approved of the assassination by guerrillas of Augusto Vandor, leader of the Metallurgical Workers Union, who reportedly had threatened Peron's control of the labor movement.

The ban on El Descamisado was vacated by a Buenos Aires court July 13 on the ground that the magazine had not tried to promote chaos, as the government had charged.

Militancia subsequently reappeared as El Peronista, but the government June 4 banned its publication and sale as well as the appearance of any publications that might replace it.

Troubles in Cordoba

Conflict between left-wing and right-wing forces resulted in a police revolt in Cordoba, where right-wing police elements overthrew a left-wing provincial administration. The federal Peron government then assumed temporary administration of the province.

Cordoba government conflict. Cordoba Province Gov. Ricardo Obregon Cano, a left-wing Peronist, charged Jan. 18 that unnamed federal officials had mounted a campaign against his administration. The assertion followed a call by the Cordoba city intendant, Juan Carlos Avalos, for federal intervention in the provincial government.

Avalos, a right-wing Peronist, had charged in letters to President Peron and Interior Minister Benito Llambi Jan. 6 that the provincial vice governor, Atilio Lopez, was leading a Cordoba city transport workers strike for political reasons. The stoppage, by the Automotive Streetcar Union, was called Jan. 4 and settled Jan. 7 when the government granted the strikers higher wages. Lopez, a former secretary general of the union, had endorsed the strike Jan. 6.

Lopez was expelled Jan. 14 from the association of Cordoba's 62 Peronist organizations, dominated by orthodox Peronists. Both he and Obregon Cano had long been attacked by conservatives in the Peronist movement.

Cordoba police revolt. An estimated 800 right-wing policemen seized control of the city of Cordoba late Feb. 27 and ousted the elected provincial government, dominated by left-wing Peronists.

The rebels, representing more than a third of the city's police force, acted with the apparent approval of President Juan Peron. They seized the provincial Government House and arrested Gov. Ricardo Obregon Cano, Vice Gov. Atilio Lopez and some 80 other officials including provincial Cabinet ministers and legislators. All were released two days later but were prevented from returning to their government posts.

Peron initially refused to intervene in the situation, but he asked Congress March 2 to remove Obregon from office and let the president name a successor. Congress was dominated by conservative Peronists sympathetic to the Cordoba rebels.

The revolt was touched off Feb. 27 when Obregon dismissed the city police chief, Lt. Col. Antonio Navarro, who was accused of organizing bombing attempts against left-wing Peronists, including Vice Gov. Lopez. (A former deputy police chief, Lt. Col. Julian Chiappe, had charged Feb. 15 that Navarro had used police funds and vehicles improperly and had conspired against the provincial government.)

Navarro refused to resign and led officers loyal to him in seizing the Government House, arresting the officials, surrounding police stations throughout the city and taking over all radio and television stations. The rebels broadcast a message asserting they had "decided to put an end to the uncontrolled Marxist infiltration in the province" and were prepared to defend the decision "to the ultimate consequences."

The insurgents also attempted unsuccessfully to blow up the printing presses of the city's leading newspaper, La Voz del Interior, which apparently had angered them by detailing charges against 19 policemen accused of executing five innocent farmers in January after mistaking them for left-wing guerrillas.

The rebels were immediately supported by the city's right-wing unions but denounced by the leftist regional leadership of the General Labor Confederation (CGT). A communique signed by CGT Secretary General Roberto Tapia and Adjunct Secretary Agustin Tosco placed union members on "alert" and charged that "reactionary... forces have appealed to the police chief to create a situation of rebellion, chaos and violence that would provoke the fall of the government elected by the people . . ."

Snipers fired on the rebels in different parts of the city Feb. 27–28.

Cordoba was paralyzed Feb. 28 as right-wing unions struck to support the rebels and right-wing civilians joined policemen in patrolling the streets. Two policemen and a bystander were killed in a clash between police and civilians, and the home of a judge was badly damaged by a bomb explosion. Some 250 federal police were sent in from Buenos Aires, but they were not put into action.

The Cordoba Justice Ministry declared Obregon out of office Feb. 28 and installed in his place the president of the provincial Chamber of Deputies, Mario Dante Agodino. Agodino pledged new gubernatorial elections for September. He subsequently met with captive Obregon in an effort to resolve the general conflict, according to police sources.

Obregon and the other officials were released March 1, and many of them immediately went into hiding. Left-wing labor leaders also were in hiding, and right-wing unionists took advantage of their absence to elect a new regional CGT leader, Bernabe Barcena of the Millers Union. Labor Minister Ricardo Otero flew in from Buenos Aires to view the election and confirm Barcena in his new office. (The election also was endorsed by national CGT Secretary General Adelino Romero, who at the time was in Cuba, according to the French newspaper Le Monde March 3.)

Cordoba remained paralyzed March 1; shooting was heard throughout the city, and Obregon's vacant home was bombed. In Buenos Aires, Peron discussed the situation with his Cabinet, and the opposition leader, Ricardo Balbin of the Radical Civic Union, met with Interior Minister Benito Llambi and Secretary to the Presidency Vicente Solano Lima. Balbin later said that the Cordoba revolt was "subversive" and that Obregon should be reinstated.

Clashes between civilians and rebel police continued in Cordoba March 2 as the death toll rose to five. Police raided offices and homes of leftists, and there was a shootout in front of the office of the Socialist Workers Party. A policeman was killed in a raid by civilians on the Los Cocos police station in the interior of the province.

Peron asked Congress to dismiss Obregon and his government, charging they had "tolerated and at times even fomented diverse conflictive situations which provoked a growing climate of public unrest." Obregon declared from hiding that he did not intend to resign.

Cordoba government removed. The federal government took over the government of Cordoba Province March 12 after Congress voted the action to end the police revolt.

President Peron then named a conservative follower, Diulio Brunelli, to replace Cordoba Gov. Ricardo Obregon Cano, whose left-wing administration had angered right-wing policemen and other orthodox Peronists. Brunelli most recently had worked for Social Welfare Minister Jose Lopez Rega, one of Peron's most conservative advisers.

Obregon and Cordoba Vice Gov. Atilio Lopez had resigned March 8 after fighting for more than a week to retain their posts. Obregon charged in his letter of resignation that the "conspiracy" against his government had "the support of officials of the national government, especially the interior minister and the labor minister."

Interior Minister Benito Llambi had ignored Obregon's repeated calls for federal intervention against the police rebels, and Labor Minister Ricardo Otero had approved the conservative take-over of the regional General Labor Confederation during the revolt.

Peron's request to replace the Cordoba regime had been approved by the Senate March 5 and by the Chamber of Deputies March 8, in each instance after long hours of debate in which the opposition parties, principally the Radical Civic Union (UCR), opposed the action as unconstitutional. UCR leader Ricardo Balbin had said March 4 that "the problem of Cordoba is strictly seditious and a federal intervenor should be named to reinstate in their offices the legitimately elected authorities. . ."

The final intervention measure included, as a concession to the opposition parties and Obregon, an article demanding that Lt. Col. Antonio Navarro and other leaders of the Cordoba revolt be tried for sedition. Navarro resigned as Cordoba police commander March 13.

A new Cordoba police chief, Lt. Col. Juan Carlos Landa, assumed office March 21.

The Communist Party had vigorously opposed Obregon's removal, asserting in its organ Nuestra Palabra March 7 that the police revolt marked the beginning of a "Chilean-style coup, with its criminal methods and genocidal objectives," in Argentina. Police raided Communist offices in Cordoba March 8 and arrested eight persons.

Unrest continues. Violence continued in Cordoba both before and after the ouster of the left-wing regime and the federal takeover.

Three more persons were killed March 3 as the strike and unrest continued. A police station at Los Reartes outside Cordoba was briefly occupied by civilian attackers.

Heavy firing between snipers and police and civilian patrols was reported for the fourth consecutive night March 4, but no casualties were reported. The next day, as right-wing trade unions lifted their general strike in support of the police rebels, snipers fired on police and radio stations occupied by the rebels.

Eighteen bombing incidents were reported March 8. An affiliate of at least one U.S. firm, Goodyear Tire and Rubber Co., was among the targets. Several more bombs exploded in the city March 10, and in Salsipuedes young supporters of Gov. Obregon threw incendiary bombs at the town hall.

Unknown persons threw Molotov cocktails into crowded streets in Cordoba March 11, provoking a shootout. Leaflets were found near the scene in which the People's Revolutionary Army (ERP), the major left-wing guerrilla group, denounced the "police-fascist coup" that deposed Obregon.

Four bombings were reported March 12, and five the night of March 15–16. A group of avowed ERP members briefly occupied and then dynamited Cordoba's LV2 La Voz del Pueblo radio station March 16.

Two bomb explosions were reported early March 22. The Buenos Aires newspaper La Prensa said other bombings had occurred almost daily during the previous week. Three policemen had been wounded early March 20 in a shootout with unknown ambushers.

Unidentified terrorists unsuccessfully tried to occupy the transmitting plant of the radio station LV3 Radio Cordoba March 26. Later the same day a policeman and a terrorist were wounded in a gun battle in another part of the city.

Bombs were thrown at three private homes in Cordoba March 27. An army lieutenant colonel and a union lawyer were among owners of the homes. Several more bombings were reported April 3.

Juan Martin Guevara, brother of the late revolutionary leader Ernesto "Che" Guevara, was placed under preventive detention by order of a Cordoba federal judge July 15. The judge ruled that there was sufficient evidence for an unlawful association indictment against Guevara, who was arrested late in April.

Peron's Final Months

Peron returns to Government House. President Peron resumed working in the Government House in Buenos Aires April 15, after living and performing almost all his presidential duties in his suburban residence for more than three months.

Peron's seclusion in his residence had sparked insistent rumors that he was in failing health. However, his aides now said his health was "excellent."

Despite the events in Cordoba and other recent setbacks, left-wing Peronists apparently continued to support the government. Some 40,000 Peronist youths held a rally at a Buenos Aires soccer stadium March 11 and chanted marching songs and slogans in praise of the president. Speakers denounced the powerful right-wing trade unionists and recent government policies and appointments, but reiterated their loyalty to Peron.

Allende elected to Senate post. Jose Antonio Allende was elected president pro tempore of the Senate, second in line of succession to the presidency, it was reported April 30. The election had the blessing of President Peron, whose wife, the vice president, was first in line to succeed him.

Allende was a member of the small Popular Christian Party, of the government's Justicialista Liberation Front coalition. He represented Cordoba.

Military intelligence chief quits. Brig. Gen. Haroldo Pomar, head of the armed forces' intelligence service, resigned May 10 under apparent pressure from the government.

Pomar was an old political enemy of President Peron and a close friend of retired Lt. Gen. Alejandro Lanusse, whose military regime yielded to the Peronist government in May 1973. Pomar had recently been reprimanded by Defense Minister Angel Robledo for attending a ceremony of the leftist state oil workers' union.

Robledo had warned Lanusse May 9 against meeting with army officers and staying at military garrisons when he traveled about Argentina. Another high government official had recently warned that "the danger of a military conspiracy is always present," the Miami Herald reported May 11.

Pomar was succeeded June 5 by Brig. Gen. Eduardo Episcopo.

Top police officers quit. The seven members of the federal police general staff asked to be retired May 13 rather than serve under Luis Margaride, appointed deputy police chief by President Peron May 10. Twenty-one police officers of the next highest rank also resigned in protest.

Margaride, an enemy of the Peronist left, had won notoriety under the supplanted military dictatorship when, as chief of the morals squad, he staged frequent raids in downtown hotels in search of adulterous couples. He was dismissed when his officers seized a number of high-ranking government officials.

Acting federal police chief Alberto Villar had been named permanent chief May 10. He was the first non-military man to hold the position since 1955.

Villar replaced Gen. Miguel A. Iniguez, who, before resigning, according to reports cited by the newsletter Latin America May 3, had tried to arrest Margaride (then head of the political police) and had had serious differences with Villar, then his second in command. Iniguez was believed to have complained that senior government officials, faced with serious political problems, "resorted to indiscriminate police repression to solve them," Latin America reported.

Social Welfare Minister Jose Lopez Rega, a retired police corporal, was named police commissioner general in a surprise decree May 3. The promotion, a jump of 15 ranks, was attacked May 11 by Sen. Amadeo Frugoli, of the Mendoza Democratic Party, who called it a "flagrant attack on the force" and a "clear case of personal favoritism." Lopez Rega was among President Peron's closest advisers, and was a bitter enemy of the Peronist left.

Solano Lima quits presidency post. Vicente Solano Lima resigned as secretary general of the presidency June 4. He was named an adviser to President Peron with ministerial rank, and replaced in his old post by army Col. Vicente Damasco.

Solano Lima, a former vice president, also remained rector of Buenos Aires University. He had assumed that post April 2, after Congress passed a law giving rectors complete authority in all administrative and ideological questions on their campuses. The measure, approved March 14, also forbade political proselytizing on campus—a provision apparently aimed at leftist activists.

Solano Lima resigned after failing in an attempt to prevent the conservative labor minister, Ricardo Otero, from designating the State Employes Association as the only union allowed to organize Buenos Aires University's 10,000 workers, the London newsletter Latin America reported June 14.

The majority of non-teaching personnel at the university were members of another union that generally supported the radical views of a majority of the students and teaching staff, Latin America reported. Solano Lima had seen Otero's interference as an obstacle to reconciliation within the troubled university and had used his position as secretary general of the presidency to argue his case, according to the newsletter.

Economic policy attacks & resignation threat. President Peron June 12 threatened to resign unless he got full public support for his economic policies, which were under increasing attack from businessmen, newspapers and workers. He withdrew the threat after an estimated 100,000 workers from Peronist labor unions gathered outside the Government House and urged him to stay on.

The government's wage and price controls, embodied in the "social pact" signed in 1973 by Peronist labor and management groups, had been threatened by inflation, shortages, wildcat strikes, a growing black market and criticism from non-Peronist newspapers and from businessmen who claimed they were being driven to bankruptcy.

Workers had been given a general 13% wage increase March 28, but this was followed by larger increases in the prices of gas, electricity, gasoline and public transport. The inflation rate, which the pact had reduced from 80% to 12%, according to government figures, reportedly tripled in May, and price-controlled foodstuffs such as eggs, milk and sugar were reported scarce.

An estimated 240,000 public school teachers staged three strikes for a 100% wage increase—a 24-hour stoppage May 23 and longer walkouts May 28–29 and

June 4–6. Policemen, railway and industrial workers, and newspaper employes struck at various times (on June 1, stoppages were reported at four newspapers, a television station, the subway and railway systems and two steel plants.) The staff of the daily La Nacion received a $120 monthly wage increase after it struck May 30, the journalists and printing workers for La Prensa received a $138 increase to end their five-day stoppage June 5.

Businessmen charged that the price controls were causing the scarcity of goods and raw materials, forcing them to buy on the black market. The newspaper Clarin, of ex-President Arturo Frondizi's Desarrollista movement, severely criticized the social pact, and the conservative Review of the River Plate accused Peron May 31 of imposing greater state control over the economy "than that ruling in Chile at the time of the fall of [President Salvador] Allende."

The Review and other conservative publications also attacked the government for granting a large credit to Cuba and for establishing joint enterprises with state-owned firms from Eastern Europe. The Review charged that the government, in its deals with Cuba, was "lightening the costly burden of maintaining the spearhead of the Soviet regime on American territory."

Peron went on radio and television June 12 to make an emotional denunciation of all opponents of the social pact, including businessmen, dissident union leaders, black marketeers, "oligarchic newspapers" and feuding sectors of his own political movement.

He asserted that he had returned to Argentina in 1973 to "liberate the country from foreign dependence" and "to unite" Argentines. "If I find that this sacrifice is in vain," Peron said, "I will not hesitate one instant in yielding [the presidency] to those who can occupy it with better chances of success."

Peron asked for strong public support for the social pact. He received it within hours, as the General Labor Confederation (CGT) called a 10-hour strike, virtually paralyzing Buenos Aires, and massed some 100,000 workers into the Plaza de Mayo, in front of the Government House, to ask Peron to stay in office. Peron obliged, saying he would fulfill his duties "until I take my last breath."

Peron's attack on conservative critics succeeded in strengthening support for the government among Peronist leftists. Mario Firmenich, a leader of the Montoneros organization, praised Peron's speech and urged the government to step up its attack on "imperialism and the oligarchy."

The entire Cabinet and the government's economic council offered to resign June 12 to give Peron a free hand, but he rejected the offer June 13. The government immediately moved to bolster the social pact.

The Chamber of Deputies June 12 passed a bill containing strong penalties for businessmen who sold goods above the official prices or hoarded products for sale on the black market.

The economic council, after meeting with Peron June 13, gave producers and distributors 72 hours to submit a sworn statement giving an inventory of all stocks that would be subject to production and storage controls. The government June 14 announced a program, called "Operation Pygmy," to fight the black market, and officials announced the confiscation of 150,000 hams and an equal quantity of cheeses hoarded in different stores.

Leaders of the General Economic Confederation (CGE), the Peronist management group, expressed renewed support for the social pact after meeting with Peron June 18.

Peron's Death

Peron dies, wife assumes presidency. President Juan Domingo Peron died of a heart attack July 1. He was 78. His death left Argentina in a state of great uncertainty, with deep political divisions and growing economic problems.

The presidency was assumed by Peron's widow, Maria Estela (Isabel) Martinez de Peron, who became the first woman chief of state in the Americas. Mrs. Peron announced her husband's death in an emotional radio address in which she called him "a true apostle of peace and nonviolence."

Mrs. Peron had assumed executive powers June 29, when doctors ordered Peron to take "absolute rest" while they treated him for what they said was infectious bronchitis with heart complications. Peron was first reported ill June 18, when he failed to go to his office because of a "grippe condition."

Most political groups and military leaders had pledged their support for Mrs. Peron June 29–30, citing the Constitution's provisions for the vice president to rule if the president was incapacitated. The commanders of the three armed forces sent messages to all military bases June 30 stating that "there is no other political solution than that which is founded in the total and absolute respect for the Constitution and its laws."

The 250,000-member left-wing Peronist Youth Organization announced its unconditional support for Mrs. Peron June 29, and the Montoneros guerrilla group, also on the Peronist left, said it backed the vice president "as long as Gen. Peron is not in the physical condition to continue exercising the presidency." Both groups previously had criticized Mrs. Peron for favoring her husband's most conservative advisers, including Social Welfare Minister Jose Lopez Rega, whom the Peronist left called a "fascist."

Hundreds of thousands of citizens lined the streets of Buenos Aires July 2 to watch Peron's body be transported from the presidential residence to the Metropolitan Cathedral for a requiem mass and then to Congress to lie in state. Citizens viewed the body in Congress until July 4, when it was returned to the presidential palace for burial.

The mass was celebrated July 2 by Antonio Cardinal Caggiano, archbishop of Buenos Aires and primate of Argentina's Roman Catholic Church, who called Peron a "Christian," a "humanist" and an "enemy of violence." The religious services were attended by Mrs. Peron, government and labor leaders, and foreign dignitaries including Uruguayan President Juan Maria Bordaberry.

Two other Latin American presidents, Gens. Hugo Banzer Suarez of Bolivia and Alfredo Stroessner of Paraguay, paid their last respects to Peron in Congress July 3. Heads of state throughout the continent expressed sorrow at Peron's death.

The right-wing Brazilian regime declared three days of mourning July 2, while Cuban Premier Fidel Castro declared a similar mourning period and called Peron's death "a blow to all of Latin America."

President Nixon said July 1 that Peron had been "a source of inspiration to his countrymen." In the Soviet Union, Premier Alexei Kosygin, President Nikolai Podgorny and Foreign Minister Andrei Gromyko visited the Argentine embassy July 5 to express their condolences to the ambassador.

Virtually all Argentine sectors, including the armed forces and the opposition political parties, expressed sorrow at Peron's death and support for Mrs. Peron's presidency July 2–4. Only one newspaper, La Prensa, an old foe of Peron, attacked the president in its editorial July 2. (In retaliation, the Peronist Newspaper Vendors Union "broke relations" with La Prensa—implying it would cut off the paper's distribution—and Peronists attacked the newspaper's offices in Cordoba and Rosario July 6.)

The Montoneros organization, the acknowledged leader of the Peronist left wing, expressed support for Mrs. Peron July 2 but warned that "the political vacuum left by Gen. Peron's absence may be filled by adventurists and unscrupulous persons who already are making plans to take power." The Montoneros apparently referred to Social Welfare Minister Jose Lopez Rega, a close adviser of both Peron and his widow whom they considered reactionary.

Lopez Rega went on national radio and television July 1 to appeal for national unity. He was the only government official aside from Mrs. Peron to make a national broadcast in the days following Peron's death.

In a slap at the Peronist left, Lopez Rega barred Vicente Solano Lima, a presidential adviser and former vice president, from expressing his condolences to Mrs. Peron July 1. Solano Lima recently had given consideration to the views of leftists at the University of Buenos Aires, of which he was rector. He resigned his posts as presidential adviser and university rector in indignation July 1.

Mrs. Peron said she would follow her husband's national and international policies "without an iota of change." "Everything that General Peron considered good will also be considered good by me," she asserted July 8

Mrs. Peron President, Violence Resumes

Mor Roig slain. Peron's death was followed by a brief lull in political hostilities as the nation paid him its last respects and virtually all sectors expressed full support for his widow and successor, President Maria Estela Martinez de Peron.

However, political violence soon resumed and culminated in the assassination July 15 of ex-Interior Minister Arturo Mor Roig. In addition, economic uncertainty continued as Mrs. Peron declared a general wage bonus July 8, weakening her husband's "social pact," and the moderate leader of the General Labor Confederation (CGT), Adelino Romero, died of a heart attack July 14.

Mor Roig was shot to death in suburban Buenos Aires July 15.

Mor Roig had been in office in August 1972, when officers at the Trelew naval air base in Patagonia killed 16 leftist guerrillas, many of them members of the outlawed People's Revolutionary Army (ERP). The ERP had vowed to kill every official in the chain of command at that time and had subsequently assassinated Rear. Adm. Hermes Quijada, who had chaired the joint chiefs of staff at the time of the killings.

The search for Mor Roig's murderers proved to be a bloody one.

Police in Buenos Aires reported July 16 that two men and a woman had been killed when they exchanged gunfire with officers seeking to search their automobile.

Interior Minister Benito Llambi announced July 18 that four suspects had been killed and 28 arrested since the assassination, and all were members of the ERP or of other left-wing extremist groups. However, the ERP denied responsibility for Mor Roig's death in a press communique July 18.

(Ex-President Alejandro Lanusse, in whose Cabinet Mor Roig had served, charged the Peronist Montoneros organization had committed the assassination, the French newspaper Le Monde reported July 21.)

Two more suspects were killed July 20 in a shootout with police. Police claimed to have found arms and "subversive" literature in the suspects' automobile.

Intervention in Mendoza. President Peron July 12 asked Congress to approve legislation ordering federal intervention in the government of Mendoza Province. Mendoza Gov. Alberto Martinez Baca had been impeached and suspended from office June 5 by the provincial Chamber of Deputies, which accused him of mismanaging the state-owned Giol winery. Martinez had asked July 11 that certain members of the provincial Senate, which would try him on the Chamber's charges, be disqualified for having already made judgments against him in the case.

Mrs. Peron's request for federal intervention—allowed where the security or stability of a provincial government was in jeopardy—was criticized by opposition politicians, who called it "a new violation of the Constitution and the laws," the Mexican newspaper Excelsior reported July 14. The Argentine Federalist Forces, which grouped together Mendoza's major provincial parties, noted that intervention was unnecessary when "the mechanisms of the Constitution are acting to resolve the conflict."

Martinez Baca was linked with left-wing Peronists, as was the third provincial governor to lose his post in 1974, Cordoba's Ricardo Obregon Cano.

Catamarca governor quits. Hugo Alberto Mott, moderate Peronist governor of Catamarca Province, resigned July 18 in a dispute with right-wing Peronist labor union leaders.

Mott quit after officials of the local General Labor Confederation (CGT) and the "62 Organizations," both dominated by conservative Peronists, demanded that he fire the provincial government and social welfare ministers. The rightists charged the ministers had offended decorum and public morality, had made "arbitrary" appointments at high levels, and had allowed foreign ideologies to infiltrate public offices.

Violence. Alleged Peronist rightists July 6 raped and beat to death a pregnant woman who belonged to the left-wing Peronist Youth (JP). The JP charged July 8 that rightists also had killed another of its members, identified as Eduardo Romero.

Leandro Salato, a high official in the Social Welfare Ministry, was shot and seriously wounded by unidentified persons near Buenos Aires July 12.

Unidentified gunmen fired on an army convoy outside Buenos Aires July 16, wounding a junior officer and a soldier. Later that day, unidentified persons opened machinegun fire on the suburban Buenos Aires home of Juan M. Courard, president of Ford Motor Argentina. A powerful bomb exploded in a Buenos Aires building housing offices of the Lawyers Guild July 17, wounding at least four persons. The Guild was well-known for its defense of leftist political prisoners and its lawsuits against right-wing labor unions.

David Kraiselburd, chairman of the board of the news agency Noticias Argentinas and publisher of the La Plata newspaper El Dia, was shot to death July 17 as police closed in on the house in La Plata where he was held by kidnappers. Police wounded and captured one abductor, identified as Carlos Starita, an alleged member of the left-wing Peronist University Youth. Kraiselburd had been kidnapped June 25, but his captors had not contacted his family nor made a ransom demand.

Jorge H. Ferrari, an official in the Economy Ministry, was assassinated by unidentified persons in the Buenos Aires suburb of San Justo July 20.

Rodolfo Ortega Pena, the leading left-wing Peronist congressman, was assassinated in Buenos Aires July 31. Martin Salas, a young right-wing Peronist, was shot to death in La Plata Aug. 5, and four leftist Peronists in that city were killed in apparent retaliation Aug. 6-7.

Ortega Pena, a journalist and lawyer who had vigorously defended imprisoned guerrillas under the supplanted military dictatorship, was the first congressman to be killed in recent years.

An estimated 350 persons were arrested Aug. 2 when police used tear gas to disperse a crowd attempting to witness Ortega Pena's burial. Police declared, over the widow's objections, that only members of Ortega Pena's family could attend the interment.

A group calling itself "Montoneros Soldiers of Peron" claimed responsibility for Ortega Pena's murder in a communique to the press Aug. 3. A United Press International report Aug. 3 said the group was an offshoot of the left-wing Peronist Montoneros guerrillas, but the London newsletter Latin America reported Aug. 9 that the group was right-wing Peronist and had no connection with the Montoneros. Another communique to the press Aug. 7 claimed Ortega Pena had been assassinated by a rightist group identified as Argentine Anticommunist Alliance (AAA).

ERP members briefly occupied a naval installation in La Plata July 29 and stole arms and uniforms.

Guerrillas fought a gun battle with an infantry unit in Jujuy Province July 30. Members of labor unions were the targets of several bomb and machinegun attacks in Buenos Aires and the interior the same day. No casualties were reported.

Separate ERP bands wearing army uniforms attacked army installations in Cordoba and Catamarca Provinces before dawn Aug. 11. At least five persons were killed as police and soldiers fought off the guerrillas, according to press reports.

In Cordoba, about 60 guerrillas attacked a military arms factory at Villa Maria, escaping with weapons, uniforms and two military hostages. Two policemen and one guerrilla were killed in the fighting, according to official sources. At about the same time, an estimated 40 guerrillas attacked an infantry post outside the city of Catamarca, northwest of Cordoba; two guerrillas were reported killed in the fighting there.

Immediately after the raids, security forces sealed off the Bolivian border and began an intensive search for the guerrillas. Police in Catamarca spotted a guerrilla band Aug. 12 and engaged it in battle, reportedly killing 16 insurgents. Police claimed Aug. 13 that 23 guerrillas had been captured since the Aug. 11 attacks. Combined security forces pursued a guerrilla column in the province's mountains Aug. 13–15, killing or arresting at least 27 insurgents. The ERP acknowledged Aug. 28 that it had suffered a "serious defeat" at the hands of police and soldiers in Catamarca.

ERP leader Roberto Santucho asserted Sept. 18 that his group would stage "indiscriminate executions" of army officers in retaliation for the alleged execution by the army of 14–16 guerrillas captured during an ERP raid on an infantry post in Catamarca Province in August.

The ERP was held responsible for the murders of an army colonel in Cordoba and an army lieutenant in Rosario Sept. 25 and for a machinegun attack in Buenos Aires Sept. 30 in which two army officers and a non-commissioned officer were wounded. ERP members also killed a policeman and a civilian Sept. 21 when they briefly occupied the northwestern town of Santa Lucia, near Tucuman.

Meanwhile, bombings and assassinations of Peronist leaders continued. An estimated 50 bomb explosions were reported in Buenos Aires and other parts of the country Aug. 22, the second anniversary of the killing of 16 leftist guerrillas at the naval air base at Trelew, and more than 100 bomb blasts were reported Sept. 16–17. Other bombings occurred daily, many at dealerships of IKA-Renault, an automobile company involved in a bitter labor dispute.

Four members of the left-wing Peronist Youth organization were killed in suburbs of Buenos Aires Aug. 22–23. At least seven Peronists were killed in a wave of assassinations Sept. 16–18. Among the victims were Atilio Lopez, a leftist union leader and former vice governor of Cordoba Province, killed Sept. 16; Alejandro Bartoch, a rightist doctor, Sept. 17; and Dante Balcanera, a rightist union leader, Sept. 18.

President Peron Sept. 18 held another emergency meeting on curbing violence, attended by Cabinet members, Congressional leaders and the president of the Supreme Court.

In addition to the bombings and assassinations, there were several kidnappings by presumed leftists. Retired army Capt. Carlos Arteaga was wounded and kidnapped Aug. 24; he apparently died of his wounds in captivity, and his body was found Aug. 29. Retired navy Capt. Eduardo Griffin, who was imprisoned in 1951–55 for participating in an abortive coup attempt against the late President Juan Peron, was abducted Aug. 30.

Labor disputes flare—A number of labor conflicts contributed to the tension and violence in Argentina in August and September.

The worst was in the industrial city of Cordoba, where 12,000 members of SMATA, the mechanics workers union, worked to rule and staged a number of strikes against the two plants of IKA-Renault, the local affiliate of the French automobile firm Renault, to support demands for a 60% wage increase.

The increase was rejected Aug. 1 by IKA-Renault and by the Labor Ministry, which claimed it would undermine the Social Pact, the basic instrument of Peronist economic policy. The job action that ensued threatened $100 million worth of export contracts that IKA-Renault had signed with Cuba, Poland, Libya and Chile.

SMATA's Cordoba local was led by Rene Salamanca, a member of the Revolutionary Communist Party, and was at odds with the union's national leadership, composed of moderate Peronists. The SMATA local was supported by the Cordoba Light and Power Union, led by leftist Agustin Tosco.

IKA-Renault locked out its workers Aug. 3, but it was persuaded to abandon the lockout Aug. 5 by Labor Minister Ricardo Otero. However, Otero allowed federal police to guard the IKA-Renault plants, causing SMATA workers to strike in protest Aug. 8. IKA-Renault resorted to another lockout Sept. 3 as partial strikes and work to rule continued.

IKA-Renault dealerships were bombed in different parts of the country in August, presumably by leftists. The Peronist Armed Forces (FAP), a small guerrilla group, claimed responsibility for a number of the bombings and for the murder Aug. 27 of IKA-Renault's labor relations manager, Ricardo Boya. SMATA's Cordoba lawyer, Alfredo Curuchet, was assassinated by presumed rightists Sept. 11.

IKA-Renault finally granted the demands Sept. 17.

Cabinet shuffle. President Maria Estela Martinez de Peron shuffled her Cabinet Aug. 13 in what was widely interpreted as a shift toward more conservative policies.

Mrs. Peron accepted the resignations of Interior Minister Benito Llambi, Defense Minister Angel Robledo and Education Minister Jorge Taiana, replacing them with men who had served in the second administration of her late husband, President Juan Peron, in the 1950s.

Alberto Rocamora, a former president of the Chamber of Deputies, was named interior minister; Oscar Ivanissevich, a former education minister, reassumd that post; and Adolfo Savino was appointed defense minister. Rocamora and Savino were close associates of Social Welfare Minister Jose Lopez Rega, the most conservative member of the Cabinet and the official closest to Mrs. Peron, according to the London newsletter Latin America Aug. 23.

The other five Cabinet ministers, including Economy Minister Jose Gelbard, who was reported to be at odds with Lopez Rega, retained their posts.

(Gelbard, the Cabinet's chief defender of the wage-price freeze embodied in the Social Pact, had suffered a setback July 23 when he was forced to dismiss his commerce secretary, Miguel Revestido, and his industrial development secretary, Alberto Davie, and replace them with more "orthodox" Peronists, according to Latin America July 26. However, Gelbard succeeded Sept. 3 in forcing the resignation of Central Bank President Alfredo Gomez Morales, a right-wing Peronist with whom he had long been at odds.)

The replacement of Taiana as education minister was denounced by left-wing students at Buenos Aires University, some 800 of whom occupied six faculties and the rector's office Aug. 14. The rector's office was cleared peacefully later in the day.

Taiana had been accused by right-wing Peronists of allowing the left to "take over" the university. The new education minister, Ivanissevich, said Aug. 14 that there would be no change in the government's university policy "for the time being."

Ex-Defense Minister Robledo was named ambassador to Mexico and ex-Interior Minister Llambi ambassador to Canada, it was reported Aug. 23.

Leftist publications closed—In a further move toward the right, President Peron banned the last two newspapers representing the Peronist left, Noticias and La Causa Peronista.

Police invaded the Noticias building in Buenos Aires Aug. 27, seizing all copies of the newspaper, expelling its editorial staff and allegedly confiscating several firearms. Interior Minister Rocamora said the publication was being closed for not "collaborating in the national pacification." No one was arrested, but Mrs. Peron later ordered Noticias' editors prosecuted, according to a report Sept. 5.

Noticias, strongly identified with the Montoneros organization, had published in its last editions a story in which a left-wing Peronist youth, Carlos Baglietto, charged two of his companions had been killed and he had been seriously wounded by men claiming to be plainclothes policemen. Noticias had previously printed reports that policemen or right-wing trade unionists with strong links to the police had attacked left-wing Peronists.

La Causa Peronista was banned Sept. 6, two days after it printed a story in which Mario Firmenich and Norma Arrostito, leaders of the Montoneros, described how they and five other Peronist guerrillas kidnapped, tried and executed ex-President Pedro Aramburu in 1970. Firmenich and Arrostito would be prosecuted despite receiving an amnesty for the crime in 1973, the news agency LATIN reported Sept. 6.

La Causa Peronista had denounced the government in recent editorials. It charged Aug. 13 that since Gen. Peron's death, right-wing "anti-fatherland forces" in the government had sought to "do away with everything." The paper asserted Aug. 20 that the government was "detached from the real struggle of the people" and that the people would consequently "have recourse to all the weapons of struggle . . . to identify the enemy." The latter editorial was titled, "Has the Hour of the Guerrilla Arrived?"

It soon became clear that Peronist guerrilla factions were prepared to mount terrorist actions in opposition to Mrs. Peron.

Montoneros resume guerrilla warfare. The Montoneros, the left-wing Peronist guerrilla group, returned underground.

The Montoneros, accused by officials of murdering ex-Interior Minister Arturo Mor Roig and newspaper executive David Kraiselburd, were increasingly critical of the rightists who influenced President Maria Estela Martinez de Peron, particularly Social Welfare Minister Jose Lopez Rega. Montoneros leader Mario Firmenich had said Aug. 12 that Mrs. Peron was not the "heir" of her late husband, President Juan Peron, because "the leadership of the masses cannot be inherited."

An alleged Montoneros internal document disseminated among journalists Aug. 3 said the guerrillas should restructure their ranks for a "resistance stage" because there was no longer any "reason" to support Mrs. Peron. A "formal break" with her government would "depend on circumstances," the document stated.

Firmenich said at a press conference Sept. 6 that his movement had begun a "people's war" against the government, which, he claimed, had been "captured by imperialists and oligarchs" since Juan Peron's death. Firmenich charged that Mrs. Peron's administration had made it impossible for leftists to operate legally, leaving armed warfare as their only alternative.

Firmenich said the Montoneros had assassinated two anti-guerrilla security officers, kidnapped an engineer and carried out a number of machinegun and bombing attacks against automobile dealerships and other targets in recent days. Montoneros in Tucuman claimed credit for the murder of sugar executive Jose Maria Paz Sept. 7.

Firmenich said the Montoneros were not yet strong enough to battle police and military units, but he expected they would be strong enough "in several weeks." He did not rule out the possibility of joining forces with the ERP, which was leftist but not Peronist. "There is no need to confuse political ideologies," he said. "We will have to see what their policy is . . . if it is like ours, we can act together . . ."

The Montoneros' decision to resume guerrilla warfare was supported by the other organizations of the Peronist left, although they chose to remain aboveground. It was denounced by the rightwing Peronist newspaper Mayoria, which asserted the Montoneros were now out of the Peronist movement, and by the independent daily La Opinion, which said the guerrillas were out of touch with reality.

The strongest support for the Montoneros came from leftist students at Buenos Aires University, where Peronist youths had occupied all but one of the faculties since Aug. 14. The University's interim rector, Raul Laguzzi, openly backed the Montoneros. Laguzzi and his wife were seriously injured and their four-month-old son was killed Sept. 7 when their home was bombed by presumed right-wing Peronists.

President Peron met with the commanders of the armed forces and leaders of anti-guerrilla operations Sept. 7 in an apparent effort to devise a strategy against the Montoneros and militant students. Mrs. Peron replaced Laguzzi Sept. 17 with Eduardo Ottalagano, a right-wing Peronist and presidential staff member, who immediately closed the university for a week on grounds that it had become a focus of "subversion against the national powers."

Three Montoneros in Rosario were killed Sept. 9 when a bomb they were carrying detonated prematurely.

The Montoneros killed two persons Sept. 19 in kidnapping Juan and Jorge Born, directors of Bunge & Born Co., one of the largest international trading conglomerates in Latin America. A Montoneros communique later demanded $50 million in ransom for the Born brothers and said they would be "tried for the acts committed against the workers, the people and the national interest by the monopolies to which they belong." The communique said the two persons killed—the Borns' chauffeur and the manager of one of their companies—had tried to prevent the kidnapping.

ERP-Montonero accord. The major left-wing guerrilla groups—the People's Revolutionary Army (ERP) and the Montoneros—agreed to coordinate operations in the future despite their serious ideological differences, the London newsletter Latin America reported Sept. 27.

The ERP magazine The Combatant announced Sept. 26 that the ERP was "prepared to collaborate with the Montoneros in the military field, to stage joint attacks against the armed forces, the police and the repressive forces in general, and the

imperialist corporations." However, the ERP said the two groups could not form a "joint military force" because the Montoneros were not a "revolutionary organization" but a group with "erroneous populist concepts at the service of a bourgeois illusion."

Rightist violence increases. Political violence continued in Buenos Aires and other cities Sept. 19-30 as a right-wing group, the Argentine Anticommunist Alliance (AAA), stepped up its campaign to murder several dozen prominent leftists.

The AAA (erroneously identified in early reports as Argentine Anti-Imperialist Action) had been organized by the federal police chief, Alberto Villar, with the cooperation of Eduardo Ottalagano, rector of Buenos Aires University, and Carlos Frattini, an official in the Education Ministry, according to the newsletter Latin America Nov. 29.

The AAA threatened Sept. 5 to kill 10 liberal and leftist federal deputies for "infamous treason against the fatherland." Two of the legislators, Leonardo Bettanin and Miguel Zavala Rodriguez of the Peronist Youth, resigned Sept. 12 to protest conservative government policies.

Members of the AAA then assassinated Julio Troxler, a leftist former deputy police chief of Buenos Aires, Sept. 20. In a communique Sept. 21, the group said it was responsible for the murders of four other prominent leftists, including Atilio Lopez, former vice governor of Cordoba Province, and that it intended to kill 12 more leftists, including ex-President Hector Campora, former Buenos Aires University Rector Raul Laguzzi and Congressman Hector Sandler. A report in El Nacional of Caracas Sept. 28 said the AAA had a "black list" of 49 persons to be assassinated, most of them left-wing Peronists.

The AAA communique said Troxler had been killed because he was "a commie and a bad Argentine." It added: "Five are down and the lefties will continue to fall wherever they are."

The AAA was held responsible for the murders of a leftist construction worker in Bahia Blanca Sept. 22; a magazine editor, a television employe and a third person in Buenos Aires Sept. 26; and two relatives of former President Arturo Frondizi Sept. 27. Silvio Frondizi, brother of the ex-president, was dragged from his Buenos Aires home and later found dead outside the city. His son-in-law, Luis Mendiburu, was killed trying to prevent the abduction. Frondizi was a Marxist lawyer and essayist; his brother ran a small political party that, according to the newsletter Latin America Sept. 27, was near a break with the government.

Several people who were on the AAA's death list or feared they might eventually appear on it fled Argentina. Rodolfo Puiggros, the liberal former rector of Buenos Aires University, took asylum in the Mexican embassy Sept. 24—an unusual step since he was not being sought by the government—and was flown to Mexico City the next day. Laguzzi, who had recently been wounded in a terrorist attack, fled to Mexico Sept. 28. (The current rector of Buenos Aires University, Eduardo Ottalagano, a rightist, survived an assassination attempt in Villaguay Sept. 23. Ottalagano was unharmed, but his assailant and a local hotel owner were killed and two policemen were wounded in the incident. The assailant's political affiliation was not revealed.)

Two prominent actors, Norman Briski and Nacha Guevara, fled to Peru Sept. 28, two days after the AAA threatened to kill them and three other well-known performers. The Argentine Actors Association struck Sept. 27 to protest the threat.

Former presidential candidate Oscar Alende, leader of the small Popular Revolutionary Alliance, demanded Sept. 22 that the government "identify" the AAA's members and investigate their "connections," particularly any possible links to the U.S. Central Intelligence Agency.

(The independent newspaper La Opinion wondered in an editorial Sept. 25 what the objectives of the CIA in Argentina might be. Hector Sandler, the congressman on the AAA's death list, asked the government Sept. 25 to call in U.S. Ambassador Robert Hill and question him on local CIA activities. Hill had been called a "CIA agent" by left-wing Peronist publications before he arrived in Argentina early in 1974.

The AAA added several additional persons to its death list Sept. 30–Oct. 1, threatening to kill each if he did not leave the country. Army Gen. Juan Carlos Sosa, leftist union leader Armando Cabo and former Bishop Jeronimo Podesta were threatened by the AAA Sept. 30. The next day the rightists threatened three legislators from the Radical Party—Deputy Mario Amaya and Senators Hipolito Solari Yrigoyen and Humberto Perette—and a dean and three professors at the state university in Rosario. With these the AAA had passed "death sentences" on 61 persons, 19 of whom had been killed in the past two months, according to El Nacional of Caracas Oct. 2.

The AAA's threats caused an exodus of leftist politicians, artists and intellectuals. Former Interior Minister Esteban Righi, a reputed leftist, and his wife took asylum in the Mexican embassy Sept. 30 and were flown to Mexico, it was reported Oct. 2. Ex-Bishop Podesta said Oct. 3 that he was leaving the country because the government would not protect him.

Another man threatened by the AAA, leftist Deputy Hector Sandler, took up residence in his congressional office Oct. 9 because police had refused to protect his home.

According to the London newsletter Latin America Oct. 11, it was generally assumed that AAA members included soldiers and police, with the police in ultimate control. Montoneros leader Roberto Quieto charged at a clandestine press conference Oct. 4 that the AAA was "organized by the federal police chief, Alberto Villar," and that its "inspiration and political orientation" came from the government itself. Latin America noted that AAA victims such as Julio Troxler and Atilio Lopez had offered no resistance to their assassins, indicating they had been stopped by men they took to be police.

(Two Uruguayans who claimed to have been kidnapped and tortured by the AAA in September asserted in Stockholm Nov. 4 that the AAA was composed of Argentine and Uruguayan police and that it was "directed by the government, by people who include President Isabel Peron and [Social Welfare] Minister Jose Lopez Rega." The Uruguayans, who had taken asylum in Sweden after being released by the AAA, said three of their comrades had been murdered by the rightists.)

Quieto said Oct. 4 that the Montoneros were prepared to negotiate a truce with the government if it would grant emergency wage increases, end its intervention in the trade unions, restore freedom of political expression, repeal repressive security legislation, stop the AAA assassination campaign and fire Villar and his deputy chief, Luis Margaride. The ERP offered a truce of its own Oct. 6, asking the government in return to free all political prisoners, repeal the new anti-subversion act and restore the ERP to legality.

The AAA killed two more persons Oct. 8—Rodolfo Achem, administrative secretary at La Plata National University, and Carlos Miguel, director ' of the university's planning department.

The AAA raided headquarters of the Communist Party in Cordoba Oct. 9 and severely beat several persons. A woman kidnapped during the raid was later murdered, according to the Cuban newspaper Granma Oct. 21. The Communist Party charged Oct. 23 that AAA terrorism in Cordoba was "sanctioned and tolerated" by the provincial government.

The AAA later added dozens of new names to its death list. It threatened to kill 44 leftists in Entre Rios Province, north of Buenos Aires, according to a report Oct. 21. In Tucuman Province, the deans of law and economics at the state university resigned Oct. 22 after both were threatened by the AAA and after the law dean's home was bombed.

Anti-terrorism bill. Congress Sept. 28 passed an anti-terrorism bill that was submitted by President Peron and backed by the armed forces. The law provided stiff prison terms for persons who disseminated subversive propaganda or tried to change the nation's political structure "by means not laid down by the Constitution," and it restricted news reporting of activities by illegal groups.

Observers said the wording of the bill indicated it was designed primarily to fight leftist guerrillas, although the government said Sept. 27 that it would also be used against rightist assassins.

Citing the news curb, the Association of Argentine Newspaper Enterprises, the nation's leading press group, charged the law "affects freedom of the press," the Mexican newspaper Excelsior reported Oct. 3. The law set prison terms of two to six years for persons who possessed,

published or reported "facts, communiques or photographs related to terrorist actions."

Mrs. Peron had charged Sept. 26 that leftist guerrillas were trying to provoke a military coup, and she pledged to the armed forces that her government would press a full battle against subversives.

In an attempt to gather support amid the increasing violence, Mrs. Peron held a rally in Buenos Aires Sept. 20. Only 30,-000-50,000 persons attended even though the huge General Labor Confederation called an eight-hour nationwide strike to enable workers to see the president. The crowd, composed almost exclusively of conservative Peronists, chanted slogans against the Montoneros as Mrs. Peron denounced "those who only know how to kill, . . . those who obstruct the road to liberation and national pacification."

Assassinations continue. Assassinations by rightist and leftist commandos continued in Buenos Aires and other cities Oct. 1-14.

Three alleged members of the People's Revolutionary Army (ERP), the Marxist guerrilla group, were killed in a shootout with police in Cordoba Oct. 1. The next day ERP members killed army Capt. Miguel Angel Paiva in Buenos Aires. Mario Eduardo Favario, an alleged ERP leader, was arrested in connection with the murder Oct. 3.

The Montoneros, the left-wing Peronist guerrillas, were held responsible for the murder of Jose Maria Russo, a civil servant, in Santa Fe Oct. 1. Teodoro Vivas, a former left-wing Peronist, was killed in Tucuman Oct. 3, presumably by the Argentine Anticommunist Alliance (AAA).

Army Maj. Jaime Gimento was assassinated Oct. 7, and police announced the same day that 138 persons had been arrested in raids against subversives. Army Lt. Juan Carlos Gambande was assassinated in Santa Fe Oct. 11. Two newsmen were found shot to death outside Buenos Aires Oct. 13, and a Peronist leftist, Juan Carlos Leiva, was murdered in La Plata Oct. 14.

President Maria Estela Martinez de Peron made a number of appeals to end the violence, and she was supported by a 15-minute general strike called Oct. 11 by the General Labor Confederation, the nation's largest labor group. In a televised message Oct. 8, Mrs. Peron vowed to "definitively eradicate all expressions of terrorism and subversion" without "sliding into authoritarianism." In a speech in Santiago del Estero Oct. 12, she called terrorists "mercenaries at the service of foreign interests."

Leftists were held responsible for other assassinations and terrorist attacks in late October. Army Lt. Col. Jose Francisco Gardon was shot to death in San Miguel, Buenos Aires Province Oct. 23; conservative Peronists Juan Carlos Mariani and Juan Vera were killed in San Martin, Buenos Aires the same day; and the rightist university professor Bruno Jordan Genta was murdered in Buenos Aires Oct. 27. The August 22 faction of the ERP claimed to have slain Jordan Genta.

In other attacks attributed to the ERP, an army lieutenant was shot and wounded in Cordoba Oct. 18, and a retired lieutenant colonel was gravely injured in Buenos Aires Oct. 25. The ERP vowed to kill 14 army officers in retaliation for the alleged murder of 14 guerrillas by police in Catamarca Province in August.

The Montoneros raided a cemetery in Buenos Aires early Oct. 16 and stole the body of Gen. Pedro Aramburu, whom they had assassinated in 1970. They said they would hold the corpse until the remains of Eva Peron were repatriated from Spain. Observers said the Montoneros sought to prevent the government from transferring Aramburu's body to a planned mausoleum for heroes of Argentine history. (The embalmed remains of Eva Peron were returned to Argentina Nov. 17, and the Montoneros returned Aramburu's body the same day.)

Prats killed—Retired Gen. Carlos Prats Gonzalez, the former Chilean army commander, and his wife were killed early Sept. 30 when a bomb exploded in or under their car as they drove to their Buenos Aires home.

A close friend of Prats, quoted by the Washington Post Oct. 1, said Prats had said recently that he had received information of a plan to kill him. Prats had said the assassination would be made to look like the work of the AAA but would be staged by Chilean or U.S. rightists.

Leftist union raided—Police in Cordoba raided the headquarters of the militant Light and Power Union Oct. 9 and arrested more than 70 persons. They claimed to have found arms and ammunition allegedly used by union members, but this was denied by Agustin Tosco, the union's former secretary general, according to the newsletter Latin America Oct. 18.

The raid reflected the government's aim of isolating leftist guerrillas from their natural bases of support—particularly the universities and the radical unions—in preparation for a major police and military campaign against them, according to Latin America.

The Light and Power Union, the Cordoba mechanics union SMATA and the Buenos Aires Typographers Federation (FGB) had recently been taken over by pro-government unionists who ousted their leftist leaders. Raimundo Ongaro, the ousted FGB leader, was arrested Oct. 30 and charged with illegal arms possession.

Party & university posts. Among political developments:

President Maria Estela Martinez de Peron accepted the presidency of the Justicialista Party National Council Sept. 29. In practice, her duties would be performed by Raul Lastiri, president of the Chamber of Deputies.

The Justicialista council had replaced its regional leaders in five provinces—Santiago del Estero, La Rioja, Salta, Chubut and Jujuy—Sept. 27.

At Buenos Aires University, the nation's largest, Rector Eduardo Ottalagano was conducting a massive purge of leftist professors, it was reported Oct. 20. Raul Zardini, recently named dean of exact sciences at the university, had caused a furor by telling a Buenos Aires newspaper that he admired Italian fascism and that he considered democracy a "juridicial invention," it was reported Nov. 1.

Police occupied the state university in La Plata and forced the resignation of the rector and the suspension of classes, it was reported Oct. 18.

Economy minister quits. Jose Gelbard, who had directed the Argentine economy since the Peronists returned to power in May 1973, resigned as economy minister Oct. 21. His departure was seen by many as signaling the end of the Social Pact, the wage-price freeze through which he had greatly reduced Argentina's annual inflation rate.

Gelbard was replaced by former Central Bank President Alfredo Gomez Morales, who had repeatedly criticized his policy. Gomez Morales, a right-wing Peronist, was backed by Jose Lopez Rega, the reactionary social welfare minister and private secretary to President Maria Estela Martinez de Peron.

Gelbard said in his resignation letter that he was quitting because "we have entered a phase in which political circumstances and definitions have acquired increased significance. [These] should always be facilitated by those of us who embrace the cause of national unity for reconstruction and liberation." His economic team resigned with him.

Gelbard most recently had opposed Mrs. Peron's plan to call a national meeting to consider wage increases demanded by the General Labor Confederation (CGT), the nation's largest labor group. Gelbard had predicted such increases would set off an inflationary wave.

In addition to the CGT, Gelbard had alienated conservative political and economic groups, particularly the wealthy rural landowners. A draft agrarian reform law supported by Gelbard had been bitterly attacked by landowners in July because it provided for land taxation according to potential productivity and expropriation of unfarmed or badly farmed land, according to a report July 26.

Conservatives also had criticized Gelbard's commercial agreements with Socialist nations, including the Soviet Union and Cuba, but Mrs. Peron and government spokesmen said Oct. 21 that Argentina would continue to ignore ideological barriers in choosing its trade partners.

Police Chief Villar slain. Federal Police Chief Alberto Villar and his wife were killed Nov. 1 when left-wing terrorists set off a bomb in a cabin cruiser on which they were sailing off the Argentine coast at Tigre, 20 miles north of Buenos Aires.

The Montoneros, the Peronist guerrilla group, took credit for the assassination Nov. 2. It had frequently accused Villar and his deputy, Luis Margaride (who became police chief Nov. 4), of encouraging the torture and murder of political prisoners.

Villar was the first high government official assassinated since the Peronists returned to power in May 1973. His murder increased pressure on President Maria Estela Martinez de Peron to crack down on terrorism before it provoked a military coup.

Police began an intensive search for leftist subversives immediately after the assassination. Four persons were reported arrested in connection with the murder Nov. 2, but seven policemen were wounded the same day when a bomb exploded in an uncovered leftist hideout.

The Argentine Anticommunist Alliance (AAA), the right-wing terrorist group, assassinated four leftists Nov. 3 in apparent retaliation for Villar's murder. The victims were Juan Carlos Nievas, Ruben Boussas and Arturo Robles Urquiza, all members of the Socialist Workers Party in Buenos Aires, and Alberto Della Riva, a left-wing Peronist professor at the state university in La Plata.

The AAA had murdered five other persons Oct. 31, according to press reports. Two of the victims were Carlos Llerena Rojas, a civil servant who belonged to the small Leftist Popular Front, and Isaac Valeriano Yorke, a leader of the left-wing Peronist Youth.

State of siege imposed. President Maria Estela Martinez de Peron placed the nation under a state of siege Nov. 6 as political assassinations and other terrorist attacks continued.

Constitutional guarantees were suspended, and security forces were empowered to search and detain without warrant and to hold prisoners without charges. Detainees had the right to choose exile over eventual trial.

Mrs. Peron acted after meeting with the three armed forces commanders.

She sent a bill to Congress Dec. 6 asking for power to call up the armed forces to fight subversion and to set up a centralized national security program under her office.

Journalists arrested—Police in Corrientes Nov. 11 arrested Jose Romero Feris, publisher of the newspaper El Litoral, and editor Gabriel Feris for allegedly violating a law against printing statements by terrorist groups.

Ernesto Carmona, a Chilean editor with the Buenos Aires newspaper El Cronista Commercial, had been reported arrested Oct. 30. Ulla Allgier, a West German journalist who had been threatened by the right-wing Argentine Anticommunist Alliance, had been seized along with Carmona, according to the London newsletter Latin America Nov. 8. Another West German, radio correspondent Walter Hanf, had been arrested without explanation Oct. 29.

Terrorism continues—Violence continued to take lives throughout Argentina. Army Maj. Nestor Lopez was shot down in Santa Fe Nov. 7, and Lt. Roberto Carbajo was murdered in San Nicolas Nov. 12. Both assassinations were attributed to the ERP.

Police Sgt. Joaquin Casas, a bodyguard for the new deputy federal police chief, was killed by unknown guerrillas in Buenos Aires Nov. 9. Another police sergeant was murdered in the capital Nov. 13.

At least 38 assassinations and more than 500 arrests were reported between mid-November and mid-December, although the AAA seemed to remain immune from arrest.

Most of the arrests were aimed at destroying the ERP. The ERP killed two more army officers—Lt. Col. Jorge Ibarzabal Nov. 19 and Capt. Humberto Viola Dec. 1—but the guerrillas abandoned their campaign against the army Dec. 12 because Viola's young daughter had accidentally been killed along with him.

Four alleged ERP members were killed in a shootout with police in Cordoba Nov. 20, and three more suspected guerrillas died in similar fashion in Buenos Aires Nov. 21. The bullet-riddled bodies of six presumed guerrillas were found by police in Buenos Aires Dec. 5, and six others were found Dec. 13. These last 12 alleged guerrillas were presumably killed by the AAA after they were arrested by police or soldiers. The wife of captive ERP leader Oscar Montenegro was murdered in Tucuman Dec. 2, and their son was assassinated Dec. 6.

Other leftists not directly linked to the ERP were also killed. Two lawyers who had defended political prisoners were found shot to death in Santa Fe Province Nov. 18, a few days after they were arrested by local security forces. Two elementary school teachers were assassinated in Tigre Dec. 13, after they were arrested there.

Other leftist victims included a member of the Peronist Youth (JP), killed in Buenos Aires Dec. 5, and a member of the Revolutionary Communist Party, murdered in La Plata Dec. 7. Rodolfo Galimberti, a major JP leader, disappeared and was feared dead, the Buenos Aires newspaper La Calle reported Nov. 30.

The Montoneros, the leftist Peronist guerrillas, assassinated Ruben Dominico, a right-wing Buenos Aires city councilman, and his bodyguard Dec. 7. Leftist guerrillas were also presumed responsible for the murder Dec. 4 of Ramon Samaniego, personnel manager of a Buenos Aires metal plant, and the assassination Dec. 14 of Antonio dos Santos Larangeira, a fishing industrialist of Portuguese origin.

In other terrorist action, avowed members of the left-wing Liberation Armed Forces used firebombs to destroy at least 18 army buses in a factory lot outside Buenos Aires Nov. 7. An estimated 25 bombs exploded in front of the homes of police officials in Cordoba Nov. 9.

Among recent bombings, leftists were held responsible for explosions at a branch of First National City Bank of New York and two General Motors Corp. showrooms in Buenos Aires Nov. 25, and rightists were given credit for firebombing a movie set in the capital Nov. 17. The movie was about Jewish gauchos in 19th century Argentina. Anti-Semitic slogans had been shouted at a recent Buenos Aires rally by rightists demanding the return to Argentina of the remains of Juan Manuel de Rosas, the 19th century Argentine dictator who died and was buried in England.

Police in La Plata claimed Nov. 26 to have discovered the headquarters of the Liberation Armed Forces, a small Marxist guerrilla group, and arrested several members.

Soldiers guarded numerous elementary schools in and around Buenos Aires Nov. 12–13, following repeated threats against teachers and pupils by unknown persons. Citizens reportedly had been alarmed by the threats, by recent sexual assaults on young girls in their schools and by the kidnapping of three students who were told by their captors to convey death threats to their teachers.

U.S. woman reported tortured—Olga Talamante, a U.S. citizen under police detention for four weeks, charged she had been beaten and given electric shocks in custody, the U.S. embassy in Buenos Aires reported Dec. 9.

Police said Talamante had been arrested with 12 Argentines in a house in Azul, south of the capital, that contained firearms and "other subversive material."

Santa Cruz governor ousted. The federal government took control of the government of Santa Cruz Province Oct. 7, ousting Gov. Jorge Cepernic, who had been accused of leftist sympathies.

Copernic was replaced by Augusto Pedro Saffores.

Salta government replaced. The government of Salta Province was taken over by the federal government Nov. 22 on orders of President Peron. Gov. Miguel Ragone, known as a left-wing Peronist, was succeeded by Jose Alejandro Mosquera, a Cordoba lawyer.

The action was denounced by the Radical Civic Union, the major opposition party, which called it "another provincial raid" by the Peronist administration. Five provincial governments had been taken over in 1973, and the governors of two other provinces had been forced to resign.

The rector of Salta University had been arrested Nov. 13 for alleged violations of the anti-subversive law. A policeman had been wounded the night before when two bombs exploded on the university's campus.

Foreign Relations

U.S. envoy called CIA agent. The left-wing Peronist weekly El Descamisado charged Jan. 8 that the new U.S. ambassador to Argentina, Robert C. Hill, was a member of the Central Intelligence Agency (CIA). Hill's appointment had been approved by President Peron, but the envoy had not yet arrived in Buenos Aires.

Hill was a former vice president of W.R. Grace & Co. and a former director of the United Fruit Co.—whose operations had been bitterly criticized by Latin American nationalists—and had been directly linked, in testimony before the U.S. Senate, to the CIA-planned coup that overthrew Guatemalan President Jacobo Arbenz in 1954.

Argentina and the U.S. were nevertheless enjoying warm relations, as shown by the signing in late 1973 of a $756 million loan pact with the Inter-American Development Bank, which would have been impossible without U.S. support, the newsletter Latin America noted Jan. 4.

The U.S. Export-Import Bank approved a $21.6 million loan for a Buenos Aires steel mill expansion project, it was reported July 18.

Libyan oil deal. An Argentine trade mission headed by Social Welfare Minister Jose Lopez Rega visited Libya Jan. 26–Feb. 4 and signed a number of agreements including one for Libya to supply Argentina with 3 million tons of oil in 1974 and as much or more in 1975.

The oil, which began arriving in Argentina in March, was bought at a very high price—$18.72 a barrel—but was of high quality, according to the Andean Times' Latin America Economic Report Feb. 22. The purchases were financed first by a group of Italian banks and subsequently by Chase Manhattan Bank of New York, the London newsletter Latin America reported May 17.

As its part of the oil deal, the Argentine mission to Libya offered to set up a vehicle assembly plant near Tripoli, help build an oil refinery and a liquid natural gas plant, and help construct half a million Libyan schoolrooms and 2,000 apartments.

A Libyan mission to Argentina signed agreements in Buenos Aires March 1 to import 30,000 metric tons of Argentine sugar, 96,000 tons of bread wheat, 15,000 tons of corn and 24,000 tons of barley. The Argentine National Bank later signed a $40 million agreement to export motor vehicles, irrigation pipes and beef to Libya, it was reported April 12.

Social Welfare Minister Jose Lopez Rega announced Nov. 2 that Libya would grant Argentina a $200 million loan to purchase agricultural and livestock goods.

Libya would buy $200 million worth of Argentine grain and sugar in 1975 and spend another $200 million for Argentine ships in the next few years, the London newsletter Latin America reported Nov. 29. Libya would supply Argentina with 300 million cubic meters of oil annually.

OAS & Cuba sanctions. At the general assembly of the Organization of American States, held in Atlanta, Ga. April 19–May 1, U.S. Secretary of State Henry A. Kissinger sought to mollify Argentina and other Latin American governments on continuing OAS sanctions against Cuba.

To prepare for the assembly, Kissinger had met privately in Washington April 17–18 with the foreign ministers of 24 hemispheric nations. Their talks stressed economic issues, particularly trade, but also touched on sensitive political issues such as the continued isolation of Cuba from the inter-American system.

In moves to defuse the Cuba issue, the U.S. agreed April 18 to issue export licenses to Argentine subsidiaries of three U.S. automobile firms—General Motors, Ford and Chrysler—to sell several hundred million dollars worth of cars and trucks to Havana.

The U.S. insisted that its approval of the export licenses did not presage a change in its Cuba policy, and officials said the decision responded to threats by Argentina to nationalize the U.S. subsidiaries if they were not allowed to sell to Cuba.

Argentine Foreign Minister Alberto Vignes called for an end to the OAS' blockade of Cuba, describing it as "unrealistic and anachronistic."

When the OAS foreign ministers met again in Quito, Ecuador, the OAS Nov. 12 upheld its diplomatic and commercial embargo to Cuba.

Argentine deals with Cuba. More than 200 Argentine businessmen and government officials had gone to Havana Feb. 25 to consolidate purchasing agreements under a $1.2 billion credit granted to Cuba by Argentina in 1973.

A resolution to lift the embargo failed to gain the required two-thirds majority of the 21 nations which signed the Inter-American Treaty of Reciprocal Assistance, or Rio Treaty, under which the sanctions were imposed. Twelve countries voted for the resolution, three voted against, and six—including the U.S.—abstained.

The favorable votes were cast by Venezuela, Colombia and Costa Rica, which jointly introduced the resolution Nov. 10, and Argentina, Ecuador, El Salvador, Honduras, Mexico, Panama, Peru, the Dominican Republic and Trinidad & Tobago. Chile, Paraguay and Uruguay voted against the resolution, and Brazil, Bolivia, Haiti, Guatemala and Nicaragua joined the U.S. in abstaining.

The mission, headed by Jose Gelbard, then Argentine economy minister, included executives of the Argentine subsidiaries of three U.S. automobile firms—General Motors Corp., Ford Motor Co. and Chrysler Corp.—which were negotiating contracts to sell Cuba 44,000 vehicles.

Argentine plants of the French firm Citroen and the West German concern Mercedes-Benz had already signed sales contracts with Cuba, it was reported Feb. 26. The Argentine subisidary of Italy's Fiat Motor Co. signed a contract Jan. 16 to ship to Cuba $81 million worth of railroad cars and equipment.

The U.S. affiliates started signing contracts with Cuban negotiators after the U.S. government, which maintained an economic blockade of Cuba along with most members of the Organization of American States (OAS), granted them special export licenses.

Under a $24.2 million agreement signed in Buenos Aires April 23, Chrysler would ship 9,000 sedans to Havana over the next three years and establish a sales and maintenance service in Cuba. Under Ford's $30 million contract with Cuba, signed in the Argentine capital April 30, 1,000 cars and 500 heavy trucks would be shipped to Havana in 1974 and an equal number would be exported in 1975–76. General Motors agreed to sell 6,000 taxis to Cuba for about $30 million, it was reported June 26.

In Buenos Aires, the decision had been hailed as a major victory for Argentine foreign policy and evidence that Cuba's enforced isolation was doomed. The newspaper Cronica asserted the U.S. had been forced to admit that the export of cars to Cuba was "a sovereign Argentine decision." The English-language Buenos Aires Herald said the decision "undoubtedly signals the eventual end of the economic blockade of Cuba."

The U.S.' attempt to make the final decision on the auto exports had been denounced by Gelberd March 28 and by the Argentine Congress April 4.

Cuba had become Argentina's principal trade partner in Latin America, having purchased more than $500 million worth of Argentine products in less than a year, it was reported July 11.

Soviet credit report denied. Argentine sources in Moscow reported May 7 that the Soviet Union had pledged $600 million in credits to help Argentina double its power generating capacity by 1977. But Economy Minister Gelbard admitted May 22 that the report was incorrect.

The report was made during a visit to the Soviet Union by a 135-member Argentine mission headed by Gelbard. The delegates visited the U.S.S.R. May 5–8 before leaving for other East European countries.

The credit had been sought to finance purchase of Soviet equipment for hydroelectric projects at Salto Grande on the Uruguay River (undertaken jointly by Argentina and Uruguay) and at Alicura in Mendoza Province, and for expansion of the Chocon Dam and construction of two thermal projects in La Plata and Rosario.

The sources said the Argentine delegation also had cemented a number of commercial deals, including the sale of Argentine meat, rice, fruits and juice concentrates, shoes, chemicals and wines to the Soviet Union. Other agreements signed in Moscow included ones for cooperation in the fields of trade, economic and technical-scientific development, according to the Andean Times' Latin America Economic Report May 17.

A Soviet delegation had visited Argentina for 10 days in February, signing on Feb. 13 agreements on trade, payments and technical cooperation which involved $200 million.

Gelbard met with Soviet Communist Party General Secretary Leonid Brezhnev after arriving in Moscow May 5. He conferred the next day with Soviet President Nikolai Podgorny and Premier Alexei Kosygin. All three Soviet leaders were awarded Argentina's highest decoration. Juan Peron had accepted an invitation to visit the Soviet Union in the fall.

A joint Soviet-Argentine communique issued May 10, after Gelbard's departure, asserted relations between the two countries were improving and Argentina was interested in establishing contact with COMECON, the Communist economic bloc.

The Argentine mission proceeded May 8 to Warsaw, where Gelbard met with Polish President Henryk Jablonski, Communist Party First Secretary Edward Gierek and other officials during a two-day visit. Four agreements to improve Argentine-Polish trade relations were signed May 9, including ones for Poland to supply technical equipment and machinery on credit terms. Gelbard said Peron would visit Poland after his visit to the Soviet Union.

Gelbard went on to Czechoslovakia May 10–12 and Hungary May 13–14. Argentina and Czechoslovakia had signed a trade agreement Feb. 24 under which the Czechoslovak firm Skoda would supply turbines and generators for four Argentine thermal and hydroelectric power stations, and launch a joint venture with Argentina for a turbine manufacturing plant.

Gelbard said May 22 that the mission to Eastern Europe had produced trade agreements worth about $4 billion.

Argentina also had signed agreements with Rumania March 8, at the end of a four-day visit to Buenos Aires by Rumanian Communist Party First Secretary Nicolae Ceausescu. They included a $100 million credit for Argentine purchase of Rumanian equipment and capital goods.

The government said the Soviet Union had arranged to buy 12,000 tons of meat from Argentina, it was reported July 9.

An Argentine economic mission in Moscow Sept. 20 signed an agreement under which Argentina would sell 90,000 tons of meat to the Soviet Union over the next three years.

Torrijos visits. Brig. Gen. Omar Torrijos, Panama's military ruler, visited Argentina Jan. 15–19, conferring with President Peron and other officials.

Peron said Jan. 16 that Argentina fully supported Panama's demand for sovereignty over the Panama Canal and Zone. Torrijos said Jan. 17 that Peron was a "leader of America, from whom we soldiers who came after have much to learn."

Bolivian exiles arrested. A number of prominent Bolivian exiles were seized by Argentine police May 3 and held until May 7, apparently at the behest of the Bolivian government, which accused them of plotting to overthrow Bolivian President Hugo Banzer Suarez.

The detainees, according to the Washington Post May 5, were Juan Lechin Oquendo, former Bolivian vice president and still leader of Bolivia's militant mineworkers; Jorge Gutierrez Mendieta, his political secretary; Edil Sandoval Moron, ex-president of the Bolivian Chamber of Deputies; Col. Samuel Gallardo, former Bolivian army chief of staff, and Ted Cordova-Claure, former press secretary to exiled President Juan Jose Torres and currently foreign editor for the Buenos Aires newspaper La Opinion.

The Argentine government news agency TELAM reported May 7 that Lechin, Cordova-Claure, Sandoval and two other Bolivians not cited in earlier reports—Felipe Malky and Victor Levy—had been freed by police that day, but Gutierrez would remain in jail. No mention was made of Gallardo.

Most press reports alleged the arrests had been made at the request of the Bolivian government, which reportedly had sent a list of exiled enemies to the Argentine government the week before. However, the Bolivian embassy in Buenos Aires denied requesting the arrests, and Argentine Defense Minister Angel Robledo claimed May 9 that the exiles had been detained solely "for trafficking in alkaloids."

Ayacucho declaration signed. Representatives of eight Latin American countries, including four heads of state, met in Ayacucho, Peru Dec. 9 and signed a declaration of political and economic solidarity.

Military leaders of the countries signed a separate document pledging to limit armaments and stop acquiring offensive weapons. All of the signatories—Peru, Venezuela, Panama, Bolivia, Argentina, Chile, Colombia and Ecuador—had been involved in frontier clashes in the past, and some still claimed territory in neighboring countries.

The documents commemorated the 150th anniversary of the Battle of Ayacucho, in which South American troops decisively defeated Spanish forces, securing independence for the continent.

Economic & Other Developments

Trade income at high level. Economy Ministry figures, reported March 1, showed Argentina's export earnings in 1973 reached $2.794 billion against imports of $1.895 billion, the highest foreign trade surplus in 35 years. Revised figures released by the ministry later and reported March 15 showed export earnings at $3.05 billion.

Exports of maize and sorghum in 1974 showed increases of 93% over 1973 and 58% over 1972, it was reported July 19.

Spain signed an agreement to purchase 300,000 tons of Argentine corn and sorghum, it was reported March 26.

Argentina agreed to spend $160 million to purchase 16 boats, 10 to be built in Spain, three in Scotland and three in Argentina, it was reported May 17.

Tractor exports in January–April 1974 showed a 460% increase over the same period of 1973, it was reported June 14.

The value of mineral exports in January–July exceeded $7.7 million, compared with some $9 million for all of 1973, it was reported Sept. 6. Exports of manufactured goods totaled $375 million during January-June, up 25% over the same period of 1973, it was reported Aug. 30.

Argentine meat exports to Europe in January–September were 48.9% behind those of the same period in 1973, earning 37.9% less in foreign exchange, it was reported Nov. 8. Prices for beef on the bone reportedly had dropped from $1,300 a ton to $900 a ton during the period.

A Paraguayan mission had agreed to make important purchases of wheat, oil and industrial products in Argentina, it was reported Nov. 15.

Foreign loans. A group of U.S. banks headed by Bank of America agreed to lend Argentina $100 million (announced April 17).

The Inter-American Development Bank (IDB) authorized the largest single loan in its history—$95 million—to help finance the second stage of an Argentine-Uruguayan hydroelectric project at Salto Grande on the Uruguay River, it was reported Nov. 8. Total cost of the project was estimated at more than $950 million.

The IDB Oct. 31 had approved loans of $45 million to help improve irrigation and agricultural production in San Juan Province.

The government announced June 13 that it had arranged an eight-year floating-rate Eurodollar loan of $100 million to help support the country's economic development. A 23-bank syndicate assisted in the negotiations.

Expropriation & nationalization. The government announced April 18 that it would pay a total of $25 million to three U.S. banks, a West German Bank and a Spanish bank for Argentine interests expropriated by the government in September 1973.

Morgan Guaranty Trust Co. would be paid $7.93 million for its controlling interest in Banco Frances del Rio de la Plata; First National City Bank of New York, $3.5 million for its branch in Bahia Blanca and $1.27 million for its share capital in Banco Argentino del Atlantico in Mar del Plata; and Chase Manhattan Bank of New York, $3.8 million, to be shared with Dresden Bank of West Germany for their majority interest in Banco Argentino de Comercio.

Chase Manhattan called the compensation offer "considerably below what we would consider fair value."

The government Aug. 1 took control of five television stations—three in Buenos Aires, one in Mendoza and one in Mar del Plata—attaining an objective announced by President Juan Peron before his death.

Trustees representing the regime had unofficially run the stations since October 1973, when their licenses expired.

Although there was general agreement that the stations should be nationalized, opposition parties protested that television policy would be formulated exclusively by the executive branch, without the participation of Congress. President Maria Estela Martinez de Peron maintained the executive was empowered to do so, and she was supported by the Peronist majority in Congress.

The take-overs followed raids on two of the stations in July by armed men claiming to represent employes who favored nationalization. One raid was led by Jorge Conti, the government trustee running the invaded station, the New York Times reported Aug. 1. Conti was a close associate of the rightist Social Welfare minister, Jose Lopez Rega.

(In a censorship order, the government Sept. 24 banned "Mannix," "Kung Fu," "Mod Squad" and other imported television shows that "promote violence by Oriental and Western means.")

The government Aug. 23 ordered the nationalization of oil marketing but postponed expropriating the foreign oil refineries. Gasoline service stations were ordered nationalized Aug. 28. Until these measures were taken, the state oil firm YPF had marketed about 50% of Argentina's oil.

Mrs. Peron said at a rally attended by 80,000 persons in Buenos Aires Oct. 17 that three major foreign electronics companies would be "Argentinized." She did not elaborate on the term.

The firms were Standard Electric Argentina Co., a subsidiary of International Telephone and Telegraph Corp. of the U.S.; Siemens S.A., a subsidiary of the West German concern Siemens A.G.; and the Italo-Argentine Electricity Co., controlled by Swiss capital.

A presidential decree Sept. 30 had annulled partially completed contracts worth $225 million between Standard Electric, Siemens and the Argentine state telephone company ENTel. The pacts, to modernize Argentina's telephone system, had been signed in 1969 by the military regime of Gen. Juan Carlos Ongania. The

Senate had voted unanimously Sept. 5 to annul them because they overcharged ENTel and were "manifestly immoral." The government Sept. 20 ordered Standard Electric to pay it $23 million in indemnities.

(The Chamber of Deputies had annulled the government's contracts with ITT as "a fraud against the country." Congressional investigators had charged that ITT's Standard Electric Argentina had made considerably more profit in its sales to ENTel than in its other operations in Argentina, it was reported July 19.)

Petrochemical plants, oil discovery. The General Mosconi petrochemicals plant at Ensenada outside Buenos Aires had been formally inaugurated at the end of June, in another step toward Argentine self-sufficiency in petrochemicals, it was reported July 12. Petrochemical exports had been suspended to increase domestic supply, it was reported June 28.

The Italian chemical firm Montedison S.p.A. announced May 21 that it had signed a long-range $1 billion agreement with Argentina to design and construct a huge petrochemical complex at Bahia Blanca, south of Buenos Aires.

The state oil company YPF announced the discovery of oil reserves worth an estimated $5 billion in Mendoza Province, it was reported June 21. They would be developed using Rumanian technology.

Drought cuts grain yield. A persistent drought in the major grain producing areas threatened the nation's agricultural production and its ability to help relieve the world's acute food shortage, the New York Times reported Dec. 15.

Leading farmers' organizations said the drought had already cut the grain crop in southern Buenos Aires Province and La Pampa Province by one-third and the yield in Entre Rios Province by half. The three provinces produced more than half of Argentina's wheat, corn and sorghum.

Argentine wheat production for the 1973-74 season totaled 6.5 million tons, a drop of 17% from the previous year's figure, it was reported June 21. The area sown was down by 24.4%, and production in Buenos Aires Province, the principal wheat producer, was down by 24%. Sowing of barley and rye also had fallen.

The food situation was further complicated by extensive smuggling of grain into neighboring Bolivia, Chile and Paraguay, where merchants offered higher prices than the Argentine National Grain Board, the only authorized buyer of crops in Argentina.

Other economic developments. Among developments reported:

Construction of the nation's largest shipbuilding yard would begin in Punta Este, Patagonia at a cost of nearly $100 million, it was announced July 12. Production of 150,000-ton boats was scheduled to start in 1976.

New copper discoveries were made in Neuquen Province, it was reported July 19.

An Anglo-Italian consortium would build a plant to produce newsprint from sugar cane waste in Tucuman Province, with an annual capacity of one million tons, 70% of which would be exported, it was reported Aug. 2.

The largest aluminum plant in Latin America was inaugurated in Puerto Madryn, Chubut Province, under the management of the firm Aluminio Argentina, it was reported Aug. 2. It was expected eventually to produce 144,000 tons of aluminum annually, enough to cover internal demand and leave some for export.

The government planned to increase copper production to 150,000 tons a year by the end of 1977, and simultaneously increase its zinc and lead output, it was reported Aug. 23. Metals imports currently exceeded $350 million annually.

Work was progressing slowly in Sierra Grande, Patagonia, where by 1976 3.5 million tons of iron ore would be mined annually and processed into two million tons of concentrated magnetite in a Japanese-built plant, according to the Aug. 23 report. The government announced it would import 100 million tons of iron ore and two million tons of manganese ore from Brazil for the Argentine steel industry, it was reported Sept. 27.

There were fewer bankruptcies in Argentina in January-June than during any six-month period in the previous 14 years, it was reported Aug. 9. Economy Minister Jose Gelbard said this reflected a recovery of liquidity, a more hopeful business climate and greater solidity in the economic situation in general.

The government's revenues rose by almost 100% in January-August, but the budget deficit remained at 50%, it was reported Sept. 20.

Argentine floods. At least 60 persons died and over 100,000 were left homeless in three northwestern provinces in Argentina following severe flooding, it was reported Feb. 17.

Wages & prices. President Maria Estela Peron July 8 announced a bonus of a month's wages for all workers, pensioners and retired persons, to be awarded later in July, to compensate for rising prices and the government's prohibition of strikes. The bonus reportedly had been agreed to June 29, before Juan Peron's death. It was a blow to the wage-price freeze embodied in the labor-management social pact.

Wholesale prices in Argentina had risen by an average 4.2% in May, the highest increase for any month since the Peronists returned to power in May 1973, it was reported July 5. Prices of imported goods continued to rise faster than those of domestic products (5.6% against 3.9%), and importers complained that the government's price controls were making it unprofitable to import a number of essential goods, according to the London newsletter Latin America.

President Peron later (Oct. 31) granted a 15% wage increase to all Argentine workers and an equivalent raise in payments for their dependents.

Labor developments. Adelino Romero, the moderate secretary general of the General Labor Confederation (CGT) died July 14.

Romero, leader of the Textile Workers Union, had been re-elected to his CGT post July 12, but three of his supporters on the federation's executive council had been replaced by more conservative unionists, giving the conservatives a majority of the council. Segundo Palma, the rightist Construction Workers Union leader, was elected deputy secretary general, and he became secretary general upon Romero's death.

The increase in the rightists' power was engineered by Lorenzo Miguel, leader of the Metallurgical Workers Union and an ally of Social Welfare Minister Lopez Rega. Miguel's union recently had won large wage increases for its members, in defiance of the social pact.

The Buenos Aires Typographers Federation (FGB) announced Aug. 29 that it would increase the strikes and partial work stoppages it had staged against two newspapers, Cronica and La Razon, to demand higher wages and other benefits. Labor Minister Ricardo Otero had ended recognition of the union Aug. 28 for its "continuous attacks on the Social Pact."

The FGB's leader, Raimundo Ongaro, a left-wing Peronist, called Otero "a servant of imperialism" Aug. 20 and announced Sept. 2 that FGB would join Cordoba's SMATA affiliate, its Light and Power Union and other "rebel" labor organizations in forming a new group to oppose the Peronist General Labor Confederation, the nation's most powerful labor alliance.

More than 200,000 primary and high school teachers struck across the country Sept. 4–5 to demand higher wages and a better retirement plan.

A collective transport strike called in Buenos Aires Nov. 28 ended the next day after the government arrested the transport union's leader.

Latin sugar cartel formed. Twenty nations in Latin America and the Caribbean formed a sugar producers' union to protect world sugar prices, currently at record levels.

Formation of the cartel, called the Group of Latin American and Caribbean Sugar Exporting Countries, was announced Nov. 28 by Francisco Cano Escalante, president of the Mexican National Sugar Commission, following a meeting of representatives of the member nations Nov. 25–27 on the island of

Cozumel, off Mexico's Caribbean coast.

The members included Mexico, the Dominican Republic, Argentina, Barbados, Brazil, Colombia, Costa Rica, Cuba, Ecuador, El Salvador, Guatemala, Guyana, Honduras, Jamaica, Nicaragua, Panama, Paraguay, Peru, Trinidad & Tobago and Venezuela.

1975: Argentina & Mrs. Peron

Government & Politics

Faced with growing discontent and violence, Argentina's new president was reported early in 1975 to be relying on the aid of a group of relatively few officials in her efforts to govern Argentina. The most powerful member of this very influential group was said to be Jose Lopez Rega.

Lopez Rega promoted. President Maria Estela Martinez de Peron Jan. 3 promoted Social Welfare Minister Jose Lopez Rega to the rank of secretary to the presidency, formalizing his power as her closest adviser.

The promotion allowed Lopez Rega to coordinate the President's activities and control all access to her. It also allowed him to require any information from any Cabinet minister or other public official, according to the London newsletter Latin America Jan. 10. Lopez Rega's power had grown steadily since Mrs. Peron's accession to the presidency in July 1974.

Misiones government removed. The federal government took over the government of Misiones Province Jan. 18, asserting the province's population was "unhappy" and the provincial administration "inefficient." It was the sixth time since 1973 that the federal administration had removed an elected provincial government.

Montoneros form party. The Montoneros, the left-wing Peronist guerrilla group, launched a new political party with a platform similar to that of the Peronist coalition which won the March 1973 elections, the newsletter Latin America reported Jan. 17.

The party, to be called Peronismo Leal (Loyal Peronism), would bring together all the Peronist elements which had been progressively excluded from participation in the government since the resignation of ex-President Hector Campora in July 1973, Latin America reported.

Government under attack. Mrs. Peron's government found itself increasingly under political attack as 1975 advanced.

The Authentic Party had held its first national constituent assembly in Buenos Aires March 11, with some 200 delegates attending, among them many former Peronist government officials. Messages of support were sent by other former officials, including ex-Gov. Alberto Martinez Baca of Mendoza Province, and by the Montoneros, the Peronist guerrilla group.

Delegates to the meeting drafted a

137

document titled, "Peronism Returns to Authentic Peronism," which supported "the revolutionary definition of Peronism given us by our unforgettable comrade Evita [Peron]." This definition was upheld by the platform that Frejuli (the ruling Justicialista Liberation Front) had adopted in the 1973 elections but later had abandoned. This definition of Peronism implied "a struggle against monopoly, participation of workers in the control and planning of the economy, denunciation of the commitments contracted by imperialism behind the people's back, and protection of the small- and medium-sized producer," the document stated.

The document charged that the government had taken "contradictory" measures since its election in 1973, violating Peronist ideals and assuring Argentine "dependency." Loyal Peronist "comrades are being massacred and shot," the document added.

"It is a strange paradox," the document continued, "that the present administration has taken the same principles as [Gen. Alejandro] Lanusse when he was in charge of the military government [before the 1973 elections], carrying out an economic plan that punishes the poor sectors of the population, the small- and medium-sized producers, the businessmen, the teachers and the professionals. It has organized repression by letting the army do it directly, and has called elections in Misiones in an attempt to constitutionalize a representation it lacks."

Social Welfare Minister Jose Lopez Rega called the Authentic Party a "deformation" March 12, characterizing its members as "traitors to the sentiment for the greatness of the fatherland." President Peron denounced the party April 4, and the government expelled from the Justicialista movement 13 Peronist leaders who had supported the Authentics, including Alberto Martinez Baca and two other former governors; Oscar Bidegain of Buenos Aires Provice and Jorge Cepernic of Santa Cruz.

(In a related development April 22, ex-President Hector Campora was also expelled from the official Peronist party. Although he lived in self-imposed exile in Mexico, Campora was widely reported to

be favored as a 1977 presidential candidate by Peronist leftists.)

In addition to the Authentic Party, another group of former government supporters, the Integration and Development Movement (MID), also attacked the Peronist administration. A MID statement issued March 14 accused the government of pursuing economic policies that went "contrary to the national interest" and were "inspired by . . . monopolistic groups." the MID had been a member of Frejuli.

(Walter Goes, a correspondent for the Brazilian newspaper Jornal do Brasil, reported March 21 that he had seen a "secret document" of Argentina's security forces implicating MID leader Arturo Frondizi, a former president, in a subversive plot with ex-President Lanusse. Lanusse asserted the report was false; and Goes was expelled from Argentina April 4.)

(Richard Gott, correspondent of the British newspaper The Guardian, reported April 9 that a military coup in Argentina was "imminent," and that the army would take a government defeat in the Misiones elections as its signal to seize power. The London newsletter Latin America reported April 11 that "even the dogs were barking" about conspiracies against the government by Lanusse, Frondizi and conservative Peronist labor leader Lorenzo Miguel.)

Government wins provincial vote. The ruling Justicialista Liberation Front (Frejuli) won elections for a new governor and legislative assembly in Misiones Province April 13. The vote was considered a referendum on the administration of President Maria Estela Martinez de Peron.

Official results gave Frejuli 46% of the ballots, to 38% for the opposition Radical Civic Union and 9% for two dissident left-wing Peronist groups, the Authentic Party and the Third Position. Frejuli candidate Miguel Angel Alterach was elected governor, and Frejuli members won 16 of 32 seats in the legislature. Radicals won 13 seats, the Authentic Party won two, and the Third Position, one.

Seven other parties competed unsuccessfully in the elections, which were necessitated by the death of Misiones' governor and deputy governor in an airplane crash in November 1974.

Frejuli leader Demetrio Vazquez called the elections a victory for Mrs. Peron, who, he said, "has shown that she is the sole legitimate heir to [President Juan] Peron and Eva Peron." However, observers noted that Misiones was not representative of Argentina, being less populated and more agrarian than the average province, and that the Radicals had considerably cut into Frejuli's popularity since the 1973 elections. Frejuli's vote total fell by 14% from its level in the second round of the 1973 elections, while the Radical total rose by 9%.

Both the Radicals and dissident Peronist leftists had charged before the elections that the government was buying votes. The government had announced new farm credits and raised the prices of key crops, while Frejuli candidates had distributed mattresses, clothes, household products and money to voters.

Frejuli gubernatorial candidate Alterach said the government's generosity in Misiones was "part of a plan that will be put into effect throughout the country and just happens to coincide with the election."

The showing by the Authentic Party and the Third Position was unexpectedly poor, according to press reports. The newsletter Latin America noted April 18 that the Authentic Party was officially forbidden to use its name or any labels or slogans identifying it as a Peronist splinter group, and was forced to run as "List 12."

Economic action. The Peron administration took various actions in the economic sector to defuse widespread criticism.

The commerce unit of the General Economic Confederation (CGE), a management group which normally supported the government, criticized the government's economic policies in a statement March 14. It charged that Economy Minister Alfredo Gomez Morales had helped fuel inflation, reduce production and encourage hoarding by first approving a wage raise and then freezing prices and devaluing the peso.

The regime March 1 had announced a wage increase of $40 a month for all employes to offset the high inflation rate,

which reached 43.5% in 1974 and 13.4% in the first two months of 1975. It decreed a 50% devaluation of the peso against the U.S. dollar March 4, and accompanied this with a new mechanism to authorize price increases. Gomez Morales denied the mechanism amounted to a price freeze, but the CGE, which had gone along with the wage increase, withdrew in protest from the National Commission on Prices, Income and Standard of Living.

The peso devaluation was designed to stimulate Argentine exports. The nation had enjoyed a $650 million trade surplus in 1974, according to Gomez Morales, but agricultural production was expected to drop sharply in 1975 because of weather conditions, mounting costs, labor disputes, and hoarding by producers. The Agriculture Ministry foresaw a 26.8% drop in wheat production, falling short of Argentina's domestic and export needs.

The 1974 budget deficit was $2.74 billion, $800 million higher than the 1973 deficit, despite a 52.3% increase in income, the newsletter Latin America reported Jan. 31.

Violence

Assassinations continue. Political assassinations and associated killings continued on into 1975.

The victims died in ambushes attributed to three terrorist organizations—the rightist Argentine Anticommunist Alliance (AAA), the Marxist People's Revolutionary Army (ERP) and the left-wing Peronist Montoneros group—and in shootouts between the terrorists and police.

Most of the murders were presumed committed by rightists. Press reports noted that although police had arrested thousands of alleged leftist assassins under the state of siege, they had seized no rightists. Police were widely assumed to participate in right-wing terrorist attacks.

A policeman died Jan. 2 after being shot by presumed leftist guerrillas in Buenos Aires Dec. 30, 1974. He was the 227th victim of political violence in Argentina since the beginning of 1974, according to United Press International. The majority of the victims were leftists, UPI reported.

Rightist labor leader Alberto Bayarsky was assassinated in Bahia Blanca Jan. 24, and two young men apparently linked to the ERP were killed in Tucuman the next day.

Fortunato Canziani, a high official in the Labor Ministry, was killed by ERP members in Buenos Aires Jan. 28. His bodyguard also was killed.

Oscar Lallia, a conservative Peronist and union leader in La Plata, was assassinated Jan. 29. Rodolfo Chavez, a labor leader in Tucuman, was murdered along with three bodyguards Feb. 4, and Antonio Muscat, an executive in the Bunge & Born trading conglomerate, was murdered in Quilmes, Buenos Aires Province Feb. 7. The Montoneros, the left-wing Peronist guerrillas, claimed to have killed Muscat and kidnapped Carlos Goguei, another Bunge & Born executive, Feb. 7.

Hipolito Acuna, a right-wing Peronist deputy from Santa Fe, was assassinated Feb. 14. The same day two leftist labor leaders were killed in San Justo, outside Buenos Aires.

Presumed members of the AAA killed and then blew up the body of newsman Jaime Luciano outside Salta Feb. 16.

One policeman was killed and three others were wounded by terrorists in Buenos Aires Feb. 19. Teodoro Ponce, a right-wing Peronist labor leader in Rosario, was assassinated Feb. 21.

One policeman was killed in Cordoba and another in Rosario in ambushes by unknown persons Feb. 23. A civilian bystander was killed in La Plata the same day during an attack on a passing police car. In Salta, the police chief said he had arrested three persons who had allegedly plotted to kill the provincial governor, the mayor of the capital, and the local Justicialista Party chief.

Adolfo Cavali, a former petroleum union leader and Justicialista official, was murdered March 1.

Unidentified gunmen March 2 gravely wounded Eustaquio Tolosa, a Peronist port workers' leader in Buenos Aires. The same day a soldier was killed when a bomb exploded in his car in Tucuman, and the body of a Buenos Aires Province official was found outside the capital.

Two policemen were killed and two more wounded March 8 in a shootout with guerrillas in Buenos Aires. A police coroner was reported killed in Rosario March 9, a police officer was assassinated in Tigre (Buenos Aires Province) March 10, and two more officers were murdered in a suburb of the capital March 11.

Police in Buenos Aires found the bullet-riddled bodies of five young men in a vacant lot March 12. Two of the five were later identified as members of the Socialist Workers Party, and their murder was tentatively attributed to the AAA. A member of the left-wing Peronist Youth was killed in La Plata March 13, presumably also by the AAA. Two more bullet-riddled bodies were found in La Plata March 14.

A policeman was killed in Cordoba March 13 when he refused to hand over his gun to men who intercepted him as he descended from a bus. The same day in Buenos Aires police killed three men who resisted when asked for identification.

Two sailors were wounded March 16 when unidentified gunmen attacked a naval station in Berisso, south of Buenos Aires. The next day police killed three alleged leftist guerrillas in San Antonio de Padua, just west of the capital.

A policeman and a female guerrilla were killed in separate shootouts in Buenos Aires March 18. The next day police found the bullet-riddled and burned bodies of four persons in a garbage dump in a suburb of the capital.

Amid the bloodshed, the government announced that it had broken up a "vast subversive terrorist operation" designed to assassinate labor leaders and to paralyze production in the industrial belt along the Parana River northwest of Buenos Aires.

Security forces subsequently arrested hundreds of persons, including many workers and labor leaders belonging to a dissident leftist branch of the Metallurgical Workers Union (UOM), which was run by conservative Peronists and strong supporters of the federal government. To protest the arrests, hundreds of workers struck March 20-22 at steel plants and other factories in San Nicolas (Buenos Aires Province) and in Villa Constitucion and Rosario (Santa Fe Province).

The national leadership of the UOM recently had been losing the support of workers in the Parana belt who were disgruntled over economic conditions, the New York Times noted March 22.

According to the government, the alleged plotters had planned to take over trade union headquarters in the area and to prevent workers in key posts from carrying out their duties, thus "paralyzing the most important production lines" in every company, the Times reported March 21. The plot "clearly specified the use of terrorism in all its forms, including the physical elimination of people who opposed the conspiracy," the government asserted.

The alleged plot was discovered as the current wave of political violence culminated in 24 killings March 20-22. The victims included a left-wing Peronist councilman, a priest and several trade unionists and policemen in La Plata, Buenos Aires, Mar del Plata, Tucuman, Cordoba and Bahia Blanca.

In Mar del Plata, the bullet-riddled body of a university administrator was found by police March 24, and a left-wing Peronist medical student was found murdered March 28. The killings were attributed to the AAA.

Presumed leftist guerrillas killed army Col. Martin Rico in a suburb of Buenos Aires March 27. A policeman was killed in Santa Fe Province March 29, reportedly by the ERP, and a policeman and army colonel were shot to death in Buenos Aires April 2 in an assassination attempt by presumed leftists against Gabriel Morales, an aide to Social Welfare Minister Jose Lopez Rega. Morales was seriously wounded.

Police killed two presumed leftists in Buenos Aires Province March 29, and they announced the arrest of 19 ERP and Montoneros guerrillas in Cordoba April 2. The army reported killing two ERP members April 3 when the guerrillas tried to ambush a military patrol.

Police in Buenos Aires reported killing two ERP members and arresting some 50 leftists April 3, including 20 members of the Tupamaros guerrilla group of Uruguay.

Jose Chirino, a conservative leader of the Metallurgical Workers Union, was murdered April 5.

Police found six bullet-riddled bodies April 6 on the road from Buenos Aires to Ezeiza International Airport. Next to the victims was a placard, attributed to the AAA, saying: "We were from the ERP, the Montoneros and the FAR." The last group, the Revolutionary Armed Forces, was a leftist guerrilla band. Police said April 8 that four of the victims were Chilean.

Chilean journalist Ernesto Carmona reported in the Venezuelan newspaper El Nacional April 26 that Argentine security forces were carrying out a "pogrom" of Chilean leftists who had taken refuge in Argentina after the 1973 military coup against the late Chilean President Salvador Allende. The persecution and murder of Chileans in Argentina was carried out in collaboration with the Chilean embassy in Buenos Aires and the Chilean military intelligence service, Carmona charged.

Police announced the arrest April 17 of three prominent leaders of the left-wing Peronist Youth (JP)—Juan Carlos Dante Gullo, Dardo Cabo and Emiliano Costa— for allegedly plotting to assassinate Chilean President Augusto Pinochet Ugarte during Pinochet's visit to Argentina April 18.

Police killed four alleged ERP guerrillas in a shootout in the Buenos Aires suburb of San Justo April 11, and they killed five alleged Montoneros in the suburb of Campana the next day. Guerrillas killed an army colonel in a raid on an army arsenal outside Rosario April 13, and they killed two policemen in Jujuy April 17. Two guerrillas were killed in the Rosario incident and two more in the Jujuy attack.

Police reported killing seven ERP members in a shootout in Salta April 20 and another five guerrillas in Buenos Aires April 22. The second group reportedly was preparing a jail break for imprisoned comrades.

The AAA distributed leaflets April 25 threatening to kill 16 prominent newsmen and actors unless they left the country by April 28. The 16, who included the well-known Uruguayan writer Mario Benedetti, went into hiding rather than emigrate, the London Times reported April 29.

Bombings reported. Police reported a series of bombings Jan. 2 in Tucuman,

Santa Fe and Mendoza Provinces. The explosions caused considerable property damage but no casualties.

The bombing targets included the Hebrew Society in Rosario (Santa Fe), and the home of a Communist Party leader in Mendoza and a university administrator and a professor in Tucuman.

The bodies of five persons were blown up in two separate bomb explosions in Buenos Aires Province Jan. 10. University student sources later said the victims were members of the left-wing Peronist Youth.

The home of the publisher of El Diario, an apolitical newspaper in La Plata, was bombed by unknown assailants Jan. 24. The explosion caused some property damage but no injuries.

Eleven bombs exploded in Rosario early Feb. 1, damaging the homes of several political officials and business executives. In San Luis, explosions partly destroyed the homes of Sen. Carlos Franco and Deputy Luis Cazanza, critics of the provincial government.

At least four persons were killed in Tucuman March 4 when a bomb exploded in their car. Four bombs exploded March 8 at the homes of councilmen in Santa Fe, but they caused only property damage.

The Buenos Aires branch of the Italo-Belgian Bank was damaged April 4 by a bomb presumably detonated by leftists. Leftists were also held responsible for the bombing the same day of the home of Norberto Kozaim, a Social Welfare Ministry official.

A policeman guarding the home of the British ambassador in Buenos Aires was killed April 25 when a bomb exploded in front of the residence.

Terrorists active. Much of the violence was blamed on full-time terrorists, although it was reported that many violent crimes, especially kidnappings for ransom, were committed by professional criminals taking advantage of the prevailing political turbulance.

Rodolfo Saurnier, manager of an automotive parts factory, was kidnapped outside Buenos Aires Jan. 8 by professed Montoneros guerrillas. There had been more than 100 abductions in Argentina in 1974, most by common criminals imitating leftist guerrillas and demanding large ransoms, according to UPI.

Other Montonero members Feb. 28 kidnapped the president of the Buenos Aires Province Supreme Court, Hugo Alfredo Anzorreguy, saying they would hold him until the government freed Sergio Schneider, an imprisoned guerrilla. Anzorreguy was freed by his captors March 5 after the government released Schneider, who was deported to Peru March 3.

Schneider belonged to the small Liberation Armed Forces (FAL), which collaborated with the Montoneros in Anzorreguy's abduction. It was the first time the two terrorist groups had worked together, according to the London newsletter Latin America March 7. Schneider declared in Peru that his group sought "the creation of a socialist state in Argentina through the only alternative, a revolutionary war."

Alfonso Marguerite, an executive of the Bunge & Born trading conglomerate kidnapped in 1974, was freed March 8 after a ransom of $500,000 reportedly was paid to his captors, presumed to be Montoneros.

Aldo Tedeschi, an automobile parts factory owner also kidnapped in 1974, was also freed March 8. No ransom was reported.

A leftist Montonero guerrilla was mortally wounded Jan. 15 in a suburban Buenos Aires factory where he and nine comrades forcibly rounded up workers for a political indoctrination session. The same day, the left-wing People's Revolutionary Army (ERP) sent a message to the press asserting it would kill a businessman or government official for every "revolutionary" slain by authorities.

A group of ERP guerrillas killed a Buenos Aires policeman Jan. 17 when he attempted to prevent one of them from distributing subversive pamphlets. The next day a police intelligence officer was murdered by presumed leftists in the Buenos Aires suburb of San Justo.

Police spokesmen said Feb. 24 that two ERP members had been killed outside Buenos Aires Feb. 21 while resisting arrest for distributing subversive literature. Two more ERP members were killed by police in Cordoba Feb. 24.

Montoneros killed three policemen in

an ambush in Buenos Aires Feb. 28. Another policeman died in a bomb explosion in Tucuman.

Police in La Plata announced the arrest of 14 ERP guerrillas Jan. 29, asserting they included two French citizens and four Paraguayans. The ERP said in a communique the next day that if 19 captured guerrillas were not proved to be "safe and sound" within 72 hours, it would "indiscriminately execute officials of the government and leaders of the ruling party." Twelve more ERP members were arrested Jan. 31 in Cordoba and Santa Fe, according to police.

Twenty-one ERP guerrillas were arrested in Mar del Plata and another 12 were seized in Cordoba Feb. 11, authorities reported.

Security forces carried out a nationwide sweep against alleged subversives Feb. 15, reportedly arresting about 1,000 persons in Buenos Aires, Cordoba, Mendoza and Santa Fe Provinces.

The government news agency Telam reported April 7 that police had arrested 13 leftist subversives in Mendoza Province and 17 in Comodoro Rivadavia. Police in Buenos Aires announced April 10 that they had discovered a leftist arms factory in Moron and arrested four Argentine and 21 Uruguayan guerrillas who were meeting to coordinate subversive activities by the ERP, the Tupamaros, the Revolutionary Left Movement of Chile and the National Liberation Army of Bolivia.

Unrest in Cordoba. Political unrest and violence continued in the troubled province of Cordoba during 1975.

About 15 ERP members briefly seized a television station in Cordoba Jan. 20 and broadcast a message denouncing the federal government and its take-over of the Cordoba provincial government in 1974.

The governor appointed by the federal administration, Gen. Raul Lacabanne, had instituted virtually indiscriminate repression which helped him combat leftist guerrillas but alienated all political parties, including the governing Justicialista Party, according to the London newsletter Latin America Jan. 17.

Cordoba's provincial police chief, Hector Luis Garcia Rey, had resigned a week earlier. The government said he quit to protect his family, which was allegedly threatened by leftist guerrillas, but Latin America reported he was dismissed because members of the provincial police had beaten a federal police official to whom one of their victims had threatened to complain.

Some 30 members of the Argentine Anticommunist Alliance (AAA), the right-wing assassination squad, invaded the plant of the moderate Cordoba newspaper La Voz del Interior Jan. 23 and blew up its printing presses, causing an estimated $600,000 in damages. The paper, Cordoba's largest, had angered many policemen in 1974 by detailing charges against 19 police officers accused of executing five farmers after mistaking them for guerrillas. Employes of La Voz said they recognized one of the AAA attackers as a police official, according to the New York Times Jan. 24.

ERP guerrillas engineered the escape of 26 female political prisoners in Cordoba May 25. Three policemen were murdered in Cordoba June 12, presumably by guerrillas, and two guerrillas were killed by police there June 24, according to official reports.

U.S. aide assassinated. The U.S. honorary consul in Cordoba, John Patrick Egan, was kidnapped by Montoneros guerrillas and murdered after the government refused to negotiate for his release.

Egan, a retired businessman, was seized by the Peronist insurgents at his suburban home Feb. 26. A communique to the press the next day said he would be "executed by firing squad" at 7 p.m. Feb. 28 unless the government proved that four recently arrested Montoneros were "safe and sound" by showing them on television. The note called Egan "the principal representative of Yankee interests" in Cordoba and it accused the government of "subjecting the people to economic exploitation and to police and army repression while it hands our country over to the Yankees."

Interior Minister Alberto Rocamora said Feb. 28 that the government would not negotiate with the guerrillas "for any reason." That night Egan's body was found at the side of a road outside

Cordoba, shot once through the head and wrapped in a Montoneros flag.

The Montoneros issued a "war communique" March 1 blaming the government's intransigence for Egan's execution and accusing the regime of "sending its own accomplices to their deaths."

U.S. Secretary of State Henry Kissinger denounced the murder Feb. 28 as "a senseless and despicable crime which shocks the sensibilities of all civilized men." President Ford March 1 called the assassination "a vicious act which will be condemned by men of decency and honor everywhere."

U.S. aides in Argentina made unofficial protests to the government because Egan's police protection had been withdrawn a few days before the kidnapping, the Washington Post reported March 4. The U.S. embassy staff, cut from 200 to 90 persons during the wave of violence in 1974, was expected to be cut further in the wake of the assassination, according to press reports.

Army pursues guerrillas. President Maria Estela Martinez de Peron Feb. 9 ordered the army to destroy a "rural column" of the left-wing People's Revolutionary Army (ERP) in Tucuman Province.

Some 3,500 soldiers began pursuing the guerrillas in the Tucuman mountains, joined later by 1,500 more troops and police. They occupied towns and villages and patrolled roads, but fought few clashes with the insurgents. One clash, reported Feb. 15 near the locality of Pueblo Viejo, left one soldier and three guerrillas dead, and three soldiers wounded. Some 50 insurgents were reported arrested by Feb. 19.

The military campaign, supported by a $5.1 million federal contribution to the Tucuman provincial treasury, was endorsed by virtually the entire Argentine press, according to the Washington Post Feb. 20. Reporters were not allowed into the military operation area.

(Ricardo Balbin, leader of the opposition Radical Civic Union, said Feb. 17 that ERP leader Roberto Santucho had declared a 620 mile "liberated zone" in Tucuman and demanded international protection for its borders as well as

treatment of captured guerrillas as prisoners of war.)

Soldiers in Tucuman Province, the center of ERP operations, fought two battles with the Marxist guerrillas May 30, in which one insurgent and five soldiers were reported killed. The army announced June 24 that soldiers had killed seven ERP members in Tucuman in the previous 48 hours.

Protests against violence. There was increasing public protest against the unceasing bloodshed.

In the first government criticism of the AAA, Interior Minister Alberto Rocamora Jan. 28 had denounced the AAA attack on the Cordoba newspaper La Voz del Interior.

In a protest against the mounting terrorism, federal deputies from the opposition Radical Civic Union demanded April 2 that the government tell the Chamber of Deputies what "measures are being taken to discover the assassins of policemen and soldiers as well as the authors of the barbarous killings that occurred in Temperley, Lomas de Zamora and Mar del Plata." Police in those three localities recently had found the dynamited bodies of 13 persons kidnapped earlier, presumably by the AAA.

The Radicals noted that while the government was effectively combatting "violence unleashed by the extreme left," it had not arrested a single member of the AAA. "This impunity," they declared, "cannot be attributed to the inefficiency of our security organisms, and it compromises the government itself."

"Bodies appear by the hundreds along public roads, but so far the government has not investigated a single case or arrested one culprit or suspect," the deputies asserted. These bodies usually bore the accepted "signatures" of the AAA—signs of torture, dozens of bullet wounds and, often, mutilation by fire or explosives.

Responding to the Radicals' demand, the armed forces commander, Lt. Gen. Leandro Anaya, briefed legislators on the ERP April 17. He said the guerrilla group was linked to the Fourth Communist International and to the Cuban government. He added that the ERP kept in close touch with the Montoneros, despite their ideological differences, and the two groups had agreed that the ERP would operate in rural areas and the Montoneros in Argentina's cities.

Interior Minister Alberto Rocamora appeared before Congress April 19 and disclosed that the government was holding 1,117 detainees under the state of siege. He denied widespread rumors that the AAA was a parapolice group. "What makes a repressive police action [against the AAA] difficult is that it acts ... against the left, a task in which the armed forces and security forces are also engaged," Rocamora said.

Rightist murders continue. Presumed members of the right-wing Argentine Anti-communist Alliance (AAA) assassinated at least 29 persons in May and they killed at least eight more in the first half of June despite pledging May 30 to suspend-operations for 90 days.

According to the English-language Buenos Aires Herald May 29, 503 persons had died in political violence since July 1, 1974, the day President Juan Peron died, and 277 had died in 1975.

Of the total, the Herald reported, "70 have not been identified. Of the 433 who have, 190 had left-wing affiliations, while 38 were right-wingers. The police have lost 54 men, the army 22 and 13 businessmen have been killed. A total of 91 persons were killed in gunfights (all of them presumed left-wing terrorists). Four innocent children have been killed, one diplomat, and 20 people who cannot be fitted into any category."

Setting aside the right-wingers, the gunfight victims and the military and police officers, the remaining 285 victims were presumably killed by the AAA. However, the newsletter Latin America reported June 6 that a "more likely calculation" would put the number of AAA victims at 800–1,200, the great majority having died in 1975.

The Buenos Aires press tended to report only those murders that occurred in the major cities, and to concentrate on the assassination of prominent lawyers, politicians and liberal journalists, Latin America noted. However, AAA terror was relatively indiscriminate, potentially affecting anyone who appeared to be non-conformist, including laborers, priests, students and teachers, the newsletter reported.

Among recent AAA victims was Jorge Money, financial reporter for the Buenos Aires newspaper La Opinion, whose bullet-riddled body was found May 18 near Ezeiza airport outside Buenos Aires. Journalists and typographers in the capital went on strike to protest the murder May 20, closing down five of the city's eight newspapers.

The AAA also threatened other prominent liberal journalists, forcing at least three—an economic specialist of La Opinion and the editor and publisher of the Roman Catholic magazine Christian Family—to leave the country, it was reported May 24. In addition, presumed AAA members May 24 blew up the front of the building of the newspaper La Voz del Pueblo in Monte Grande, south of Buenos Aires.

AAA actions against liberal journalists coincided with new government restrictions on the press, protested vigorously by the Association of Argentine Newspaper Enterprises. A decree enacted May 20 forbade Argentine publications to print reports on Argentina by foreign news agencies, and ordered all news agencies and their correspondents to register with an unspecified government agency within 90 days. The government also specifically attacked La Opinion and the Buenos Aires daily El Cronista Comercial, implying in a television broadcast May 18 that they aided subversives.

Protests against AAA terrorism grew in May, particularly among legislators and leaders of the opposition Radical Civic Union. A Radical document released May 24 charged: "The fear that anguishes and enervates is taking over the body of the republic," and "the authors of [AAA] violence act amid an evident impunity."

Interior Minister Alberto Rocamora May 27 denied charges from Radicals and others that the government was protecting the AAA, whose members were rumored to be police and military officers. Social Welfare Minister Jose Lopez Rega, whom many observers linked directly to the AAA, asserted May 29 that the government "will not tolerate" terrorism from any group and that it would investigate the "motives" and "members" of the AAA.

The next day news agencies in Buenos Aires received a communique signed by the "Federal Command" of the AAA pledging an end to terrorism for 90 days while the group decided on new methods to "combat adequately the Marxist guerrilla." In the meantime, the communique said, the government should order the death penalty or life imprisonment for terrorists and their direct or indirect supporters.

Despite this pledge, another communique signed by the AAA "National Executive Board" and sent to news agencies June 3, pledged to kill four prominent military men and politicians who were found to be "incompatible with the final objectives of our movement and the interests of the fatherland." The four were Adm. Emilio Massera, the navy commander; Gen. Jose Videla, an army division commander; Francisco Manrique, a right-wing politician and former presidential candidate; and Raul Alfonsin, a Radical leader who was particular critical of the AAA's freedom of operation.

Montoneros free Born brothers. Juan and Jorge Born, top executives of the Bunge & Born trading conglomerate, were released after their company paid a reported $60 million ransom to the Montoneros guerrilla group, which had kidnapped them in September 1974.

Jorge Born was freed June 20 at a clandestine press conference held by Montoneros leader Mario Firmenich. Juan reportedly had been released more than a month earlier after suffering psychological problems in captivity. Both brothers had been treated well by the Montoneros, according to family sources.

The massive ransom distressed government and military officials. The government ordered an investigation of the payment June 23 to determine whether it violated tax or foreign exchange laws. (Much of the ransom was presumed smuggled into Argentina in U.S. dollars.) Seven Bunge & Born executives were arrested June 25–26, according to police.

In addition to the $60 million (a figure Bunge & Born neither confirmed nor denied), the company also distributed $1.2

million worth of food and clothing in poor neighborhoods around the country—some of which the police claimed to have intercepted—and it paid for the publication June 19 of a Montoneros statement in Argentine and foreign newspapers.

The statement accused Bunge & Born of having exploited Argentine workers and having supported the 1955 military coup against the late President Juan Peron. The Born brothers had been "tried" on these charges and sentenced to one year in prison, reduced to nine months, and their company had been sentenced to pay the ransom and to immediately resolve labor conflicts it had experienced since the brothers' abduction, according to the statement.

At his press conference June 20, Firmenich asserted the ransom money would be used to create "people's power; to develop an integral war against imperialism, and to establish definitive national liberation." The money "stolen from the people is being returned to the people," he said.

Firmenich unexpectedly criticized the late President Peron, asserting Peron had committed "many errors for which we are now paying dearly." Among these was allowing the rise to political prominence of Social Welfare Minister Jose Lopez Rega, whom the Montoneros had "condemned to death by firing squad," Firmenich declared.

Labor & Economic Troubles

Steel strike. Labor discontent with the Peron administration's economic policies was highlighted by a two-month strike at the Villa Constitucion steel mills. Beginning March 23 and not ending until May 20, when the strikers reportedly yielded to a tacit threat of military intervention, the walkout crippled Argentina's steel output and threatened to halt automobile production.

The two leading auto firms, IKA-Renault and Ford Motor Argentina, announced April 10 they would have to shut down their plants if steel production did not resume. The other seven car companies in the country were also reported running out of essential steel products.

The Villa Constitucion strikers demanded that authorities release some 150 persons, including 46 labor leaders, who had been arrested in March for allegedly plotting to disrupt production in the industrial belt along the Parana River northwest of Buenos Aires. Most observers felt the alleged plot was an excuse devised by the government to arrest leftists who had legally gained control of the local branch of the Metallurgical Workers Union (UOM).

A slate of leftist and moderate dissidents had easily won the local UOM elections in November 1974, defeating a slate backed by Lorenzo Miguel, the union's conservative national leader. Miguel was said to have great influence in the federal government, particularly with Labor Minister Ricardo Otero, a former UOM official. Residents of Villa Constitucion said armed right-wing unionists had accompanied police during the March arrests, pointing out dissident leaders for detention, it was reported April 13.

Police occupied the steel plants and arrested a number of strikers March 27 in an unsuccessful effort to end the strike. In an apparent demonstration of support for the strikers, members of the Peronist Montoneros guerrilla group killed the Villa Constitucion police chief March 23. Alleged guerrillas attacked the local police station the next day.

Wide dissent. The steel strike coincided with other protests against the government's economic policies. Subway workers in Buenos Aires struck for higher wages April 7–9; the government declared the strike illegal and police arrested 49 picketers. Farmers in the five major agrarian provinces—Buenos Aires, La Pampa, Entre Rios, Santa Fe and Cordoba —had struck for higher agricultural prices and lower taxes March 3, refusing to send animals to slaughter or grain to market.

Even conservative Peronist labor leaders, considered the backbone of the government, expressed displeasure with its policies. Leaders of the powerful General Labor Confederation (CGT) circulated an internal document calling for the resignation of Economy Minister Alfredo Gomez Morales and Social Welfare Minister Jose Lopez Rega, the advisers closest to President Maria Estela Martinez de Peron. CGT leaders also acknowledged holding talks with ranking military officers, although they denied discussing a possible coup against the government, the New York Times reported March 28. [See above]

(Both the CGT officers and their military contacts were opposed to Lopez Rega, who was considered the strongman of the Peron administration, the Times reported. In recent months Lopez Rega had kept labor leaders from the president, remaining virtually the only government figure with direct access to her, according to the Times.)

In an effort to regain CGT support, Mrs. Peron visited union headquarters in Buenos Aires April 4 and promised to consult with labor leaders more often. She denounced unidentified "traitors" in the government and said she would hand over to the CGT the Mayo publishing company, which had put out the Peronist newspaper "Democracia" during the first two Peronist administrations in the 1940s and 1950s.

The 62 Organizations, the Peronist umbrella group, declared their support for Mrs. Peron April 9, asserting that in her speech to the CGT she had "fully exercised the political bossism which is appropriate to those elected."

Lopez Rega's power grows. As economic troubles mounted, the Argentine government's strongman, Social Welfare Minister Jose Lopez Rega, took firm action to increase his own power.

Lopez May 31 forced the resignation of Economy Minister Alfredo Gomez Morales and replaced him with Celestino Rodrigo, who had been his assistant for social security in the Social Welfare Ministry.

Lopez had already made his son-in-law, Raul Lastiri, first in line to succeed Mrs. Peron. He secured the resignation April 25 of the Senate president, Jose Antonio Allende, and persuaded the Peronist bloc in the Senate not to elect a successor to Allende, thus leaving Lastiri, as president of the House of Representatives, next in line for the presidency.

In further enhancement of his power, Lopez secured the army command for a close military associate, Gen. Alberto Numa Laplane. Army Commander Gen. Leandro Anaya resigned May 13 after disagreeing with Defense Minister Adolfo Savino and President Peron on several issues, including potential military intervention against steel strikers. The strikers reportedly ended the strike in order to avoid a confrontation with Numa Laplane, who was said to favor military intervention.

Labor crisis. The economic situation and labor discontent reached crisis proportions by late June as thousands of workers struck in protest against high living costs and government austerity measures, including a rollback of wage raises that had been negotiated earlier.

The crisis had been preceded June 4 by an announcement of the new economy minister, Celestino Rodrigo, of an emergency program to deal with the severe economic problems, including an estimated 100% annual inflation rate. The program included a 50% devaluation of the peso, sharp increases in interest rates and in the prices of fuel, gas, electricity, water and transportation, and a 38% ceiling on wage increases. (The ceiling also constituted a wage offer.)

The ceiling would revoke wage increases negotiated recently in a number of industries, some as high as 100%–135%. Labor leaders rejected the ceiling June 5 and strikes began, starting with automotive workers in Cordoba. Rodrigo raised the ceiling to 45% June 12, but the CGT rejected this the next day.

Strikes and antigovernment demonstrations were reported June 17 in Mendoza, Cordoba, Mar del Plata, Rio Negro and Bahia Blanca, and workers at General Motors plants were reported on strike June 18. Workers at certain industrial plants accepted 45% wage increases June 19–20, but others stayed on strike.

About 200,000 teachers struck across the country June 26 to demand wage raises, and workers at the General Motors plant in Cordoba seized 20 executives and held them hostage to press wage demands.

The CGT and the "62 Organizations," the Peronist umbrella group, called a general strike June 27, virtually paralyzing Buenos Aires, Cordoba, Santa Fe, Tucuman, La Plata and Rosario. In the capital some 80,000 workers marched on the government palace to demand the resignation of Rodrigo and of Social Welfare Minister Jose Lopez Rega, widely acknowledged to be the most powerful man in Argentina.

Mrs. Peron responded to the workers' demands June 28 by offering a final wage increase of 50%, with further 15% raises in October and in January 1976. The only alternatives to her offer were accelerated inflation and mass unemployment, she declared.

Labor Minister Ricardo Otero resigned immediately after Mrs. Peron's declaration, and the opposition Radical Civic Union announced its support for labor demands, declaring them "legitimate and necessary."

The next day local CGT leaders in Lanus and Avellaneda, two industrial centers in Buenos Aires, called strikes and withdrew their allegiance from Mrs. Peron as head of the Justicialista Party, the Peronist political movement. Members of the Peronist bloc in the Senate attempted to meet with the president but were rebuked; they immediately voted to elect a new Senate president, upsetting Lopez Rega's arrangement for the succession, with debate on the election beginning June 30.

Hundreds of thousands of workers struck June 30 in defiance of Mrs. Peron's orders to return to their jobs and accept the 50% raises. The CGT's regional offices called general strikes in Cordoba, Mendoza and Chubut Provinces, and strikes paralyzed the auto, metals, textile and construction industries in Buenos Aires.

President Peron met that night with the CGT's national leadership and pledged further meetings to end the crisis. (The CGT leaders met with her cabinet July 2.) The labor leaders asked workers to return to their jobs July 1, but thousands of workers continued to strike, notably in Cordoba—the nation's automotive center—and La Plata, where Peronist insurgents had seized the local CGT leadership and vowed to continue fighting for higher wages.

The Peronist bloc in the Senate and the eight minor parties associated with the Justicialista Party declared their support for labor leaders demanding an end to the wage rollback and the dismissal of Rodrigo and Lopez Rega.

The Cordoba CGT called an indefinite general strike July 3, and the national CGT called July 4 for a 48-hour general strike to begin at midnight July 6. The National Statistics Institute reported July 4 that the cost of living had risen by 21.3% in June, for an official annual inflation rate of 110%.

The armed forces threw their weight on the side of the protesters July 3, recommending cabinet changes and giving Mrs. Peron a military report which linked Lopez Rega to the Argentine Anticommunist Alliance (AAA), the right-wing assassination squad. The armed forces commanders subsequently leaked the report to the newspaper La Opinion, and they rejected Lopez Rega's suggestion that they intervene against the CGT.

La Opinion cited the report on Lopez Rega July 6 and reported that the military chiefs were concerned over a number of issues, including the lack of dialogue between the executive branch and other "factors of power" including the armed forces; the "lack of representativeness" of the government and its growing separation from the political parties; government control over the information media and excessive government propaganda campaigns; adherence "in certain official circles" to "pseudoreligious" sects (a reference to Lopez Rega's membership in an Afro-Brazilian spiritualist sect called Umbanda; he was also a practicing astrologer); use of government funds for political campaigns; the impunity under which right-wing terrorists operated, and the general insecurity among Argentines and lack of confidence in the police and armed forces; and the government's serious mismanagement of the economy.

To combat these problems, La Opinion reported, the armed forces had recommended the dismissal of "the most irritating figures and those considered responsible for a long series of errors that have carried the country to the brink of a grave institutional conflict"; the immediate opening of "a broad political dialogue which would include all sectors of national life, to study a series of emergency measures"; and "the fullest

observation of the institutions, as determined by the Constitution."

Lopez Rega's Fall

Mrs. Peron yields, ousts Lopez Rega. Under intense pressure from Congress, the armed forces and the labor unions, President Peron cancelled the wage rollback and dismissed Jose Lopez Rega.

Mrs. Peron July 8 approved recently negotiated industrial wage increases of 100%–135% after a 38-hour general strike by the General Labor Confederation (CGT) paralyzed Buenos Aires and other cities. The strike, the first of its kind against a Peronist government, followed 10 days of protests by teachers, bank and railroad employes, and workers in the automotive, textile and metals industries.

The military chiefs met with Mrs. Peron several times before she agreed to abandon the wage rollback July 8. After her concession the CGT immediately called off the general strike, and pledged that workers would give the government a day's pay for each month of their new contracts to help speed an economic recovery. The strike crisis reportedly cost the country $804 million from its beginning June 27 until work resumed July 10. (July 9 was a holiday marking Argentine independence.)

The armed forces, the political leadership and the labor movement all pledged their support to Mrs. Peron's presidency, but work continued against Lopez Rega and his policies. The Senate elected itself a president July 8, upsetting the arrangement under which Raul Lastiri, the Chamber of Deputies president and Lopez Rega's son-in-law, was first in line to succeed Mrs. Peron. The new Senate president, now first in the line of succession, was Italo Luder, a Peronist who reportedly had good relations with labor, the armed forces and the opposition parties.

In a further slap at Mrs. Peron and Lopez Rega, the Senate heavily amended and sent to the Chamber of Deputies a law on the succession introduced by the executive. Under the Senate's version, if the president died or left office the president of the Senate would rule the country until a joint session of Congress elected a new president from among its own members and the provincial governors. Mrs. Peron's version would have passed the presidency to the president of Congress, a new post to which she hoped Lastiri would be elected, and allowed the subsequent election of cabinet ministers to the presidency. The Senate's version was approved by the Chamber July 12.

Peronist Deputy Jesus Porto proposed the impeachment of Lopez Rega July 10, calling him the "instigator and intellectual author" of AAA terrorism, accusing him of "fraud against the state" in the purchase of oil from Libya for allegedly excessive prices, and noting he had officiated at an Umbanda ceremony in Buenos Aires in defiance of the Constitution, which made Roman Catholicism the state religion. Porto had recently survived an assassination attempt by the AAA, as had another deputy, Santiago Raico, who publicly challenged Lopez Rega to a duel July 5 and again July 6.

Mrs. Peron July 11 reluctantly accepted Lopez Rega's resignation as social welfare minister, secretary to the presidency and personal secretary to the president. She made three other cabinet changes, but her cabinet remained dominated by associates of Lopez Rega, including Economy Minister Celestino Rodrigo and Labor Minister Cecilio Conditti, both of whom were reappointed to their posts.

(The entire cabinet had resigned late July 6 in an unsuccessful attempt to head off the general strike. In her cabinet shuffle July 11 Mrs. Peron named Carlos Villone as social welfare minister, Jorge Garrido as defense minister and Ernesto Corvalan as justice minister, and she shifted Antonio Benitez from the justice portfolio to the interior ministry. Of the eight cabinet ministers, five—Villone, Rodrigo, Conditti, Education Minister Oscar Ivanissevich and Foreign Minister Alberto Vignes—were considered close to Lopez Rega. Villone's brother Jose Maria was named personal secretary to the president.)

Miguel Radrizzani, a Buenos Aires lawyer, filed charges against Lopez Rega in court July 14, accusing him of being the AAA's "political supervisor." Radrizzani cited the military report, which, he said, named Luis Almiron, head of Mrs. Peron's bodyguards, and Juan Ramon Morales, chief of Lopez Rega's bodyguards, as military heads of the AAA.

Labor and congressional protests continued despite the wage increases and cabinet changes, as the government sought to salvage its economic austerity program and prices continued to rise.

Political, congressional and labor leaders July 12 denounced the retention of Rodrigo, who was considered to have devised the unpopular austerity program with Lopez Rega. In a continuation of the program July 15, the government devalued the peso by 18%.

Strikes were reported July 15 by 300,-000 teachers and by transit, paper, chemical, pharmaceutical, sugar, telephone and judicial workers across the country who sought wage increases comparable to those of the CGT. The CGT charged the increases were already being eaten up by price increases, which had brought the annual inflation rate to 200%, according to unofficial sources cited in press reports.

Some 300 employes of Ford Motor Argentina had been fired July 14 for striking to protest recent price increases which they put at 300%. Public transport fares were increased by 200% that day and the prices of cigarettes and of telephone, postal and shipping rates were doubled.

Shakeup continues. President Peron was forced to make additional changes in the cabinet and military leadership as the armed forces' role in the government grew.

The first changes, demanded by the military and by the Peronist labor movement, removed the cabinet officials linked to Lopez Rega, who left for Spain July 19 despite a travel ban imposed on him by Congress because of impeachment procedures begun against him in the Chamber of Deputies and court charges filed against him for allegedly leading a right-wing assassination squad.

Economy Minister Celestino Rodrigo, a close associate of Lopez Rega, resigned July 18 after the General Labor Confederation (CGT) said it would begin a 72-hour strike unless he quit along with

Social Welfare Minister Carlos Villone and Labor Minister Cecilio Conditti. Villone and Conditti were close to Lopez Rega, and Conditti had been appointed labor minister without the customary consultation with the CGT.

Villone resigned July 21 and was replaced by Rodolfo Roballos, another associate of Lopez Rega. Pedro Bonanni, a conservative Peronist and former finance minister, was named economy minister July 22. He declared an immediate price freeze, but the freeze did not head off strikes for higher wages by doctors, airline pilots and telephone workers July 22–24.

In another slap at Mrs. Peron and Lopez Rega, the Chamber of Deputies July 23 voted out its president, Raul Lastiri, who was Lopez Rega's son-in-law and favored candidate to succeed Mrs. Peron. Lastiri was also forced to resign as vice president of the Justicialista (Peronist) Party, which he ran for Mrs. Peron.

The Authentic Peronist Party, a leftist group linked to the Montoneros guerrillas, July 22 called for Mrs. Peron's resignation, new general elections and a return to the center-left policies on which Peronist candidates campaigned in 1973. The Montoneros demanded July 25 that Mrs. Peron resign.

Labor agitation increased at the end of July and beginning of August as more than 250,000 layoffs were reported in Buenos Aires Province. The cost of living rose by 34.7% in July, according to government figures reported Aug. 9. (The increase for August was 22.1%, for a total rise of 238.6% since August 1974, it was reported Sept. 4.)

Julio Broner, head of the General Economic Confederation (CGE), a management group, said few businesses were "in a condition to pay salaries for the second half of July" or to restock raw materials and supplies, it was reported Aug. 3. Auto and manufacturing companies reported sales down by 45%–80% since June, when the government tripled the price of gasoline and halved the value of the peso, causing a rise in prices which in turn caused successful demands by workers for higher wages. Wholesale prices rose by 42% in July, according to the Aug. 3 report.

The government suspended imports of about 100 items Aug. 5 and suspended export duties on wool, leather, rice and frozen chickens in an apparent attempt to gain foreign exchange. The peso was devalued by an average 16% Aug. 9.

The CGT, which demanded a greater role in the government, particularly in the economy and social welfare ministries, urged Mrs. Peron Aug. 7 to declare a state of economic emergency and a freeze on layoffs for 90 days. Economy Minister Bonanni called the same day for a wage-price "truce," but this was rejected by the CGE Aug. 9 on grounds that it would "condemn businessmen to bankruptcy."

Mrs. Peron revised her cabinet Aug. 11. She reappointed only two officials—Defense Minister Jorge Garrido and Justice Minister Ernesto Corvalan—and she left the economy portfolio temporarily vacant. The five new appointees were Pedro Arrighi as education minister, Carlos Emery as social welfare minister, Carlos Ruckauf as labor minister, Angel Robledo as foreign minister and Vicente Damasco, an army colonel, as interior minister.

The appointment of Col. Damasco, a former military aide to the late President Juan Peron, raised a furor in the armed forces. Senior military leaders reportedly were consulted on the appointment of all cabinet ministers except Damasco, with whom the Peronists apparently hoped to forge an alliance with the armed forces.

A number of army generals, despite insisting on a say in the appointment of cabinet ministers, felt the presence of Damasco in the cabinet unwisely tied the armed forces to the government's faltering policies. Officers in the navy, the most conservative of the armed forces, reportedly feared that Damasco had presidential ambitions and left-wing Peronist sympathies.

A number of military officers Aug. 13 asked Mrs. Peron to fire Damasco. Ten army generals met to debate the issue the next day, and Gen. Alberto Numa Laplane, the army commander, forged a compromise in which they accepted Damasco's appointment but declared the army's "total independence" from the cabinet. They added that, in compliance with army rules, Damasco must leave the cabinet or retire from the army within two months.

However, the controversy continued

after the compromise, with increasing hostility in all armed services toward Damasco and Numa Laplane. Five leading army generals, including the commanders of three of the nation's five garrisons, joined the navy and air force chiefs Aug. 26 in demanding that Damasco and Numa Laplane resign. Mrs. Peron agreed to fire Numa Laplane but proposed to replace him with Gen. Alberto Caceres, the most junior of the generals, whose appointment would force the retirement of all generals opposing Damasco. The generals rejected this Aug. 27. They placed their garrisons on alert, and Gen. Carlos Delia Larroca, the most senior general next to Numa Laplane, declared himself army commander. Mrs. Peron, fearing a military coup, then fired Numa Laplane and named as the new army chief Gen. Jorge Videla, next in line after Delia Larroca, whose retirement was thus forced.

Videla, a reputed opponent of military involvement in politics, began a purge Aug. 30 of officers considered close to the Peronist movement. The retirement of Gen. Caceres was confirmed that day, as was the dismissal of Col. Jorge Sosa Molina, chief of the presidential military guard and a supporter of Damasco.

Meanwhile, Mrs. Peron appointed a new economy minister, Antonio Cafiero, Aug. 14. Cafiero, a former Argentine envoy to the European Economic Community, announced a program Aug. 25 to stem the growing unemployment rate, currently estimated at 7%. Government credits would be made available quickly to businesses and public agencies, even at the risk of added inflation, Cafiero said.

(One reason for Argentina's inflation was the printing of huge amounts of money without the backing of treasury funds, it was reported Aug. 26. The extension of new government loans to enterprises presumably could spur the inflationary rate.)

Cafiero also pledged an effort to contain inflation through cuts in government spending, but he rejected sudden "shock" measures that would create a stronger recession. He said controls would be imposed on basic necessities to aid working-class families, but there would be no return to the widespread price controls of the past two years.

The peso was devalued again Aug. 25, by an average 3.43%.

Cafiero and Casildo Herreras, the CGT secretary general, departed for the U.S. Aug. 30 to seek new foreign loans and renegotiate payment of Argentina's huge foreign debt, estimated at $10 billion.

President Leaves for Month

Mrs. Peron takes leave. President Maria Estela Martinez de Peron began a month-long leave of absence Sept. 13, ostensibly for health reasons. Senate President Italo Luder took over as interim president.

An official communique said Mrs. Peron would resume the presidency by Oct. 17, after resting at an air force club in the mountains of Cordoba Province. Foreign Minister Angel Robledo admitted she might resign while on leave, but he said she would do so only for health—not political—reasons.

Mrs. Peron had spent most of August in bed, reportedly suffering from nervous and intestinal problems. She had lost much weight during her 14 months in office, and had spent little time at her official duties since her closest adviser, former Social Welfare Minister Jose Lopez Rega, was driven from office and into exile in July.

Luder, described as a moderate Peronist lawyer who had good relations with both the armed forces and the labor movement, would exercise full presidential powers during Mrs. Peron's absence. Mrs. Peron said any major decisions made by Luder during her absence would have her support.

Luder had helped draft the 1949 Peronist constitution and had defended the late President Juan Peron against treason charges in 1955-56, after Peron's second administration was ended by a military coup. He was the fifth person to assume the presidency of Argentina since the 1973 elections.

Luder replaces officials. During his first full day in office Sept. 15, Luder accepted the resignations of Interior Minister Vicente Damasco and Defense Minister Jorge Garrido.

Damasco, an army colonel whose

resignation had been demanded by the top military leaders, was replaced by Foreign Minister Angel Robledo. The foreign affairs portfolio was temporarily left vacant. Garrido was replaced by Tomas Vottero.

After replacing the interior and defense ministers Sept. 15, Luder replaced Mrs. Peron's private secretary and her press secretary Sept. 16. The new private secretary, Luder's son Ricardo, supplanted Julio Cesar Gonzalez, the last official in the presidential palace considered to have been close to Jose Lopez Rega, the exiled former social welfare minister.

Luder Sept. 18 dismissed the right-wing governor of Cordoba Province, Brig. Gen. (ret.) Raul Lacabanne, who had waged a brutal campaign against leftist subversives but allowed unrestricted assaults by the Argentine Anticommunist Alliance, the right-wing assassination squad allegedly organized by Lopez Rega. Lacabanne was replaced by Raul Bercovich Rodriguez, a veteran Peronist party official. Luder Oct. 2 named a new foreign minister, Manuel Arauz Castex, a former law professor and Supreme Court judge who pledged to follow "the traditional Peronist attitude: a third position, between liberalism and Marxism."

Luder vowed Sept. 16 to allow reporters greater access to information and freedom of movement in the Government House. The next day left-wing Peronists were allowed to print and distribute a publication for the first time since 1974. The new magazine, El Autentico, was the organ of the Authentic Peronist Party, which had links with the Montoneros guerrilla group. Its first issue attacked the government, saying it had been dominated by the armed forces since before Mrs. Peron's departure.

Violence Continues

Political killings mount. The volume of political violence appeared to mount during Argentina's economic and government crisis. Political killings averaged about 100 a month.

The victims included policemen, soldiers and members of the two major leftist guerrilla groups, the People's Revolutionary Army (ERP) and the Montoneros. Soldiers pursued ERP insurgents in the mountains of Tucuman Province, while police fought Montoneros and ERP members in Cordoba, Buenos Aires, La Plata and other cities.

The victims also included leftist civilians presumed killed by the Argentine Anticommunist Alliance (AAA), the assassination squad allegedly organized by Jose Lopez Rega, the exiled former social welfare minister. More than a dozen bullet-riddled and burned bodies were found in areas known to be AAA dumping grounds.

In response to the violence, the government formally outlawed the Montoneros Sept. 8, forbidding any mention of the group's activities in the press. The battle against leftist guerrillas became the principal concern of the army under its new commander, Gen. Jorge Videla, it was reported Sept. 12.

Several of the guerrilla attacks were connected with the third anniversary of the killing of 16 guerrillas at the naval air base at Trelew, Chubut Province on Aug. 22, 1972. Several bombs exploded in Cordoba Aug. 22, and the Montoneros blew up a missile-launching frigate at the naval shipyard in Rio Santiago, south of Buenos Aires.

Right-wing assassins claiming allegiance to the late President Juan Peron had killed four relatives of the slain guerrilla Mariano Pujadas Aug. 15 in an apparent attempt to provoke extensive guerrilla violence that would encourage army to seize power. Guerrillas killed five policemen in Cordoba Aug. 20 in apparent retaliation for the Pujadas murders.

Policemen and soldiers claimed to have killed and arrested dozens of leftist insurgents in August and September, particularly in Tucuman. An unidentified army general in Tucuman said Aug. 30 that 800 guerrillas, including ones of Chilean and Uruguayan nationality, had been killed, wounded or arrested during the army's seven-month offensive in the province.

A bomb exploded by the Montoneros at the Tucuman airport Aug. 28 set fire to a military transport airplane carrying some 120 antiguerrilla troops. At least four soldiers were killed in the fire and 25 were wounded.

Ruben Cartier, mayor of La Plata, had been assassinated July 15.

In other terrorism, Charles Agnew Lockwood, the British financier kidnapped by the ERP and ransomed for some $2 million in 1973, was abducted again July 31. Police rescued him in suburban Buenos Aires Aug. 31, killing four of his captors, all ERP members. Frank Ingrey, an Anglo-Argentine businessman, was found dead in Buenos Aires Sept. 10. He had been kidnapped and held for 20 days in April by an unidentified guerrilla group.

Julio Larrabure, an army major kidnapped by the ERP in 1974, was found dead in Rosario Aug. 23. The ERP reported the day before that he had committed suicide in captivity. The ERP had offered Aug. 2 to free Larrabure and end all terrorist operations if the government freed all political prisoners, lifted the ERP's illegal status and revoked "all repressive legislation." The government made no reply to the offer.

At least 30 persons were killed in Formosa Oct. 5 when the Montoneros assaulted the local army garrison, the airport and the federal prison. The first two attacks were apparently intended to divert attention from the third, an unsuccessful attempt to free several jailed insurgents. The Montoneros asserted in a communique Oct. 8 that they were forming "a regular army" to help "the people take power in the country." The Formosa operation showed "the weakness of the enemy," proving there was "no place in the country, not even the most isolated garrisons, where the military forces of reaction at the service of imperialism and the oligarchy can feel secure," the Montoneros declared.

An intensive search for guerrillas began in Formosa Oct. 6 as the army commander, Gen. Jorge Videla, flew in from Buenos Aires. At least 12 Montoneros were killed in the city that day, five attempting to free wounded comrades from a hospital. At least four guerrillas were killed and 30 arrested Oct. 7.

More than 200 ERP members attacked three military garrisons in Tucuman Province and set off eight bombs in the city of Tucuman Oct. 8, killing at least 31 persons. One of the bombs badly damaged the palace of the Roman Catholic archbishop. The attacks, commemorating the eighth anniversary of the death of guerrilla leader Ernesto "Che" Guevara and the 80th birthday of the late President Juan Peron, brought a wave of arrests in Tucuman, Buenos Aires, Mendoza, Santa Fe and La Plata. Some 165 persons were reported seized in Buenos Aires and 29 ERP members were reported arrested in La Plata.

In response to earlier guerrilla violence, including the murder of the military intelligence chief Sept. 17, Interim President Italo Luder had created a National Defense Council Oct. 2 to direct security operations. The council consisted of Luder, Defense Minister Tomas Vottero and the three armed forces commanders. To carry out the council's directives, Luder Oct. 6 established an Internal Security Council composed of himself, the cabinet ministers and representatives of all security forces.

As in the past, the government took no apparent notice of murders by the AAA and other rightist commandos. Two lawyers who had defended leftist political prisoners were murdered in Rosario Sept. 30, presumably by the AAA. The next day an editorial in the Buenos Aires newspaper La Opinion, said: "In Argentina there are more executions than in Spain, but no member of the international community feels obligated to protest the 100 death sentences [carried out but] not made official in September." Marcos Osatinsky, a Montoneros leader arrested Aug. 8, was tortured and then executed in Cordoba Aug. 21, according to the French newspaper Le Monde Oct. 9.

A group of French lawyers who visited Argentina in May on behalf of the Inter-National Federation for the Rights of Man and the International Movement of Catholic Jurists, asserted Oct. 9 that repression, terrorism and torture had become "a form of government" in Argentina. Government repression was directed "only against armed groups of the extreme left," allowing rightist commandos to operate "with total impunity," the lawyers said.

In other terrorism, 10 bombs were exploded by presumed left-wing guerrillas in Cordoba Sept. 23, one severely damaging the office of Xerox Corp. of the U.S. Police reported Sept. 24 that an executive of another U.S. firm, Otis Elevator Co., had been kidnapped by the ERP July 9 and ransomed for $2 million Aug. 22. The executive, Jean Deloubieux, was a French citizen on a business visit to Argentina.

Foreign, Trade & Other Developments

OAS denounces U.S. trade law. The Permanent Council of the Organization of American States (OAS) passed a resolution Jan. 23 denouncing the new U.S. Trade Reform Act as "discriminatory and coercive."

Twenty Latin American nations voted for the resolution and the U.S. abstained. The vote came at the end of a special four-day meeting of the council to air Latin complaints against the U.S. law.

Voting for the resolution were Argentina, Barbados, Brazil, Chile, Colombia, Costa Rica, Dominican Republic, Ecuador, El Salvador, Guatemala, Honduras, Jamaica, Mexico, Nicaragua, Panama, Paraguay, Peru, Trinidad-Tobago, Uruguay and Venezuela.

When the council meeting convened Jan. 20, representatives of 16 Latin governments had criticized the trade law, which imposed restrictions on U.S. imports, including denial of preferential tariff treatment to nations that joined commodity cartels, curbed U.S. access to their raw materials, expropriated U.S. companies without adequate compensation, or inadequately controlled the narcotics traffic from their borders to the U.S.

Kissinger parley postponed. The Argentine goverment Jan. 27 indefinitely postponed a meeting between Latin American foreign ministers and U.S. Secretary of State Henry Kissinger, scheduled for March in Buenos Aires.

Argentine Foreign Minister Alberto Vignes said the reason for the action was the new U.S. Trade Reform Act, which, "by its rigidity and unfairness, damages fundamental interests of the Latin American countries."

Vignes stressed that Kissinger's avowed "new dialogue" with Latin America was only being postponed, not "interrupted." He said the foreign ministers' conference could take place as soon as the U.S. revoked provisions of the trade act which Latin American countries considered discriminatory.

'74 Soviet trade surplus. Argentine trade with the Soviet Union in 1974 totaled $330 million, with $290 million recorded in sales to the U.S.S.R., the newsletter Latin America reported Jan. 10. The largest Soviet purchase had been $50 million worth of wool.

Anti-guerrilla officers killed. Thirteen senior army and police officers who were experts in counterinsurgency were killed in an airplane crash Jan. 6 in the mountains of Tucuman Province, where leftist guerrillas were believed to be operating. One of the victims was Gen. Enrique Salgado, commander of the 3rd Army.

Mrs. Peron Back in Office

President returns. President Maria Estela Martinez de Peron returned to office Oct. 16, rejecting advice by political and military leaders that she prolong her month-long leave of absence or resign in view of the nation's continuing political and economic crisis.

Addressing a Loyalty Day rally in Buenos Aires Oct. 17, Mrs. Peron pledged to complete her term of office and urged Argentines to support the armed forces in their "battle against subversion." "Their dead are our dead," she said, referring to military casualties in clashes with left-wing guerrillas.

Interim President Italo Luder and Foreign Minister Angel Robledo had visited Mrs. Peron at her retreat in Cordoba Province Oct. 7 and urged her to extend her vacation or resign. Luder and Robledo reportedly were supported by the armed forces leadership and by sectors of the Peronist political and labor movements. Left-wing Peronists outside the official movements also urged the president to step down.

Mrs. Peron resisted, however, and returned to Buenos Aires Oct. 15. Military leaders including Gen. Jorge Videla, the army commander, accepted her decision but reportedly expressed concern that under Mrs. Peron the government would once again be run by a small group of presidential advisers isolated from Congress, the armed forces, the labor unions and other Argentine institutions.

Luder had replaced several cabinet ministers and eased restrictions on the press, but he had not decisively assumed national leadership during Mrs. Peron's absence, according to press reports. He had also given the armed forces a greater role in national security following a series of attacks on military officials and installations by leftist guerrillas.

Luder met frequently with political, labor and military leaders, but he was unable to reconcile rival factions within the Peronist political and labor movements. In Congress, some 17 members of the Peronist bloc feuded with party leaders over "verticality," the principle that Peronist legislators must abide by all decisions of the party leadership. In the labor movement a minority of leaders demanded that Mrs. Peron resign.

Victorio Calabro, governor of Buenos Aires Province and treasurer of the Metallurgical Workers Union (UOM), declared Sept. 30 that if Mrs. Peron did not resign and allow effective leadership to be restored, there would be a military coup. The 62 Organizations, the Peronist umbrella group headed by UOM secretary Lorenzo Miguel, denounced Calabro's statement as "subversive" Oct. 4. Carlos Menem, governor of La Rioja Province, said Oct. 5 that Calabro's remarks were "serious, imprudent and too suggestive of treason."

Andres Framini, an Authentic Peronist leader, called Oct. 13 for Mrs. Peron's resignation, asserting: "This is the worst government we have ever endured." However, ex-President Hector Campora, whom the Authentics claimed as a leader, had called Sept. 29 for unity in the Peronist movement. Campora had been allowed to return to Argentina Sept. 27 after a year-long, self-imposed exile in Mexico during which he was expelled from the Justicialista (Peronist) Party.

Two senators of the opposition Radical Civic Union, Carlos Perette and Fernando de la Rua, urged Mrs. Peron Oct. 3 to consider whether her return to office would do more harm than good. Ricardo Balbin, the Radical leader and former presidential candidate, had urged Luder Sept. 30 to move the 1977 elections up to 1976 to help end political uncertainty.

Index